Devolution

Vernon Bogdanor

Devolution

Oxford University Press 1979
Oxford New York Toronto Melbourne

Oxford University Press, Walton Street, Oxford OX2 6DP

OXFORD   LONDON   GLASGOW
NEW YORK   TORONTO   MELBOURNE   WELLINGTON
KUALA LUMPUR   SINGAPORE   JAKARTA   HONG KONG   TOKYO
DELHI   BOMBAY   CALCUTTA   MADRAS   KARACHI
IBADAN   NAIROBI   DAR ES SALAAM   CAPE TOWN

British Library Cataloguing in Publication Data

Bogdanor, Vernon
    Devolution. – (Opus).
    1. Decentralization in government – Great Britain – History
    I. Title   II. Series
    354'.41'082   JN329.D43   78-41055

    ISBN 0-19-219128-4
    ISBN 0-19-289115-4 Pbk

For R.B.   J.E.B.
P.S.R.B.   A.M.D.B.
who all helped

Preface

This book seeks to analyse the political and constitutional aspects of devolution in Britain from Gladstone's espousal of Home Rule in 1886 to the present day. In doing so, it may cast light both on how we are governed, and upon how constitutional ideas are affected by political realities.

Much of the contemporary material in the book is based upon interviews, and I would like to thank all those who were generous enough to spare the time to talk about devolution with me. The book was completed in August 1978, and does not take account of developments since then.

I owe an enormous debt of gratitude to my former tutor, Mr. Geoffrey Marshall, and to Mr. Philip Williams for their help and encouragement at all stages in the preparation of this book. In addition I would like to thank the following for reading and commenting upon earlier drafts: Mr. Jack Beatson, Professor R. B. McDowell, Dr. Brian Harrison, Dr. K. O. Morgan, Professor George Jones, Dr. Harry Judge, Professor F. S. L. Lyons, Professor Barry Nicholas, Mr. Michael Woods, Mr. John Dunbabin, Mr. Nevil Johnson, Sir Norman Chester, and Mr. Michael Brock. They are not, of course, to be implicated either in my arguments or my conclusions. I should also like to thank Henry Hardy and Judy Spours of O.U.P.

I was fortunate enough to be made an Associate Member of Nuffield College, Oxford while completing the book and would like to thank the Warden and Fellows of Nuffield for their kindness and hospitality.

To my own college, Brasenose, I am deeply indebted. The Principal and Fellows have given me generous sabbatical leave and paid for the expenses of typing the book, as well as putting up with all kinds of importunate questions on devolution. I am grateful to be a member of so stimulating an academic community.

I could not have written the book without my wife's constant encouragement and help. I am grateful also to my sons, Paul and Adam, for keeping me cheerful throughout.

Acknowledgments

The quotations on pp. 17 and 32 are from photostats of the originals preserved in the Royal Archives, and made available by gracious permission of Her Majesty the Queen.

I should like to thank Mr. A. J. P. Taylor for allowing me to quote from the Lloyd George papers.

Contents

1 Introduction

'Then how do you explain the growth of nationalism?' I asked.
'That is precisely the proof of what I say,' answered Franz Kafka.
'Men always strive for what they do not have. The technical advances which are common to all nations strip them more and more of their national characteristics. Therefore they become nationalist. Modern nationalism is a defensive movement against the crude encroachments of civilisation.'

Gustav Janouch: *Conversations with Kafka*.

I

The central theme of this book is that devolution, as well as being the most pressing constitutional issue of the day, is likely to have more profound effects upon the workings of British politics than any other institutional reform since the war. For devolution not only involves constitutional change of a wide-ranging and funda-mental kind: it also raises basic questions about the nature of the British state, questions such as—How is national unity best secured—through centralized government, or through the dispersal of power? Is the recognition of a sense of nationality in one of the component parts of a state compatible with the continued unity of that state? These are the kinds of issue that lie behind the contem-porary debate, just as they tormented our Victorian predecessors in the fierce and protracted arguments over Irish Home Rule.

But devolution also raises a broader question of political philo-sophy, the question of whether centralization is to be regarded as inevitable and welcomed, or whether it is something to be strenuously combatted. This of course is not a question facing Britain alone. Indeed in many other democratic countries the same issue is being debated. In France, Spain, and Belgium ethnic and linguistic pressures seem to be threatening the traditional structure of the state. In the United States of America, 'the new federalism' attempts to reverse the pressures of centralization which have been so dominant since the time of Franklin Roosevelt's New Deal; and in Canada the question has been posed whether the federal system is flexible enough to contain the pressures exerted by the *Parti Québecqois*.

Devolution is thus not just another piece of administrative scene-shifting, irrelevant to all beyond a restricted circle of constitutionalists. It is an issue with profound implications for the way in which we are governed, and for the kind of society in which we are to live. One of the main purposes of what follows is to show how the issue has arisen in British politics, how it has been dealt with in the framework of British constitutional thought, and to spell out the implications of devolving power from Westminster. But first we must look a little more closely at the concept of devolution and what it means.

II

The process of devolution involves the dispersal of power from a superior to an inferior political authority. More precisely, it consists of three elements: the transfer to a *subordinate elected body* on a *geographical basis*, of *functions at present exercised by Parliament*. These functions may be either legislative, the power to make laws, or executive, the power to make decisions within an already established legal framework. An example of a devolved government would be the government of Northern Ireland from 1921 to 1972. For by the Government of Ireland Act of 1920, Westminster established in Belfast a subordinate parliament with wide powers over the domestic affairs of Northern Ireland.

Devolution involves the creation of an elected body, subordinate to Parliament: it therefore seeks to preserve intact the supremacy of Parliament, a central feature of the British Constitution. It must, then, be distinguished from federalism, which would *divide* supreme power between Parliament and the various provincial bodies. In a federal state, the authority of the central or federal government and the provincial governments is co-ordinate and shared, the respective scope of each unit of government being defined by a written constitution, as in the United States or the Federal Republic of Germany.

Admittedly, 'federalism' like 'devolution' is a term used rather loosely in current debate; and in most of the proposals for a 'federal solution' in Britain, the term 'federal' is intended to mean not a division of power between Westminster and provincial units of government, but rather a policy of devolution applied to Britain as a whole, and not just to Scotland and Wales. We shall, therefore, to avoid confusion with the type of government in the United States or West Germany, characterize such proposals as 'federal devolution' rather than as strictly federal.

III

To secure the dispersal of power has been a central concern of political thinkers since Aristotle. Yet it is only comparatively recently that federalism and devolution have been seen as techniques for achieving this aim. The modern concept of federalism was first introduced into political discourse by James Madison, the philosopher of the American Constitution, in his contributions to the *Federalist*, a series of papers written in 1787–8 to urge ratification of the American Constitution. Madison sought to prove that, contrary to the view of Montesquieu and Rousseau, representative democracy was possible in a large state. Indeed, the federal principle allowed a happy mean to be found between a state which was so small as to be parochial, and one which was so large that it ignored local interests. The federal constitution, Madison argued in the tenth *Federalist* paper, 'forms a happy combination in this respect; the great and aggregate interests being referred to the national, the local and particularly to the state legislatures'.

The idea of devolution, however, is a peculiarly British contribution to politics. It makes its first appearance in Edmund Burke's speech on American Taxation delivered to the House of Commons in 1774. Burke wanted to show that it was perfectly possible to reconcile American demands for local autonomy with the imperial rights of Britain. The American legislatures were to have freedom to decide their own domestic policies, but they were to be strictly subordinate to Parliament. Westminster, however, was 'never to intrude . . . whilst they are equal to the common ends of their institution. But in order to enable Parliament to answer all these ends of provident and beneficent superintendence, her powers must be boundless'.[1]

Burke thus sought to give maximum autonomy to the colonies without weakening the imperial power by dividing it as in a federal scheme. His plea, although unsuccessful in the case of the American colonies, became the *leitmotiv* of the policy of responsible government adopted in Canada in the nineteenth century; and as we shall see, it exerted a profound influence on Gladstone in deciding upon Home Rule as a solution to the Irish Question.

Home Rule, the policy of devolution to an Irish legislative body sitting in Dublin, occupied the centre of the British political stage for much of the period between 1886, the year of the first Home Rule Bill, and the outbreak of the First World War in 1914. After the war, however, the Irish problem seemed to have been settled by Lloyd George, and devolution was no longer a matter of active political controversy. It is only during the last decade that it has again come to appear a subject of particular interest.

IV

In Britain, devolution has been seen primarily as a technique to deal with Scottish and Welsh nationalism in the hope that it will lead to better government in Scotland and Wales, and therefore defuse separatist feeling. Indeed, in Europe as a whole, pressure for devolution is greatest in those areas on the geographical peripheries of countries peopled by national minorities—such as Brittany, Alsace, Corsica, the Basque country, Catalonia, Scotland, and Wales. But it would be wrong to believe that the grievances which have given rise to ethnic politics are confined only to these peripheral areas. For it may well be that these grievances are felt equally strongly in areas which, lacking a distinctive ethnic tradition, lack also the nationalist parties which might give these grievances political expression. It will indeed be one of the arguments of this book that the nationalist parties have brought the issue of decentralization onto the agenda of British politics, and, in doing so, have performed a constructive function for England as well as for Scotland and Wales.

Modern ethnic nationalism has arisen as a reaction against powerful forces in the modern world, the forces of technocracy and corporatism. As the state has come to take on more and more functions, so it has come to seem more and more remote from the citizen. The vast array of responsibilities which have come to be assumed by the modern state have served to undermine traditional notions of liberal democracy. Holders of power seem to become less accountable both to the electorate and to parliament. Power seems to flow to the bureaucracy and to giant corporations representing employers and trade unions rather than to elected politicians. In place of the individualism of classical democratic theory, policy comes to seem the result of bargaining between these corporations and government, with representative institutions being kept very much at arms length.

Such a dispensation might perhaps have been accepted if it had produced tangible economic benefits, since 'The logic of centralization is economic: it is predicated on growth',[2] and the needs of economic management have provided a rationale for centralization. But the economic strains of the 1970s have put paid to the optimism of the Keynesian consensus which held that governments could, by skilful management, stabilize the economy. The state has come to seem incompetent as well as impersonal and remote, and the result has been that it has lost both legitimacy and authority. The state has long ceased to be loved; now it is ceasing even to command respect.

These trends have come to be accentuated by Britain's membership of the European Economic Community (E.E.C.), which in the view of the Memorandum of Dissent published as volume II of the Report of the Royal Commission on the Constitution (Cmnd. 5460–1) would 'remove important areas of decision still further away from the British people', 'weaken the doctrine of ministerial responsibility', and 'increase even more the power of officials' (Para. 106). Yet in the view of most politicians, entry to the E.E.C. was essential for Britain if she was to plan her economic future successfully. In the world of multi-national companies, the state too had to become multi-national if it was not to be at the mercy of external economic forces. The demands of economic and technical rationality seem to require the imposition of larger and larger units, both in government and in business.

The E.E.C., however, represents something more than the forces of bureaucracy. For it also symbolizes supra-nationalism, and therefore scepticism about the value of the traditional state apparatus. The E.E.C. may have begun to deprive the state of its fundamental rationale—its supposed self-sufficiency. If the supremacy of Parliament can be modified so as to accomodate the upward flow of power to Brussels, why cannot it also be modified in the opposite direction, so as to devolve power downwards? Indeed devolution may take on added importance for a country in the E.E.C., since it offers a counter-balance to processes which seek to centralize decision-making in Brussels. It is for this reason that George Thomson, then a member of the European Commission, linked together the issues of E.E.C. membership and devolution during the 1975 referendum campaign. 'It will be much easier,' he argued, 'to alter the United Kingdom constitution in favour of decentralization in the context of the E.E.C. than in the framework of Britain alone.' (*Western Mail,* 21 May 1975). Moreover, membership of the E.E.C. has, as we shall see when we come to examine Scottish nationalism, fundamentally altered the relative costs and benefits of independence, so as to make it a more attractive policy option. For an independent Scotland within the E.E.C. can secure the benefits of independence while avoiding the disadvantages of economic separation.

V

Modern ethnic nationalism and movements of regional decentra- lization are in essence attempts to humanize the state. Economic and technical developments whose tendency is to make men more and more alike find themselves checked by political pressures— the search for identity and the demand for participation. It was Rousseau who first understood that these emotional needs demanded satisfaction if men were to lead genuinely fulfilled lives. Indeed he insisted that the search for wealth and power corrupted society, just because it made it impossible for men to live in accordance with their real needs.

A more moderate view, however, would hold that only after some degree of affluence has already been achieved, and after the worst problems of deprivation and unemployment have been solved, can men think seriously about the more intangible needs which are essential to their happiness. When this stage has been reached, the old political ideologies cease to have meaning, class conflict declines, and there comes to be less intensity of feeling between Left and

Right. Paradoxically class conflict was a factor making for political homogeneity, since it affected voters in Glasgow as much as voters in Plymouth. But in the contemporary politics of Western Europe, and perhaps of Britain in particular, 'The weakening of old class and corporatist ideologies has created a political space in which new ideas and explanations of the world have a better chance of survival . . .'.[3] What progress are these new ideas and explanations likely to make within the constitutional framework of the United Kingdom?

VI

In Britain, what is constitutional is often as much a matter of instinct as of logic, and one of the reasons why the issue of devolution has never been fully explored is that we hesitate to make our philosophy of government explicit. The United States, as the Bicentennial reminded us, was formed on the basis of an explicit philosophy of government based upon the *Federalist* and embodied in the Constitution. In Britain, however, as Sidney Low once remarked, 'We live under a system of tacit understandings. But the understandings are not always understood.'

Perhaps the strongest of these 'tacit understandings' is the profoundly unitary nature of the United Kingdom, as expressed in the supremacy of Parliament. We find it difficult to think in terms of a separation of powers, and difficult also to think of government as a series of interdependent layers, each with its own rights and responsibilities. Britain is, amongst democracies, the largest of the unitary states, apart from Japan; for other democracies do not seek to manage the affairs of so large a population through a single Parliament. Britain is also an extremely centralized country and probably more centralized in practice than France, traditionally the paradigm of centralized government. For whatever Jacobin ideology may dictate, in practice many French mayors are extremely powerful political figures who would not tolerate the kind of central interference to which local authorities in Britain are regularly subject. Moreover France now has a regional layer of government which, although at present lacking executive power, may nevertheless come to act as a further counter-balance to the capital.

Yet when one has defined the unitary and centralized nature of

British government, one has not by any means captured the spirit in which this unitary state is administered. For the British system of government can best be characterized as one of centralization tempered by kindness. With the exception of Southern Ireland, Britain, unlike France, has always been able to accommodate subordinate identities such as those of the Scots or Welsh. It has, until recently at least, been possible for those living in Scotland and Wales to see themselves as Scots or Welsh *and* as British without these identities conflicting.

. . . British identity was traditionally multiple, embracing sets of dual loyalties. The stress has been on the form of the state as unitary—and unlike France it has not been necessary to buttress it with cultural uniformity. . . . There is, then, a difference of degree which exists in the recognition of Welsh cultural identity and the corresponding non-recognition of Breton or Basque identities.[4]

This is because the state in Britain has never been seen, as it has in France, as the guardian of the nation. It has never needed to eliminate other identities in order to fuse the population into one state. 'Without centralization,' a prominent Gaullist has asserted, 'there could be no France.'[5] Such a statement could never be made in Britain where centralization has the force of habit but not of ideology.

As a result, the structure of the United Kingdom has been able to accommodate a considerable diversity of political relationships. It has sustained a unique relationship with Scotland, whereby the Scots have been allowed to retain many of the attributes of statehood while at the same time remaining full members of the United Kingdom; and it sustained the quasi-federal parliament of Northern Ireland between 1921 and 1972, as well as much looser consti-tutional relationships with the Channel Islands and the Isle of Man.

So even if Britain is a highly centralist state, it is not dogmatically so; and British politicians have rarely allowed a theory of govern-ment to prevent them from constructing new relationships which, whatever the faults to be found in them by strict constitutionalists, nevertheless succeed in providing workable answers to practical problems.

We must begin our study of devolution, however, by looking at the one case where the attempt to construct such a practical solution broke down—the problem of Ireland. For it is impossible to understand either the nature of devolution or the political responses which it evokes without examining the Irish Question. From a consideration of the problems of Irish Home Rule, we shall be able to form a clearer conception of the preconditions for the success of a policy of devolution. Then we shall consider the only part of the United Kingdom to have actually operated a devolved administration—Northern Ireland. Here, too, we shall find lessons applicable to the contemporary problems posed by the rise of nationalism in Scotland and Wales. Then we shall analyse the structure of the new political forces produced in Britain by the nationalist parties and by the development of a politics of locality. We shall then consider the extent to which the Scotland and Wales Acts passed by Parliament in 1978 meet the grievances expressed by these new political forces, and we shall conclude by attempting to evaluate the implications of devolution for the future development of British politics. These implications are likely to be far-reaching and to transform the character of the British state.

2 Irish Home Rule

There are only three Home Rulers—Mr. G., because he is mad, John Morley, because he does not understand anything about Ireland, and myself because I want to get rid of the Irishmen.

Henry Labouchere quoted in Sir Edward Hamilton's Diary, 29 September 1893.

I

'The long, vexed, and troubled relations between Great Britain and Ireland', claimed W. E. Gladstone in April 1886, 'exhibit to us the one and only conspicuous failure of the political genius of our race to confront and master difficulty, and to obtain in a reasonable degree the main ends of civilized life'.[1] The policy of Irish Home Rule sought to secure these 'main ends of civilized life' by allowing Ireland to govern herself within the framework of the United Kingdom, and it was the most convulsive issue in British politics between 1886 and 1914.

During this period, three Home Rule Bills were introduced into Parliament. The first in 1886 was defeated in the Commons as the result of a split within the Liberal Party, and this split deprived the Liberals of the services of the leading Radical politician of the day, Joseph Chamberlain, and prefigured the eventual decline of the Party; the second Bill in 1893 passed the Commons but was defeated in the Lords, and the unwillingness of Gladstone's Cabinet colleagues to challenge the Lords was one of the factors which precipitated his retirement; the third Bill, introduced into Parliament in 1912, was twice rejected by the Lords but, under the provisions of the 1911 Parliament Act limiting the delaying power of the Lords to two years, it became law in 1914, although the outbreak of war caused its operation to be suspended; the passage of this third Bill was, moreover, accompanied by threats of direct action on the part of Ulstermen and Conservatives of a kind not seen in British politics since the seventeenth century. Indeed, in the view of some observers, if Britain had not declared war in 1914, the Home Rule issue might well have led to civil war.

Since our primary interest is the nature of devolution in a unitary state, we shall be concerned less with the political history of Irish Home Rule than with its constitutional implications. But first, it is necessary to ask why it was that British statesmen came to see Home Rule as a solution to the Irish problem; and we can best answer this question by analysing the approach to it of Gladstone, the dominant figure in the conversion of the bulk of the Liberal Party to Home Rule in 1886.

Ireland, according to Sir Robert Hamilton, the permanent under secretary in Dublin, was 'passing through a great social revolution' in the mid-1880s. Gladstone's first attempt to pacify Ireland, the disestablishment of the Irish Church in 1869, had weakened the position of the Protestant ascendancy; and his two Land Acts of 1870 and 1881, providing for fixity of tenure and regulating the rent of land, were beginning to weaken the dominant position of the landlords. 'These influences', to quote Hamilton again, which had worked 'imperfectly enough, I admit, and often tyrannically, for the guidance of local affairs, have disappeared, and nothing has been substituted for them'. There was a vacuum of authority in Ireland which was barely filled by the British executive situated in Dublin Castle, the centre of Irish government.

Although Ireland's representatives were thus, according to Gladstone, 'nominally under a free Constitution',[2] they were able to play no part in the government of their country. Ireland seemed equal to Britain in terms of its franchise laws and the formal rights of its citizens, but it was in reality in a dependent relationship with Britain because it was governed by England and not by Irishmen. Such a situation became extremely dangerous with the extension of the franchise, and in the general election of 1885, Ireland returned eighty-five Home Rulers to Westminster, M.P.s who saw themselves not as contributors to the party battle in Britain but as representing the demands of Irish nationality.

Moreover, for all but two years since the great Reform Act of 1832, Ireland had been administered by special coercive legislation which had no counterpart in Britain. Despite this special legislation, however, Gladstone argued that agrarian crime in Ireland 'is not only not rooted out, but it has more and more become habitual . . .

even at times threatening to break up the foundation of social order, and bring us to touch upon a state of things essentially belonging to civil war.' Thus the prevalence of agrarian crime was 'not so much the cause as the symptom of a yet more deeply rooted evil, that is to say a want of sympathy with the criminal law in all that relates to or bears upon the holding of land'.

Repressive legislation had, in Gladstone's view, failed. It was 'morally worn out'. The success of further coercion 'requires, in my judgment, two essential conditions, and these are the autocracy of Government and the secrecy of public transactions'. Neither of these conditions held in a liberal polity and the British public were, for Gladstone, unwilling to admit the need for further coercion until all other alternatives were exhausted. Coercion had been unsuccessful because it bore the character of an imposition by a foreign authority, and 'stamped on the Executive Government in Ireland' there was 'the aspect of a Government essentially foreign'. 'Of this state of things in Ireland one inevitable consequence is to produce in Great Britain not only disparaging and hostile judgment but estrangement of feeling from Ireland and thus to widen the breach between the countries.' Government in Ireland could be successful only if 'as in England the law is felt to be indigenous'. This meant a domestic system of government for Ireland.[3]

It was essentially these practical considerations rather than any idealistic view of the rights of small nations, which turned Gladstone's mind towards Home Rule. Like Burke, he opposed 'the opening of abstract questions respecting the indefeasibility of national rights; questions which are . . . capable of introducing confusion into affairs.'[4] He was concerned less with any supposed right of the Irish to self-government, than with the practical question whether the Irish demand could be reconciled with the principles of British government, and in particular with the central principles of parliamentary supremacy and Imperial unity.

That the demand could be so reconciled followed in Gladstone's view from three separate considerations. The first was an understanding of the true nature of Irish nationalism, the second a belief that the insights of Edmund Burke in his speeches on American affairs could be applied to the Irish question; and the third was the practical experience, both of other European countries and of the self-governing colonies, which showed 'that the concession of local self-government is not the way to sap or impair, but the way to strengthen and consolidate unity.'

Irish nationalism was, for Gladstone, not a demand for separation or for independent statehood, but a 'local patriotism . . . The Irishman is more profoundly Irish, but it does not follow that because his local patriotism is keen he is incapable of Imperial patriotism.'[5] He spoke not of Irish nationalism, but of Irish 'nationality' as a phenomenon similar to Scottish or Welsh nationality; and, just as a Scotsman's loyalty to Scotland was compatible with his loyalty to the United Kingdom as a whole, so the nationality of an Irishman could be made compatible with the British connection. For separate nationality 'does not mean disunion with England. It means closer union with England.'[6] Irish nationality was 'a nationality which has regard to circumstances and traditions . . . a reasonable and reasoning, not . . . a blind and headstrong nationality',[7] and it 'vents itself in the demand for local autonomy, or separate and complete self-government in Irish, not in Imperial affairs.'[8] It could therefore be satisfied by a judicious policy of devolution, placing Irish government on the firm foundations of consent and representative institutions.

While preparing the first Home Rule Bill, Gladstone studied the writings of Edmund Burke on Ireland and the speeches on conciliation with America. He found these 'a mine of gold for the political wisdom with which they are charged',[9] for Burke, the theorist of responsible government in the colonies, had shown how the Imperial connection could accommodate the feeling of nationality in subordinate communities.

Burke had noticed that the Imperial Parliament at Westminster performed two functions; it was not only 'the local legislature of this island', but also possessed an 'imperial character, in which as from the throne of heaven, she superintends all the several legislatures, and guides and controls them all without annihilating any.' These functions were, for Burke, separable and ought to be separated by devolving to the colonies the responsibility for local legislation. This devolution of power would show that the Imperial rights of Great Britain and the privileges of the colonists could be reconciled; they were 'just the most reconcilable things in the world',[10] and therefore Imperial supremacy was not dependent upon the centralization of all local functions in the Imperial Parliament. What Burke had shown was the possibility of two political communities, the one being supreme and the other subordinate, with the supreme authority retaining its Imperial power while the subordinate community enjoyed practical autonomy.

It was not, however, necessary to rely on the beliefs of political philosophers for a solution to the problem of reconciling Irish demands within an Imperial framework. Nor was it necessary to look for the solution in terms of abstract principles of government. For other countries had attempted to deal with the same problem— indeed the 'Last half-century (is) rich in lessons' whereby 'Unity not only preserved but strengthened':[11] and Gladstone cited the cases of Sweden and Norway and Austria-Hungary, as examples of countries which remained united without a common legislature.

If such a solution could be attempted in the case of these countries, then *a fortiori*, it would be possible for Britain which had '*greater advantages*'. For 'If two independent and nearly equal States can, by the expedient of autonomy, be made to work as an organic unity, how much slighter must be the strain, where there is no question of constitutional independence, and where in the last resort the superior Parliament retains the power to solve any and every controversy between them in such manner as it may think fit.'[12]

These advantages had been exploited in granting responsible government in the Colonies, in Canada, and in the Australian and South African states, where the concession of local parliaments had, as Burke predicted, served to retain the Imperial connection and to lessen grievances. The British North America Act of 1867 establishing the Confederation of Canada yielded an example 'not parallel' but 'analogous. It is strictly and substantially analogous,'[13] and the great lesson of Imperial history was that 'forcing uniformity and centralizing authority have caused severance', while 'local independence and legislative severance' had maintained union.[14]

Irish Home Rule was thus based upon principles that had already been applied in Britain's Imperial relations; it offered the same remedy as had been adopted in Canada. It was a policy 'especially founded on history and tradition', which aimed 'in the main at restoring, not at altering the Empire'[15] for it was an undoubted fact that . . . 'the creation of such legislatures had in certain cases been an instrument, not of dismembering, but of consolidating Empire.'[16] It was for these reasons the policy of an Imperialist and not of a Little Englander, and a policy which 'Surely . . . has high titles to a conservative character.' For 'it is a policy which, instead of innovating, restores; which builds upon the ancient foundations of Irish history and tradition; which by making power local, makes it congenial, where hitherto it has been unfamiliar, almost alien; and strong, where hitherto it has been weak. Let us extricate the question from the low mist of the hour, let us raise the banner clear of the smoke of battle, and we shall see that such a policy is eminently a conservative policy.'[17] It was conservatism of this kind that Gladstone had noticed in his mentor Peel, as 'the conviction that it is possible to adjust the noble and ancient institutions of this country to the wants and necessities of this unquiet time, without departure from the fundamental principles, not which theory, but which history ascribes to them.'[18]

But, if the principle had already been applied successfully, what modifications in its application were necessary in the case of Ireland? The application could not be the same, since the crucial factor of distance meant that the Irish Parliament would inevitably lie in a different relationship to Westminster from that enjoyed by the Parliament of Canada or Victoria. Moreover, in view of the danger from a hostile Ireland in time of war, Britain would have to retain some powers, such as control of the army, which had been devolved to the self-governing colonies.

There were, therefore, precedents for Irish Home Rule, but they were not exact precedents, and a measure had to be devised taking into account the specific problems of Ireland. In particular, special care had to be taken to ensure that parliamentary supremacy was preserved. Admittedly the supremacy of the Imperial Legislature was for Gladstone 'Essentially unlimited. Cannot alienate.' Nevertheless, Parliament could constitute against itself an obligation of honour, as it had done, for example, when promising to respect existing Scottish legal and ecclesiastical institutions in the Acts of Union of 1707. Therefore the 'same care should be exercised in constituting such obligation of *honour* as if we gave away *powers*.'[19]

The method of the Colonial Acts had been to devolve power on a plenary basis to the colonies, without retaining any reserve powers at Westminster. Imperial supremacy was preserved not through the exercise of reserve powers, but through the use of the Lord Lieutenant's veto, and the Judicial Committee of the Privy Council, which would be a final Court of Appeal on the jurisdiction of the colonial government. Moreover the Colonial Laws Validity Act of 1865 contained a declaratory clause giving notice that the Imperial Parliament would not hesitate to use its powers to legislate for the colonies if it thought its supremacy was threatened.

Gladstone, however, sought to give Ireland self-government only in domestic affairs, and to reserve Imperial subjects to Westminster. Home Rule, therefore, involved a contract by which the Irish were pledged 'to an express admission of that supremacy by the same vote which accepted Local powers', and Gladstone thus required the Irish 'to accept as a satisfactory charter of Irish liberty a document which contained an express submission to Imperial power and a direct acknowledgement of Imperial unity.'[20] In addition to these weapons of veto and reservation of powers, each of the Home Rule Bills added further prohibitions to the exercise of devolved powers, the primary prohibition being on laws interfering with religious equality. By these moves, Gladstone sought to undermine still further the Unionist contention that home rule was incompatible with parliamentary supremacy; for if it had worked in subordinate communities such as Canada and the Australian states, communities which had been given larger powers than Ireland was to be granted, then *a fortiori*, it would work in Ireland; and if supremacy was consistent with a lesser degree of subordination to Westminster, it could certainly be maintained with a greater degree of subordination.

The problem remained of defining those Imperial rights necessary to be retained at Westminster. There had to be a 'Strict and thorough severance of Imperial from Local affairs.' A 'Reservation of the first' and 'transference of the second'. And this should be based 'On the principle of Trust—which is adverse to Exceptions.'[21] But what ought to be the extent of the reserved powers? Here, again, Gladstone looked to historical precedent. There were indeed two examples of constitutions based on a division of powers which would naturally have presented themselves to him. The first, the Constitution of the United States of America was unsuitable for his purposes, because it did not secure sufficient power to the federal government, and this deficiency had led to the recent Civil War.

But the second example, the division of power between the government of Canada and its constituent provinces, was of far more relevance, both because its aim, in deliberate contrast to the United States, had been to maintain the power of the centre at the expense of the provinces, and because it explicitly asserted the supremacy of the Dominion Parliament.

Gladstone, therefore, decided to reserve to the Imperial Parliament at Westminster those powers which the British North America Act had reserved to the Dominion Parliament in Canada, and Clause 3 of the 1886 Government of Ireland Bill is taken from Clause 90 of the British North America Act, enumerating the reserved powers of the Dominion Parliament. These reserved powers were of four kinds. First, matters relating to the Crown and Defence, secondly foreign and colonial relations, thirdly 'subjects reserved on practical grounds'[22] such as patents, copyright law, and contracts, and finally 'all power of protection and differential duties'.[23] Gladstone's original intention was to allow the Irish Parliament the power to retain other revenue duties, but the Cabinet decided to reserve this also, so that this final category entailed, by the time the Bill was presented to Parliament, the reservation to Westminster of Ireland's indirect taxation.

The Bill then blended two different constitutional models into something that was *sui generis*. The idea of a devolution of power to satisfy the principle of nationality was, as we have seen, based upon the model of colonial self-government, and especially upon the granting of responsible government to Canada. The particular division of powers governing devolution was based upon the federal-type division of powers between the Canadian provinces and the Dominion Parliament.

The Bill's complexity was, however, widely misunderstood amongst supporters and opponents alike. John Morley wrote to Gladstone in January 1887 that the object of the first Home Rule Bill had been 'to bestow on the Irish body the functions of provincial legislatures in Canada.'[24] Yet the Irish Parliament would in fact enjoy wider powers than these legislatures, and it would have all the powers not specifically reserved to Westminster. In the Canadian Constitution, by contrast, the powers of the provinces were specifically enumerated and the Dominion Parliament was given all residuary powers.

The opposite criticism was made by Joseph Chamberlain who argued that the Bill, instead of being based upon the federal principle, which he could have supported, was based upon the relationship of Britain to Canada, a relationship which in his view was inapplicable to Ireland. But, as we have seen, this criticism was misconceived since the Irish Parliament, in contrast to the Dominion Parliament of Canada, was not to have control of taxation, trade and commerce, or military or defence matters. The powers of the Irish Parliament, therefore, lay between the powers of the Dominion Parliament of Canada, and the powers of the provincial parliaments of Canada such as Ontario and Quebec.

It was indeed this double aspect of the Bill which laid it open to its most damaging criticisms, criticisms which might possibly have been avoided if a clear-cut choice between two constitutional models had been made, but at the cost perhaps of producing a model which did not fit the peculiar circumstances of Ireland.

The central distinction between the two models is clear enough. For the colonial model is marked by two features which distinguish it from the federal model; the first is that the colony is no longer represented in the Imperial Parliament; the second—seemingly a logical corollary—is that the colony is no longer taxed by the Imperial Parliament. In a federal relationship, on the other hand, the different units would continue to be represented in, and contribute a share of taxation to, the federal parliament. The difference between the two models corresponds to a difference in the degree of supremacy which the Imperial Parliament seeks to exercise.

In the first Home Rule Bill, Gladstone found that he could not obtain the colonial solution for Irish finance; for, since Ireland would be receiving the benefits of the reserved services which were being retained at Westminster, it was natural that she should be asked to contribute to the costs of these services. She would, therefore, unlike the colonies, have to pay what was known in the jargon of the times as an annual Imperial Contribution, and this would be a first charge on Ireland's expenditure.

But Gladstone also decided that Home Rule implied the removal of Irish members from Westminster, as in the colonial model. At this point, however, the hybrid scheme would clearly cause complications, since the Irish would be taxed by Westminster, even though they would not be represented there. In other words, the first Home Rule Bill raised the spectre of taxation without representation, a constitutional contradiction which had led to the separation of the American colonies.

II

In seeking to evaluate the strengths and weaknesses of Home Rule as a solution to the Irish problem, we must be careful not to overrate the importance of defects in the Bills themselves as causes of their failure. A full historical account would have to give considerable and perhaps preponderant weight to wider factors, and especially to changes in the intellectual climate at the end of the nineteenth century as Gladstonian Imperialism came to be superseded by an Imperialism based upon *Realpolitik:* nor should the factor of anti-Irish prejudice be minimized, for there is ample evidence to confirm the view of L. P. Curtis that 'what really killed Home Rule . . . was the Anglo-Saxon stereotype of the Irish Celt.'[25]

There is no doubt, however, that the first Home Rule Bill in particular displayed considerable faults of constitutional logic, faults which may well have played some part in its defeat, and which must also cast doubt on the frequently made assertion that Home Rule would have yielded a permanent settlement of the Irish question. The central defects of the Home Rule Bills were of three inter-related types. The first was the failure to find a solution to the problem of how Ireland was to be represented at Westminster after devolution, a failure which was logically unavoidable; the second was the failure to divide taxation powers in a way which would allow the authority of the U.K. Chancellor of the Exchequer to be combined with the financial independence of Ireland; and this was a failure that could have been avoided, although in practice it would have been difficult to avoid, since it resulted from the peculiar economic structure of Ireland; and finally there was the doubt whether the supremacy which Westminster was to retain could be practically vindicated: this doubt was one which followed directly from the hybrid nature of the Gladstonian proposals.

The exclusion of Irish members from Westminster in the first Home Rule Bill was, according to Joseph Chamberlain, 'not a technical point, but the symbol and flag of the controversy'.[26]

Taxation without representation would inevitably lead to separation, since Ireland would not tolerate a situation whereby tariff policy and foreign policy were decided at Westminster with Ireland not represented. Sooner or later, Ireland would demand control of these functions, and this would mean separation.

Gladstone faced what in his notes for his second reading speech in 1886, he called 'The double dilemma'.

'Ireland is to have a domestic legislature for Irish affairs. ∴. *Cannot come here for English or Scotch affairs*[27] . . . The one thing follows from the other. There cannot be a domestic legislature in Ireland, dealing with Irish affairs, and Irish Peers and Representatives sitting in Parliament at Westminster to take part in English and Scotch affairs.'[28]

Could Irish M.P.s be recalled, then, solely for reserved matters, i.e. United Kingdom affairs? This proposal, the so-called 'in and out' solution, Gladstone ruled out in 1886 for two reasons. First, he argued that the distinction between Imperial and non-Imperial affairs 'cannot be drawn, I believe it passes the wit of man'.[29] The problem was not perhaps so much one of drawing the distinction, however, for, after all, in dividing powers between London and Dublin the Bill did just that; but rather that the distinction once drawn would not really assist in the solution of the problem since any proposal to spend public money, whether on U.K. or on 'local' matters would compete in terms of priorities with any other proposal. Ireland would in practice require a subsidy by the United Kingdom Parliament if her standard of living was not to show a catastrophic decline after Home Rule, but the size of this subsidy would be directly dependent upon the amount of money which English and Scottish members decided to spend upon their own local priorities. Therefore the Irish standard of living would still depend upon decisions made in a forum from which she was excluded.

There was, however, an even more fundamental objection to the 'in and out' proposal. In his notes, Gladstone wrote that it was 'Impossible (because opinion touches responsibility)'.[30] It would bifurcate the government of the United Kingdom, since there might be one government with the Irish present, a Liberal/Irish Nationalist government; and a government of an opposite political complexion—a Conservative government—with the Irish absent. It would thus completely undermine the principle of collective responsibility according to which a government must stand or fall as a whole, and therefore command a majority on all the issues that come before Parliament, rather than just a particular selection of them.

Gladstone therefore came to the conclusion that 'Irish members *cannot ordinarily* sit in the Imperial Parliament.' This conclusion was also favoured by a number of positive considerations. For if Irish members were to be retained, there would be an immediate dispute about the numbers who should be retained. 'Great Britain would not tolerate 103—Ireland would fight against 40.' Moreover, 'Painful Parly relations of later years recommend a period of inter-mission.'[31] For other liberals, there were motives of a different kind. 'The great bribe to me', wrote Granville to Hartington in December 1885, 'and I expect to England and Scotland would be to get rid of the Irish M.P.s here, who are introducing the dry rot into our institutions.'[32] If the Irish remained, then, according to John Morley, 'there is no power on earth that can prevent the Irish members in such circumstances from being . . . the arbiters and the masters of English policy, of English legislative business and of the rise and fall of British Administration.'[33] Exclusion of the Irish members, however, left Gladstone impaled on the other horn of the dilemma.

'How then is Ireland to be taxed?'[34] The powers reserved to Westminster were, as we have seen, the Crown and defence, foreign and colonial relations, various subjects reserved on practical grounds, and indirect taxation. It was this last which caused Gladstone the most difficulty.

As regards the first category, the Crown and defence, Gladstone was forced to confess 'I do not see how to modify the Bill with any advantage.' On the second item, foreign and colonial relations 'the "sentiment" presses for a change. But how could Irish members, unless always here, be enabled to participate in dealing with a class of subjects which are mainly in the hands of private members, (at least I should say in proportion of twenty occasions against one) and perfectly uncertain as to the time and method of handling?' To deal with this problem, Gladstone made two suggestions, the first a series of 'Regular communications between the British and Irish Executives . . . Foreign policy is thus managed as between Sweden and Norway.' The second suggestion was the Austro-Hungarian model of a joint delegation or standing committee from the two Parliaments, with Ireland being represented 'in some reasonable proportion such as perhaps one third . . .'[35]

This still left the difficulty of how changes in indirect taxation which affected Ireland could be made without the Irish members. But here, too, Gladstone was not without resource. First, it could be argued that 'Ireland could not be said to be taxed without representation when her representatives agreed'[36] to the provisions of the Bill. But even so Gladstone was finally willing to concede that 'When the Government makes a proposal for the alteration or repeal of any tax now levied in Ireland by the authority of Parliament, or for the imposition of any new tax' the Irish members would be granted the right to return. They would also be granted the right to return if any alteration in the Home Rule settlement was in the offing, whether desired by Westminster or by the Irish legislatures.

It might seem at this stage as if Gladstone had now reached by a roundabout route the 'in and out' solution which he had earlier said was an impossible one, but his scheme contained an important difference. According to the 'in and out' proposal, the Irish would remain members at Westminster as of right, and with the right, therefore, to participate in parliamentary votes upon what issues were to count as reserved and what as transferred. On Gladstone's 1886 proposal, however, Irish representation was possible only at the discretion of Westminster. This would lessen the possibility of Irish political leverage being applied to the very question of what was to count as a reserved matter. The decision would be that of the English and Scottish members. Admittedly, there would still be 'some inconvenience in this, as there might be intrigues with the Irish to overthrow a ministry through its Budget.'

'But we know the worst of this inconvenience now. Since the Act of Union, I think that only two Ministries (one of them already in a minority) have been overthrown, i.e. driven out, on Budgets. These cases were in 1852 and 1885.'[37] Moreover, it could be argued that on what Gladstone called a 'question of class' the Irish members might be just as divided as the English and Scottish, and that 'On any question of national interest, say of altering the organic statute (in points withheld from the Irish Chamber) . . . they would still require over 260 British M.P.s' to win a majority and 'It would not seem very unjust that they should gain their point when Ireland was unanimous on a matter primarily affecting her, or was supported by more than $^5/_{12}$ of the British representatives.'[38]

In this way, Gladstone managed to preserve some semblance of consistency in his proposals for Irish representation, but only at the cost of bringing over the Irish members to Westminster on what the jurist Anson called 'a sort of imperial or financial excursion'.[39] One cannot claim that it would not have worked; but one can claim that it would have required a great deal of goodwill and mutual forbearance on both sides if it was to work.

The alternative to exclusion or to the 'in and out' solution, which was adopted at the committee stage of the 1893 Bill, and in the 1912 Bill, was to allow the Irish to continue to attend at Westminster, and to be able to vote on all matters, but to attend in reduced numbers. This, however, raised the objection that Irish members would be deciding upon English and Scottish affairs while English and Scottish M.P.s would have no say in the domestic affairs of Ireland. The reduction of the number of Irish M.P.s was of little help in strict constitutional logic, since, as Harcourt pointed out to Gladstone in 1889, 'though it may lessen the *amount* it does not really touch the *principle* of the objection. When parties are pretty equally divided fifty Irish votes may be as decisive as 100 . . . and when you have once conceded the objection to Irish interference you don't get rid of it any more than the young woman did of the baby by saying it's such a little one.'[40]

Retention of the Irish members would deprive Britain of one of the principal advantages which she hoped to gain from Home Rule, namely the possibility of devoting more parliamentary time to the discussion of English and Scottish affairs, and less time to the Irish question. Indeed, the Irish M.P.s might prove to be just as unreasonable in a post-Home Rule Westminster as they had in the early 1880s. For they would continually be tempted to regard themselves, not as representatives of the United Kingdom, but as agents or delegates of the Irish legislature to the British Parliament. This meant that Irish issues would be fought out first in Dublin, and then at Westminster. The House of Commons would, perforce, have to re-assume the role of arbiter of Irish problems.

The retention of Irish members was thought necessary after 1886 as an 'outward and visible sign of Imperial supremacy', and Gladstone came to the conclusion that it was 'a matter of great public importance because it visibly exhibits that supremacy'.[41] But, if the Irish members were to regard themselves as agents or delegates of another legislature, retention would introduce an odd element of federalism, or even of confederalism, into the unitary structure at Westminster.

It is hardly surprising, then, that Gladstone told Parnell in 1889 that 'the real difficulty' still lay 'in determining the particular form in which an Irish representation may have to be retained at Westminster.'[42] For each of the answers to the problem of Irish representation—exclusion, 'in and out', and retention with reduced representation—suffered from crucial weaknesses. These weaknesses were unavoidable in principle resulting as they did from the attempt to graft federal or quasi-federal elements on to a fundamentally unitary constitution. This does not mean that a solution was not *practically* possible; for the survival of constitutions does not depend upon logic. What it does mean, however, is that the Gladstonian settlement would have contained many points of possible friction, so that if the potential for serious conflict still existed between Britain and Ireland, there would be no shortage of occasions for displaying that conflict. It must, therefore, be a matter for political judgement whether any of the solutions proposed would have seriously modified the causes of dispute between Britain and Ireland.

III

The attempt to discover workable and fair financial arrangements led to difficulties at least as serious as those involved in the parliamentary representation of Ireland after Home Rule. Gladstone laid down as one of the conditions of a good plan of Home Rule that there be a fair and equitable division of the financial burden. But what was Ireland's fair contribution to U.K. revenue, and how was it to be assessed? All three Home Rule Bills required a payment from Ireland in the form of an 'Imperial Contribution' to cover the cost of Ireland's share of the reserved services. It was vital, therefore, to form an estimate of what the cost of this share might be.

Unfortunately, however, there seemed no objective way of determining this sum and disagreement tended to reflect national interests with the Irish arguing that the sum required from them was excessive. Their case was that the Imperial Contribution should 'be measured by the only genuine test—how much can Ireland spare?'[43] It should be a residual and not a first charge on Irish revenue, to be paid after Ireland's local needs had been met. The difficulty with this case, however, was that the residual element would rapidly shrink to nothing since the Irish legislature would understandably seek to use its financial resources for the purposes of economic development, rather than the payment of tribute to Britain. The Irish members, indeed, submitted the argument that Ireland should be entitled to some special consideration on account of over-taxation in the past. One of the Nationalist members, Tim Healy, went so far as to suggest in January 1893 that Britain should make reparation for her ill-treatment of Ireland by not asking for an Imperial Contribution at all, a proposal which the *Economist* on 7 January 1893 dubbed 'an impudent request'.

These problems of relative taxable capacity and historic obligation were, almost certainly, 'insoluble, not in the sense that no answer to them is possible, but because so many plausible answers are possible that the number of solutions threatens to equal the number of solvers.'[44] Nevertheless, if the Imperial Contribution was fixed at a reasonable level, Irish revenue would be insufficient to meet her basic requirements; and, to quote Healy in the *Economist* again, if the Irish legislature began by saying 'We will have to impose a new tax', then, 'he would say that the members of that Parliament would deserve to be hissed out of the country.'

Gladstone, of course, was on the side of financial retrenchment. For him, one of the advantages of Home Rule was that it would stimulate economies in public expenditure. He would have agreed with the comments made by his former secretary Sir Edward Hamilton in 1893 that, after Home Rule, 'Great Britain being rid of an expensive partner will be no longer subject to the constantly growing demands of Ireland on the common purse . . .'[45] For Gladstone, the value of any financial scheme would lie, therefore, in the inducements to economy which it offered both to Westminster and to the Irish legislature. He was thus disposed to be rather inflexible to the Irish claim that a Home Rule Parliament would require further revenue, in order to improve the condition of Irish education, railways, etc. 'If the Irishmen don't like my proposals', he told Hamilton in 1893, 'they must lump it. The question for them is whether they will have Home Rule with my finance or no Home Rule.' It is not surprising that Hamilton wrote in his diary of Home Rule as 'the dissolution of a partnership in which the partner with no capital and most spendthrift habits was leaving the firm'.[46]

There was thus, from the beginning, a source of conflict over the financial arrangements by virtue of the difficulty of assessing what was a fair Irish contribution to U.K. revenues. The Irish members argued that each of the Home Rule Bills required them to contribute too much; while the British taxpayer could legitimately argue that he was wrongly being required to subsidize Irish autonomy; to him, the Irish seemed to want the benefits of self-government without wishing also to accept the corollary of total financial independence.

There was a further difficulty implicit in the financial arrangements. How precisely ought the taxing power to be divided so as to reconcile Irish autonomy with the freedom of the U.K. Chancellor of the Exchequer to manage the country's fiscal affairs. According to Sir Robert Hamilton, 'no settlement will be accepted as satisfactory to the Irish people',[47] which did not give to the Irish Parliament the power to raise its own revenue. Therefore the taxing power would have to be divided. However, three-quarters of Irish revenue was derived from Customs and Excise duties; could these duties be devolved? In 1886, Gladstone was perfectly prepared to do so, but he was unable to carry his Cabinet with him. 'I feel confident', Gladstone's Home Secretary Hugh Childers argued, 'that English and Scottish public opinion will never tolerate any plan which gives to an Irish Legislature power to impose Customs duties, to make Ireland a 'Foreign country' and trade with Ireland 'Foreign trade''.[48] Britain was a Free Trade country, and on ideological as well as material grounds would be unwilling to countenance a Protectionist Irish legislature. Yet many Irish Nationalists were coming round to the view that a tariff would be needed to stimulate economic development in Ireland.

The devolution of Customs would also mean that the Irish model of Home Rule would be incapable of becoming a model for

Scottish or Welsh Home Rule as part of the grand federal recon-
struction that some Liberals had in mind; and, indeed, it conflicted
with Gladstone's assertion that it was not 'allowable to deal with
Ireland upon any principle, the benefit of which could not be
allowed to Scotland in circumstances of equal and equally clear
desire.'[49] Moreover if Ireland was given the power to impose tariffs
against Britain and to make commercial treaties with foreign
countries, not only was this inconsistent with a federal arrangement,
but it meant that there would hardly be any state left at all.
Therefore Customs and Excise duties were retained in all of the
Home Rule Bills.

But this meant that the Irish Parliament had control of only
one-quarter of total Irish revenue. Of this quarter, a further quarter
came from the Post Office, and it was difficult to change postal
rates to any significant extent; of the remainder, roughly half was
derived from income tax. This, too, was a form of revenue which it
would be difficult to raise without being 'hissed out of the country'.
It seemed, therefore, that the structure of the Irish revenue and the
parameters of the Home Rule Bills imposed strict limitations upon
the degree of practical autonomy which Ireland might enjoy.

On both of these contentious issues—the value of the Imperial
Contribution, and the division of the taxing power—the Liberals
found themselves at odds with their Irish allies. An Irish legislature,
therefore, would certainly have done its best to reform the financial
part of the Home Rule settlement, which it would have been
unlikely to regard as final. Here also the goodwill which Home
Rule might engender would be vitiated by a continuing dispute
over finance. It would be unlikely to satisfy Gladstone's criterion
for the success of Home Rule that it be in the nature of 'a settlement,
and not of a mere provocation to the revival of fresh demands.'[50]

As with the arrangements for the parliamentary representation
of the Irish, Gladstone strove hard to overcome the financial
difficulties. In the 1886 Bill, he sought to circumvent the problem
of ascertaining Ireland's true revenue with all the ammunition for
discord which that involved. The first Home Rule Bill required
Ireland to pay a fixed proportion of a specific sum—namely
one-fifteenth of total Imperial expenditure i.e. expenditure on
reserved services in 1886. This was to be a first charge on the
Irish Exchequer. All other revenue collected in Ireland was to be

the property of the Irish Exchequer, whether or not it was properly contributed by Ireland. Moreover, the sum of one-fifteenth of total Imperial expenditure in 1886 was to remain fixed for thirty years — it was not to alter with variations in U.K. revenue, and it could only be changed by agreement between the Irish legislature and Westminster. The fixing of a maximum Imperial contribution flowed from the fact that, since Ireland would no longer be represented at Westminster, she would have no means of checking increases in Imperial expenditure, and therefore should not be made liable for such increases. These arrangements would, so it was hoped, provide Ireland with a surplus on her domestic account of £404,000, which would be sufficient for her to begin self-government with a margin to spare for necessary domestic expenditure.

Unfortunately, however, this arrangement would have led to serious difficulties for both Britain and Ireland, even apart from the fact that Parnell regarded the surplus of £404,000 as grossly insufficient, believing that a surplus of at least £1¼m. was necessary. For the U.K. Chancellor would be able to make no change in indirect taxation without disrupting Irish financial arrangements. If the Chancellor in his Budget raised customs duties, Ireland would enjoy a windfall benefit, while if the Chancellor lowered duties, she would suffer an unexpected loss.

Considering first the example of a lowering of duties, Irish revenue would fall, but she would still have to meet a fixed Imperial Contribution. The Irish government, therefore, would either have to accept a drastic reduction in its public spending, or it would have to budget for a sharp rise in Irish direct taxation which, we must remember, constituted less than one-quarter of Ireland's total revenue. Some idea of the magnitude involved is given when it is realized that a repeal of the tea duties would require a 40 per cent rise in Irish direct taxation to compensate. This would have compelled Ireland to raise her rate of income tax from sixpence to one shilling, despite the fact that Irish domestic needs would not require such an increase.

To Ireland, therefore, it might seem as if Britain was compelling the payment of a tribute while at the same time disrupting Ireland's budget through her fiscal policy. England and Ireland, therefore, would be 'brought into direct hostile collision. The rich English government appears in the light of an imperious creditor, the Irish

Government stands in the position of a poverty-stricken debtor'.[51]

In the alternative case, if Britain raised customs duties, Ireland would find herself with a windfall benefit, and revenue which she did not require. She might attempt to deal with the situation by lowering direct taxation; but this would be socially regressive, since the poor would be paying higher duties on consumption goods, whilst the rich would be relieved of income tax. Ireland would thus have forced upon her firstly a revolution in her financial arrangements which she would not want, and secondly 'a ratio between direct and indirect taxation which might be both financially unsound and socially harmful'.[52] The Irish legislature, therefore, would be bound to complain whenever the U.K. government altered indirect taxation, because it would ruin the financial calculations of the Irish Chancellor. Direct taxation, which was seemingly under Irish control, would not really be so because it would vary inversely with variations in indirect taxation.

Nor would the British budget be in a healthier situation. Suppose an increase in the cost of Imperial services meant that she required more revenue. If this revenue were to be obtained through increasing direct taxation, Ireland would be making no contribution towards it. Nor would the Irish necessarily respond to a patriotic appeal from the U.K. Government to raise direct taxation given, as Harcourt rather delicately put it, 'the ethical and patriotic temperament of the men with whom we have to deal'.[53] Therefore, to ensure that Ireland made a proportionate contribution, the revenue would have to be sought through raising Customs duties, a difficult option for a Liberal and Free Trade government to accept.

The financial scheme of 1886, therefore, would probably not have worked very well in practice. It would have involved constant financial conflict between the British and Irish Parliaments, since their finances would be hopelessly intertwined. It both restricted the freedom of the U.K. Chancellor, and eroded Irish financial autonomy almost to non-existence.

This dilemma was inevitable in any financial scheme unless it either gave to Ireland control of Customs—and this was ruled out in 1886—or alternatively credited Britain with Irish customs duties and treated the sum raised through Customs as the Imperial Contribution. This second method—the crediting of Britain with

Irish customs—was adopted in 1893. For if Irish customs, but not excise, was credited to Britain, this would provide a reasonable Imperial Contribution, and also leave Ireland with a surplus of £½m. This scheme had the great advantage of being easy to comprehend, and it meant that customs duties, attribution of which it was difficult to assign precisely, were retained as U.K. taxes. It could, moreover, be regarded as a development of existing practice, rather than an innovation, since Goschen's scheme of local government finance had required central government to pay the local authorities the proceeds from various specified taxes. For these reasons this proposal seemed to the Primrose Committee on Irish Finance which reported in 1911, the best that had been produced, because 'it would have provided a clear-cut line of demarcation between Imperial and Irish finance', and it did not require reference to the insoluble problems of relative taxable capacity or historic obligation.[54]

Unfortunately this scheme too was not without its defects. For it made the size of the Imperial Contribution almost fortuitous, dependent as it was upon the fiscal policy of the U.K. Government. Under a Free Trade Chancellor such as Harcourt, Ireland would reap an uncovenanted gain. For it was Harcourt's aim to secure a 'free breakfast table' by reducing the duty on commodities such as tea, while recouping the revenue through death duties. Ireland would then obtain the entire benefit of the reduction of tea duty while contributing nothing via death duties towards U.K. taxation. The Irishman would thus have cheaper tea at the expense of the English taxpayer. It is little wonder that Harcourt wrote to Gladstone, 'I plainly foresee that either the Budget will kill the Irish finance, or the Irish finance will kill the Budget.'[55] For Ireland's contribution would vary inversely with the Free Trade predilections of the U.K. Chancellor.

It would, however, be futile to speculate further on how this objection might have been met, since the original scheme had to be withdrawn, after 'an enormous error' was discovered 'in the computation of the Excise revenue due to Ireland and Great Britain respectively.'[56] The effect of this error was to lessen the Irish surplus from £½m. to £140,000, a sum which would have been insufficient for Ireland's domestic expenditure. This scheme was therefore dropped in committee.

A second scheme was proposed at the committee stage of the Bill. This was similar to that of 1886, except that it required Ireland to pay a variable rather than a fixed charge, equivalent to one-third of Irish revenue. It was thus open to many of the objections involved in the 1886 scheme, and had the further disadvantage of requiring an estimate to be formed of Ireland's true revenue, and this problem as we have seen was likely to prove insoluble.

By 1912, the expansion of public services was placing considerable strain upon Irish domestic accounts, which were now in deficit; and the deficit could be expected to increase with the further development of the Welfare State. If Ireland had been an independent country, she would not have been able to afford, for example, an old-age pension scheme on the British model; she would either have had to do without such a scheme entirely, or, alternatively, pay old-age pensions at a reduced rate.

If the Irish account, however, was in deficit, there could be no question of an Imperial Contribution being required from her. For if an Irish Parliament was not to be saddled with such liabilities as would make an increase in taxation its first legislative measure, the British taxpayer would be required to subsidize even her domestic services as well as her share of the reserved services for some years to come, if not in perpetuity. This meant that 'a material change in the attitude of the British taxpayer towards the question will have to be reckoned with'.[57] For here the anomaly of Ireland enjoying the unique status of self-government within the United Kingdom at the expense of the British taxpayer would tend to put him on the alert; and it would become impossible to grant Ireland any large measure of financial autonomy for as long as her domestic accounts were in deficit.

Liberal statesmen did not, then, succeed in discovering a financial settlement which could both have underwritten Irish autonomy and avoided conflict between the two legislatures. What militated against such a solution was, as we have seen, the peculiar structure of the Irish economy, in particular her dependence upon Customs and Excise duties for the bulk of her revenue. This meant that the only way to give Ireland real financial autonomy was to give her control of Customs as Gladstone had originally proposed. For only in this way would the financial provisions of Home Rule have been in line with the aim of the policy itself which was to secure 'freedom

within its own sphere for Irish nationality'. As we have seen,
however, such a proposal was unacceptable to most Liberals, and
in particular to two groups of Liberals whose support was essential
to the passing of Home Rule: the first comprised those who hoped
that a scheme for Scottish Home Rule could be constructed on the
Irish model, and the second those who hoped that Irish Home
Rule might be the prelude to a grand measure of federal recon-
struction of the United Kingdom. For these Liberals, Irish Home
Rule was a means to a wider reform of government; but it is not
clear whether such a wider reform could have recognized the
special and pressing claims arising from Irish nationality which
formed the rationale of Irish Home Rule.

IV

For Gladstonians and Unionists alike, the supremacy of Parliament
was the central principle of British government, the constitutional
cement which held the U.K. together. Indeed as we have seen
Gladstone believed that the supremacy of Parliament offered
Britain positive advantages in meeting Irish claims; since, if
Westminster's authority could be retained, there would be more
effective government than was possible in a state consisting of two
co-ordinate legislatures, as in Austria-Hungary after 1867; or in a
state where the centre was too weak to assert itself as in the United
States. Where a written constitution would merely constrain the
process of political evolution, parliamentary supremacy allowed
more flexible arrangements to be pursued.

Gladstone therefore argued that the supremacy of Parliament
formed an essential pre-condition for a successful plan of Home
Rule; although, since he also held that parliamentary supremacy
was something inalienable, 'and is in itself incapable of being
surrendered or impaired',[58] this pre-condition may not have
foreclosed his options by very much. Unionists believed that,
insofar as supremacy was retained at all, it was supremacy of a
nebulous and attenuated kind, such as could not be enforced by the
U.K. government.

For there is considerable ambiguity in the notion of 'the
supremacy of Parliament'. It can be interpreted in two different
ways. It might mean that supremacy corresponding to a real

exercise of political authority which Parliament enjoyed in relation to the United Kingdom; but it might also mean the more nominal, although not wholly nominal, degree of supremacy which Parliament held over the self-governing colonies such as Canada and the Australian States. Nor is the ambiguity resolved by substituting the phrase 'the integrity of the Empire' which Gladstone frequently used as synonymous with the supremacy of Parliament, for 'the integrity of the Empire' was frequently used in those days to mean the integrity of the United Kingdom, just as the Imperial Parliament was a synonym for the U.K. Parliament.

This ambiguity corresponded very largely to a difference in interpretation between the English Liberals and Irish Nationalists as to the meaning of Home Rule. For Parnell and Redmond the supremacy which the U.K. Parliament should exercise over Ireland after Home Rule should be a dormant supremacy, very like that exercised over Canada; for if it was a real supremacy implying the possibility of the regular intervention of the superior power, the Irish would find it irksome as something hardly compatible with their sense of nationality.

But, as we have seen, Liberals did not intend to allow the Irish so great a degree of autonomy; for the self-governing colonies were, for most practical purposes, completely autonomous by 1886. They enjoyed, for example, the power to establish their own tariffs; and, since 1862, they had been responsible for their own defence arrangements. Therefore, Liberal governments decided not to follow the Canadian precedent but to reserve certain subjects to Westminster; and that is why the financial arrangements had to be made to reflect the necessity of Ireland paying an Imperial Contribution to cover her share of the cost of these reserved services. But how were these provisions to be enforced when Britain and Ireland were divided by two such different conceptions of the precise degree of governmental authority that was being conceded? 'It was not treating the House fairly,' claimed Viscount Cranborne, 'to treat it as the Prime Minister did, and to try and persuade two Parties, which absolutely differed as to their conception of what the supremacy ought to be, to vote for the Bill on these vague generalities of the inalienable supremacy of Parliament.'[59]

After Home Rule, the U.K. government would be morally, if not legally, under an obligation of honour not to legislate for Ireland, or to alter the terms of Home Rule itself without the consent of the Irish members. The veto power which was the symbol of supremacy was not therefore an instrument for normal use, but something to be exercised only in an emergency. In effect, therefore, Parliament would be unable to exert its supremacy when this involved control over Irish domestic affairs. For as long as Home Rule worked normally, the Irish legislature would be a co-ordinate and not a subordinate body.

Nevertheless, even in an emergency, difficulties would arise since the administration of the laws of Ireland would be handed over to the Irish Government. It might well be that the Lord Lieutenant would find himself unable to secure an Irish administration commanding a majority in the Irish legislature, except one which insisted on overriding the Imperial veto. For this reason Sir Michael Hicks-Beach argued that 'the safeguards in the Bill are absolutely unreal. There is not one of them that is not at the complete mercy of the very persons against whom they are devised, and, for my part, if this measure were ever unhappily to become law, I would infinitely sooner see it without any of these safeguards at all, in the interests of our own honesty, rather than that we should pretend to retain powers which we know very well in practice we could not exercise.'[60] The situation would be aggravated if Irish members were retained at Westminster since they would be likely to act as a pressure group on behalf of the Irish legislature, and prevent Westminster's veto ever being used.

After Home Rule, therefore, there would be only two ways in which the U.K. government could secure compliance with its wishes—agreement and force; and agreement with the Irish, although more necessary after Home Rule, would also be more difficult, since Ireland, having as it were a corporate existence, would be in a far stronger position than when the Bill was enacted. Self-government worked in the colonies since they were generally content with their constitutions; and they were peopled mainly with settlers of British descent, who had little desire to separate from Britain; but, in any case, they knew that if they genuinely sought separation, it would probably not be refused them. With the Irish, however, none of these conditions were met. They were not entirely happy with their constitution; they sought revision of the financial clauses; and they would seek to use their representation at Westminster to exact further concessions for Dublin. They were therefore in a stronger position than the colonists to enforce their demands, but Westminster was unlikely to countenance separation except as a last resort. Yet, as the Primrose Committee remarked, 'there is no means, short of the employment of force in the last resort, by which an independent legislature or executive can be compelled to do something positive against its will.'[61] Would the U.K. government be able or willing to enforce its supremacy when it had devolved the judiciary and the police into Irish hands? If not, Home Rule, instead of ending the age-old conflict between Britain and Ireland, might well have multiplied both the grounds and the opportunity for further collisions.

V

The seemingly insuperable difficulties involved in any scheme of Irish Home Rule led some politicians to argue that only a 'federal solution' could reconcile the demands of Irish Nationalists with the requirements of parliamentary supremacy; meaning by federalism not a division of powers on the American model but federal devolution, the creation of a number of assemblies throughout the country, each one being strictly subordinate to Westminster.

This solution was proposed by Joseph Chamberlain in 1886 as an alternative to Home Rule, and in the years before the First World War, his son Austen attempted, on the whole unsuccessfully, to convert the Conservative Party to the idea. But many leading Liberals such as Lord Rosebery and Churchill were sympathetic to federalism, and indeed the first draft of the 1912 Home Rule Bill proposed the creation of Parliaments for England, Scotland, and Wales as well as Ireland. This part of the Bill was deleted at the request of the Irish Nationalists who saw the claims of Ireland as being prior and urgent, but nevertheless in introducing it into the Commons, Asquith spoke of it as 'only the first step in a larger and more comprehensive policy'.

Federalism thus offered the prospect of solving the Irish question by consent, rather than through an increasingly divisive party conflict. Unionists might prefer it to an Irish Home Rule Bill which they saw as separatist; and Liberals might accept it if it would pre-empt Conservative and Ulster Unionist opposition. In the view of the Conservative propagandist, F. S. Oliver, federalism represented 'the only solution of the Irish question, because it is the only means which enables nationalists to realize their ideal of Irish unity, while allowing unionists to keep inviolate the Union of the Three Kingdoms.'[62]

But federalism also offered solutions to the three constitutional problems associated with Home Rule which we have discussed. The creation of Parliaments for England, Scotland, and Wales would solve the problem of how Ireland was to be represented after Home Rule, since Westminster would become a federal Parliament, and the Irish would be represented in it on exactly the same terms as the other nationalities comprising the federal state. At the same time, federalism might help to secure a more equitable division of financial power between the various parts of the state, since each of the Parliaments would be given the same taxing powers.

Above all, however, federalism could preserve parliamentary supremacy and avert separatism, since it gave to Ireland nothing which was not also given to other parts of the United Kingdom. Speaking in the House of Commons debate on devolution in 1919, the geographer Halford Mackinder claimed that Joseph Chamberlain, in putting forward the federal idea

saw that there was safety in numbers. In the number of subordinate Parliaments there is safety, for the majority of subordinate Parliaments will be able to exercise restraint on the recalcitrant Parliament that would cut itself adrift or otherwise misbehave.[63]

This in turn might serve to conciliate Ulster which, instead of being deprived of her membership of the United Kingdom, would have it confirmed. It was for this reason that Sir Edward Carson, leader of the Ulster Unionists, argued in the same debate, 'I do not believe that devolution is a step towards separation. Indeed, I am not sure that devolution, if properly carried out, may not lead to closer union . . .'.[64] Since the Ulster issue had become by 1914 the main point of conflict between Liberals and Conservatives—a conflict which nearly led to civil war—any proposal which might succeed in preventing this terrible outcome was surely worthy of serious attention.

Yet it is easy to understand how the federal solution remained a constitutionalists's creation which was never translated into the realm of practical politics. The most obvious objection to it was that it gave to England a constitution she did not want, in order to retain Nationalist Ireland, which repudiated federalism, within the United Kingdom.

Speaking in the debate on the 1886 Home Rule Bill, Healy rejected the federal solution and quoted what a former Liberal Secretary for Ireland, W. E. Forster, had said to him in 1875:

You want a Constitution for Ireland; but you have no right to force a paper constitution upon us. You want Home Rule for Ireland for 5,000,000 people; but why should you expect that Englishmen should change a Constitution for England which we wish not to change.[65]

For there was in England no popular pressure of any kind calling for the creation of an English Parliament. 'After all,' argued Lloyd George when the federal option was put to him after the First World War, 'here is a population of 34,000,000 out of 45,000,000, and unless you have got a substantial majority of the English representatives in favour of it, it is idle to attempt it.'[66] Indeed, such little demand as did exist arose not because it was thought that an English Parliament would improve the government of England, but because it would solve the Irish question: it would, however, be difficult to persuade an English electorate that it should support the introduction of a completely new constitution, simply to conciliate the Irish.

There was, moreover, considerable doubt as to whether a federal solution would actually succeed in placating the Irish Nationalists. For they demanded not federalism but a form, admittedly ill-defined, of national self-government. The demands made by the Nationalists in 1886, in particular their request to be given the power to tax imports from England, showed that they wanted powers which were hardly compatible with a federal solution. When Parnell claimed that 'An Irish custom-house is really of more importance to Ireland than an Irish parliament',[67] he was asking for something which it was difficult to concede within a federal framework.

A federal system required each of the units within it to display at least as much loyalty to the Imperial Parliament at Westminster as would be necessary in a unitary state. Indeed, it probably required a greater degree of loyalty. For, as thinkers so different as Bagehot and Dicey had frequently pointed out, a federal system of government was more difficult to operate satisfactorily than a unitary system. Where a number of units were required to co-operate to secure successful government, friction was even more likely than in a state where there was only one strong central unit of government.

A Federal Government is, of all constitutions, the most artificial. If such a government is to be worked with anything like success, there must exist among the citizens of the confederacy a spirit of genuine loyalty to the Union. The 'Unitarian' feeling of the people must distinctly predominate over the sentiment in favour of 'state rights'.[68]

But in the case of the relationship between England and Ireland, England, the largest state in the United Kingdom, did not desire 'state rights' while Ireland, if the Nationalists were to be believed, were not enamoured of union.

The federal solution offered to the Irish the same opportunities for disrupting English and Scottish affairs in a new federal Parliament at Westminster as they had used so successfully since 1880. For Irish M.P.s, moreover, the federal parliament would be seen as an English Parliament since, on grounds of population, England would be bound to enjoy a powerful preponderance within it. If Irish M.P.s were to play the same role in the federal Parliament that they had played at Westminster hitherto, the result would not be pleasing to English statesmen. As Dicey observed, 'A sick man fears to lose a limb; he will not be greatly consoled by the assurance that his arm may be retained at the risk of his suffering general paralysis.'[69]

The federal solution thus suffered from the double drawback that most of those whom it was intended to benefit did not want it; while most Unionists believed that it would weaken the government of the United Kingdom without solving the Irish problem. Moreover, the introduction of a federal system of government for Britain would be bound to delay the introduction of Home Rule for Ireland; and yet, to practical Liberal politicians, there was a considerable difference in the relative urgency of the two proposals. Ireland's condition seemed desperate, requiring an immediate solution, and the Nationalists were certainly not willing to wait while a larger scheme was being constructed, whereas the British system of government, whatever its theoretical defects, seemed perfectly tolerable to all but a few. Considerable care would have to be taken to work out an appropriate scheme of federal government, and convert the British electorate to an appreciation of its necessity. Far from leading to consensus, therefore, federalism would probably stimulate as much debate and conflict as Home Rule. It would hardly be a non-controversial measure which could secure parliamentary sanction after a few weeks' discussion.

The difficulties of federalism were graphically illustrated by the Conference on devolution,[70] convened under the chairmanship of the Speaker of the House of Commons, in 1919. This Conference was set up in the immediate post-war period when the urge to achieve a final settlement of the Irish problem coincided with anxiety at the vastly increased responsibilities of government, to yield an intellectual movement in favour of federalism. But the Conference failed to reach agreement on any particular scheme of federal devolution, and when Lloyd George's government decided to deal separately with the Irish problem, the political dynamic which might have led to federalism entirely disappeared.

Lord Salisbury was perhaps being excessively hard-headed when he wrote in April 1889 to a correspondent who had urged the federal solution upon him. 'As to Home Rule in your sense—which is Federation—I do not see in it any elements of practicability. Nations do not change their political nature like that except through blood.'[71] Federalism might have been made acceptable to the British electorate if it could have been presented as a remedy for clearly perceived and deeply felt political grievances. In the absence of a fully worked-out critique of government, however, it was bound to appear remote and impractical.

VI

Liberal statesmen never succeeded in their self-appointed task of reconstructing the constitutional relationship between Britain and Ireland. Their failure resulted from the peculiar circumstances in which Ireland was placed, and from the very nature of the Irish national demand. Gladstone sought to reconcile Ireland to the British connection by winning her goodwill, and securing a 'Union of Hearts'. Whether he would have been successful, therefore, depended less perhaps on the constitutional logic of Home Rule than upon whether the state of Irish opinion was such that Britain could still secure her allegiance to the Union. We may remember that when Gladstone recognized Irish nationality as a factor with which government had to deal, he saw it as a purely local patriotism which was compatible with the British connection; it was a patriotism like that of Scotland or Wales, and therefore consistent with membership of the United Kingdom. Had that been the case, then the degree of consensus and goodwill required to work a system of government based upon the division of powers might well have been present. But, if Irish nationality was something rather different from Scottish or Welsh nationality, if it represented a nationalism fuelled by 'a thirst for revenge . . . that hatred, that undying hatred, for what they could not but regard as the cause and symbol of their misfortunes—English rule in Ireland',[72] then the attempt to corral it was doomed to failure. It was, to change the metaphor, an attempt to mix oil and water.

The truth is that the Liberals no less than the Conservatives were Unionists, in the sense that they sought to develop a system of constitutional rules and practices by which Ireland could be kept within the United Kingdom. They differed not on the necessity of the Union, but on the more subsidiary issue of whether the existing relationship of Ireland within the Union was a tolerable one.

Yet any scheme of Home Rule which a Liberal government was likely to propose, or the British people to accept, was bound to fall short of what Irish Nationalists demanded, even if only in symbolic terms—and of course these symbolic issues are often of the utmost importance in the relations between governments. For any scheme of Home Rule was bound to display and indeed to make explicit Ireland's practical subordination to the United Kingdom from which the Irish wished to escape. Lord Thring, for example, arguing that true federalism was very different from Home Rule, claimed that 'federation between the dominant head of the Empire and a *subordinate community* is a contradiction in terms, and never was dreamt of by the framers of the Home Rule Bill.'[73] (My italics.) But Ireland, unlike Canada, was not prepared to accept the status of a subordinate community, because her relationship to Britain was marked by hostility and not friendship.

To the student of governmental relationships, therefore, the long and fruitless saga of Irish Home Rule shows the truth of the theorem that 'no scheme of Devolution is likely to satisfy a demand for self-government prompted by national sentiment'. The Home

Rule Bills 'attempted to solve a problem in political sovereignty by a proposal for better government'. Devolution 'suggests only a means whereby better government may be secured within a single State. Its value disappears once the unity of the State is questioned.'[74]

3 Northern Ireland

In the ideally-sized unit a dissatisfied farmer anywhere within its boundaries ought to be able to travel by public transport to the administrative centre, horse-whip the responsible official, and get home again by public transport, all in the same day.

Ulsterman to Commission on the Constitution.

I

Northern Ireland is the only part of the United Kingdom to have gained practical experience of devolution. For fifty years—from 1921 when the Northern Ireland Parliament was opened by George V to 1972 when it was suspended by Mr. Heath's administration—six of the nine counties of Ulster enjoyed Home Rule, the system which Ulster had taken the lead in resisting in the thirty years before 1914. Clearly any study of devolution in the United Kingdom must ask whether the Northern Ireland model of devolved government could be adapted to other parts of the country.

Unfortunately, however, there are some limitations upon the value of the Northern Ireland example as a case-study of devolution. For two inter-connected factors make the experience of Northern Ireland very different from that of other areas of the United Kingdom. First, of course, there is the community problem, the antagonism between an entrenched Protestant majority which accepted the link with Britain and a Roman Catholic minority, many of whom sought union with the rest of Ireland. This problem would not, fortunately, be one which need concern other areas of the United Kingdom which were candidates for devolution; but we shall have to ask whether devolution helped to exacerbate the community problem, and whether alternative political arrangements might have helped to lessen the antagonism which erupted most seriously into open violence in 1968, and led to the suspension of the experiment in devolved government.

The second factor that makes Northern Ireland untypical as a case-study of devolution is that her parliament was not sought by the Ulster Unionists, but was pressed upon them by the British government as a by-product of Lloyd George's attempt to solve the Irish problem. The Parliament of Northern Ireland was not established, as such institutions generally are, to meet a nationalist or separatist threat, but on the contrary, to secure a settlement for those who asked for nothing more than to remain as members of the United Kingdom with equal rights and obligations to those in Great Britain. The circumstances surrounding the birth of the Northern Ireland Parliament were bound to condition the whole experience of devolution in the province, and we must, therefore, go into them in some detail.

In the First Reading debate of the 1912 Home Rule Bill, Sir Edward Carson claimed that every argument for giving Home Rule to Ireland was also an argument for giving Home Rule to North East Ulster. But the central aim of Irish Unionists in both the North and the South was not to establish a separate Ulster but to kill Home Rule. The 'Orange card' first played by Lord Randolph Churchill was to be used solely for this purpose; 'if Ulster succeeds, Home Rule is dead,'[1] claimed Carson on 10 October 1911, the implication being that an independent Ireland, which Unionists believed would be the inevitable consequence of Home Rule, could not be viable without the industrial wealth and strength of Belfast and its environs.

The Unionists could not forcibly prevent Home Rule in any part of Ireland except the North East; they proposed, however, once a Home Rule Parliament was established, to take over the responsibility for government in the part of Ireland which they could effectively control. If, therefore, the Liberal Government wished to avoid the threat of civil war consequent upon the coercion of Ulster, it would have to exclude Ulster from the jurisdiction of the proposed Dublin Parliament. Exclusion was thus a fall-back position for the Unionists of the North and their Conservative allies, but it was also compatible with the Liberal pledge to create a Dublin Parliament.

Partition was proposed by Mr. Agar-Robartes, a Liberal back-bencher, in an amendment to the Third Home Rule Bill in 1912. Arguing that 'orange bitters will not mix with Irish whisky' Agar-

Robartes proposed that four of the nine counties of Ulster—Antrim, Down, Armagh, and Derry—be excluded from the operation of the Bill. His amendment was defeated by sixty-one votes, but Lloyd George and Winston Churchill, although Cabinet ministers, abstained in the vote. In June 1914 Lord Crewe, the Lord Privy Seal, introduced on behalf of the government a proposal that the nine counties of Ulster could, on a basis of county option, vote themselves out of a Dublin Parliament for a period of six years after the Act came into force. Carson, however, rejected what he called 'sentence of death with a stay of execution for six years', and the Lords transformed the temporary exclusion of Ulster into permanent exclusion, a proposal which Asquith could not accept. The Bill became law in 1914, but its operation was suspended for the duration of the war with the Ulster question still unresolved.

The government decided that the only chance of satisfying the claims of Irish nationality while avoiding civil war lay in allowing Ulster to opt out of Home Rule; and in 1916 Lloyd George proposed that Ulster be excluded from Home Rule and administered by a Secretary of State. A similar suggestion was made at the ill-fated Irish Convention in 1918. A separate parliament for Ulster was not, however, proposed. Indeed it had been opposed by leading Unionists who wanted Ulster to be ruled from Westminster in the same way as any other part of the United Kingdom.

By 1918, Lloyd George's Coalition Government faced a 'situation in regard to Ireland' which was 'governed by two fundamental facts: the first that the Home Rule Act of 1914 is upon the Statute book; the second that in accordance with the pledge which has been given by me in the past, and indeed by all Party leaders, I can support no settlement which would involve the forcible coercion of Ulster.'[2] In Southern Ireland, the Sinn Fein movement had obliterated the Irish Nationalist Party of Parnell and Redmond in the General Election of 1918, and refused to take its seats at Westminster, establishing a separate Irish Parliament—the Dail—in Dublin in January 1919. Autonomy for the South and exclusion for the North was therefore the only policy compatible both with the situation in Ireland and with Lloyd George's pledges. There was one problem however:

. . . the policy of exclusion is open to one general objection of the most serious kind. It involves the retention of British rule in some part of

Ireland. There is good reason to doubt whether it would ever be possible to convince Irishmen themselves or Dominion or American opinion that Great Britain was sincere in its policy of Home Rule unless it withdrew its control from the domestic affairs of Ireland altogether. British rule in the domestic affairs of Ireland has been the root of the Home Rule movement from start to finish. If it is retained anywhere in Ireland the opponents of Great Britain will be able to say either that Great Britain is ruling nationalist majorities against her will, or that it is giving active support to Ulster in its refusal to unite with the rest of Ireland.

A separate Parliament for Northern Ireland 'gets rid of the tap-root of the Irish difficulty by providing for the complete withdrawal of British rule from the whole government. It thus meets the fundamental demand of the overwhelming majority of Irishmen ever since the days of O'Connell.' It would moreover 'enormously minimize the partition issue. The division of Ireland becomes a far less serious matter if Home Rule is established for both parts of Ireland than if the excluded part is retained as part of Great Britain. No nationalists would then be retained under British rule.'[3] At the same time everything should be done to promote Irish unity, and therefore the 1920 Government of Ireland Act proposed in addition to two Parliaments in Dublin and Belfast a Council of Ireland consisting of an equal number of representatives from each Parliament, and this Council was to have power 'by mutual agreement and joint action to terminate partition and to set up one Parliament and one Government for the whole of Ireland'. Partition was therefore not intended to be permanent; and the Northern Ireland Parliament was to be a transitional institution to be superseded once the unity of Ireland had been secured.

The solution proposed thus combined respect for self-determination together with a recognition of the force of the pledges given to Ulster and a determination to do all that was possible to secure Irish unity within the limits of these pledges.

The Act, then, consisted of an immediate temporary settlement for the two parts of Ireland, and it also provided the machinery by which a permanent solution could be secured. There was, however, only one part of Ireland where this settlement was accepted— Northern Ireland—and there the temporary settlement was accepted as a permanent one. The South rejected the settlement; for Sinn Fein demanded not Home Rule, but dominion status which was secured by the 'Treaty' of 1922. Even this, however, did not prove a final resting-place in Ireland's constitutional evolution, for gradually the ties which bound her to the Commonwealth were loosened until in 1949 her secession from the Commonwealth was recognized, and she became an independent republic.

With the rejection by Southern Ireland of Home Rule, the North was faced with three choices; the first, to join the South in a unified Ireland, was unthinkable to the majority; the second, to abandon her separate Parliament and reintegrate the province with the rest of the United Kingdom, might have seemed superficially attractive, but was in reality in the words of the Ulster Unionist Council in 1936,

a subtle move fraught with great danger. Had we refused to accept a Parliament for Northern Ireland and remained at Westminster there can be little doubt but that now we would be either inside the Free State or fighting desperately against incorporation. Northern Ireland without a Parliament of her own would be a standing temptation to certain British politicians to make another bid for a final settlement with Irish Republicans.[4]

If Northern Ireland remained a part of the United Kingdom, surrendering her separate Parliament, she would return at most thirty members to Westminster—less than five per cent of the total number. It would be easy for Ulster members to be outvoted, and for Northern Ireland to be handed over to Dublin against her wishes. During the debates on the 1920 Bill, the brother of Sir James Craig, the Ulster leader, explained why Ulster would accept the third alternative—the retention of her separate Parliament.

. . . we feel that an Ulster without a parliament of its own would not be in nearly as strong a position as one in which a parliament had been set up . . . . We believe that so long as we were without a parliament of our own constant attacks would be made . . . to draw us into a Dublin parliament . . . We profoundly distrust the right hon. gentleman the Member for Paisley [Asquith]. We believe that if either of those parties [Labour or the Liberals] or the two in combination, were once more in power our chances of remaining a part of the United Kingdom would be very small indeed.[5]

With her own parliament Northern Ireland would acquire legitimacy and could not be coerced into a united Ireland. Instead of a majority of the House of Commons being necessary to secure Irish unity a majority of the Northern Ireland Parliament would be required. Ulster's veto, therefore, would be institutionalized and the Northern Ireland Parliament would be the agency through which her continued membership of the United Kingdom would be assured.

The far-sightedness of the Unionists was soon revealed. During the negotiations with Sinn Fein which preceded the Anglo-Irish Treaty, Lloyd George attempted to barter the six counties in return for Sinn Fein acceptance of allegiance to the Crown. Once guaranteed a separate parliament, however, the North could afford to refuse all such overtures, knowing that she could never be coerced.

Northern Ireland had in Craig's words (11 November 1921, Cmnd. 1561) accepted 'As a *final settlement* and supreme sacrifice in the interests of peace' the 1920 Act, 'although not asked for by her representatives.' (My italics.) After Ireland became a republic in 1948, the position of Northern Ireland was formalized in s.l(2) of the Ireland Act of 1949, which declared that Northern Ireland would not cease to be a part of the United Kingdom without the consent of her Parliament. The Parliament of Northern Ireland thus became the body through which alone Northern Ireland could be deprived of her membership of the United Kingdom; and this constitutional provision gave meaning to the political argument that by accepting a separate Parliament, Northern Ireland could give herself the right to determine her own future, even in the face of a hostile majority at Westminster.

So was vindicated the claim that Ireland was not a political unity, first made by Lord Randolph Churchill and Joseph Chamberlain in 1886, and the part of Ireland which most strenuously resisted Home Rule came to accept and welcome it because it was the only way to ensure that she was not placed under a Dublin Parliament.

It should now be clear how the working of devolution in Northern Ireland was irrevocably determined by the circumstances of its inception. Devolution is usually conceded as a response to nationalist pressure, its purpose being to establish institutions expressing the particular national feelings of a region within a state; in Northern Ireland, however, the motivation was precisely the opposite— not to provide for different legislation from the rest of the country, but to ensure that she was governed on the same terms as the rest of the country, and that her legislation diverged as little as possible from that of the rest of the United Kingdom. Moreover, the circumstances of devolution in Northern Ireland were such as to offer a strong inducement to success, since the result of failure would be not separation but absorption into the hated Irish Free State. For her part, Britain came to feel a moral obligation to ensure that Northern Irishmen should enjoy similar standards to inhabitants in the rest of the country, and was therefore willing to contribute the financial resources to make devolution a success. Thus the pressures which led to devolution in Northern Ireland were not 'centrifugal' as they so often are, but 'centripetal'[6] and therefore likely to minimize friction between the subordinate authority and Westminster.

II

The Government of Ireland Act of 1920 became the constitution of Northern Ireland. It laid down the division of legislative and financial powers between Westminster and Belfast and provided for machinery by which Belfast could be prevented from acting in breach of the constitution. Section 1 of the Act set up a Parliament which reproduced, as far as was possible, Westminster in Belfast, and consisted of the King—represented by the Lord Lieutenant, later the Governor—and two Houses. Section 4 conferred upon this Parliament a general grant of legislative power to make laws for the 'peace, order and good government' of the inhabitants of Northern Ireland. This general grant of power, however, was made subject to specific limitations. Section 4(1), paragraphs 1–14, enumerated excepted subjects, on which it was necessary to secure uniformity throughout the United Kingdom. Responsibility for excepted subjects would remain with Westminster: they included such matters as the Crown, the Navy, Army, and Air Force, relations with foreign countries, and external trade. Because she enjoyed the benefit of a separate parliament, Northern Ireland was to be under-represented at Westminster in proportion to population being allocated only thirteen seats (twelve after its university seat was abolished in 1948) instead of the seventeen to which she was entitled.

Section 5(1) of the Act, modelled on earlier Home Rule Bills, attempted to entrench religious freedom by prohibiting laws interfering with religious equality; and Section 8(6) extended this prohibition to the executive acts of government. Sections 21 and 22 of the Act reserved to Westminster the power to levy certain taxes, including income tax, surtax, customs and excise duties on goods manufactured or produced, a business profits tax, and a general tax on capital or substantially similar taxes. These taxes would clearly be of far greater importance in raising revenue than the transferred taxes controlled by the Parliament of Northern Ireland, the most important of which was the motor vehicle licence tax. In addition, Section 25 of the Act gave the Northern Ireland Parliament the power to grant Northern Ireland taxpayers a rebate on income tax or surtax, although for reasons that will be explained, this power was never used.

The Act also provided for machinery whereby the validity of Northern Ireland legislation could be tested, and the supremacy of Westminster enforced. Sections 49 and 50 allowed for an appeal to the Northern Irish Courts, with a right of ultimate appeal to the House of Lords, and Section 51 made provision for an appeal to the Judicial Committee of the Privy Council on constitutional matters. These Sections provided for statutes of the Northern Ireland Parliament being declared *ultra vires* by the Courts; and this conception of an *ultra vires* statute was 'novel in our constitutional law',[7] since it allowed the Courts to declare an Act of Parliament, albeit a subordinate one, invalid.

Section 12 of the Government of Ireland Act required the Lord Lieutenant, and his successor the Governor, to withhold assent to legislation of the Northern Ireland Parliament when so instructed by the King. And finally Section 75 of the Act emphasized that the Northern Ireland Parliament was a *subordinate* Parliament by the declaration that

Notwithstanding the establishment of the Parliament of Northern Ireland . . . or of anything contained in this Act, the supreme authority of the Parliament of the United Kingdom shall remain unaffected and undiminished over all persons, matters and things in Northern Ireland and every part thereof.

The constitution thus seemed to provide powerful constraints upon the autonomy of Northern Ireland. Section 6 of the Act, moreover, prevented the Northern Ireland Parliament from amending or altering the Act, although Westminster retained the power to legislate for Northern Ireland, even on matters within the transferred sphere, if it so wished. The constitution was thus a rigid one from the point of view of Northern Ireland, but, in theory at least, a completely flexible one from the standpoint of Westminster.

What was the precise constitutional status of Northern Ireland under the 1920 Act? Sections 6, 12, and 75 which seemingly preserved Westminster's supremacy led Wheare in his classic text *Federal Government*, to deny that Northern Ireland lay in a federal relationship with Westminster. From the strictly legal aspect, this view is correct; but in practice, Northern Ireland gained a degree of autonomy more appropriate to that of a provincial unit in a federal system. This occurred for two reasons.

The first was that, by convention, Westminster did not attempt to legislate on matters for which responsibility had been transferred. Sir Ivor Jennings argued that it would have been 'unconstitutional' for Parliament so to legislate.[8] It is true that after 1968, Parliament used Section 75 to press reforms upon Stormont. In the words of Mr. Callaghan, Home Secretary at the time, 'Our view was that in the last resort this section gives the Parliament at Westminster supreme authority to withdraw such power as it had delegated.'[9] And Captain O'Neill, then Prime Minister of Northern Ireland, said that 'Mr. Wilson made it absolutely clear to us that if we did not face up to our problems the Westminster Parliament might well decide to act over our heads.'[10] By this time, however, the normal working of devolution had been disrupted by sectarian violence, and before 1968 the relationship was rather nearer to that suggested by Jennings than by Wheare. Mr. Callaghan's 'supreme authority to withdraw such power as it had delegated' was very different from the 'unaffected and undiminished supremacy over all persons, matters and things' mentioned in Section 75. In practice, therefore, the system of government in Northern Ireland, though not the legal relationship, can be classified as quasi-federal, in that it displayed many of the characteristics of a federal division of powers.

Moreover, the canons of constitutional interpretation adopted by the courts, when dealing with the legislative competence of the Parliament of Northern Ireland, came to be those applied in federal systems. For example Atkins J. in the leading case *Gallagher v Lynn*[11] argued (my italics):

These questions affecting limitation on the legislative powers of subordinate parliaments *or the distribution of powers between parliaments in a federal system are now familiar*, and I do not propose to cite the whole range of authority which has largely arisen in discussion of the powers of Canadian Parliaments.

Captain O'Neill, speaking as Prime Minister of Northern Ireland, claimed that the system of government in Northern Ireland was 'unique in these islands, but fairly common elsewhere in the Commonwealth', and drew an analogy between the position of Northern Ireland *vis-à-vis* Westminster, and the position of a province in the Canadian confederation.[12] Moreover, the development of services in Northern Ireland displayed yet another feature found in federal states, in that on issues of industrial and agricultural policy, co-operation between the two governments rather than a rigid division of powers became the norm.

The second reason why Westminster's supremacy was more theoretical than real was that the constitutional safeguards embodied in Sections 5(1), 8(6), and 12 proved ineffective. Neither Section 5 nor 8 was ever invoked to deal with allegations of religious discrimination against the Roman Catholic minority. It is a chastening reminder of the ineffectiveness of 'an embryonic form of a legally enforceable Bill of Rights'[13] unaccompanied by a spirit of toleration that the only area of the United Kingdom where there have ever been constitutionally entrenched safeguards against discrimination is also the only area in which discrimination was widely prevalent.

Section 12 was invoked only once, by the Lord Lieutenant in 1922 when the Northern Ireland Government proposed to abolish proportional representation in local government elections with the clear political purpose of preventing the growth of a third force between the majority Unionist and the Catholic minority parties. The Bill lay within the legislative competence of the Northern Ireland Parliament, but nevertheless assent was withheld for two months at the request of the U.K. government. Mr. Cosgrave, the Irish Prime Minister, claimed that the measure was a breach of the spirit, although admittedly not of the letter, of the Anglo-Irish Treaty of 1922. Lloyd George did not attempt to refute Cosgrave's contention but made it clear that the Bill could not be vetoed. Sir James Craig, the Prime Minister of Northern Ireland, argued that 'The Bill was clearly within the powers of the Northern Parliament, and either they must make some patched-up arrangement or his

Government must resign.' Faced with this threat, the U.K. government was forced to give way. 'The Prime Minister said there was no question of vetoing the Bill . . .'.[14] Later Winston Churchill, the Colonial Secretary, wrote to Cosgrave: 'I have come, though most unwillingly, to the conclusion that the Local Government (N.I.) Bill could not be vetoed . . . I have never concealed from Sir James Craig my opinion that the measure was inopportune.'[15]

The failure of the U.K. Government to overrule Northern Ireland doubtless encouraged Craig to abolish proportional representation for elections to the Northern Ireland Parliament itself in 1929. His aim in doing this was not the crude one of increasing Unionist representation and diminishing that of its opponents. For the first-past-the-post system did not greatly increase the number of Unionist members nor decrease the number of anti-Partition members in the Northern Ireland House of Commons. Total Unionist representation was forty in 1921, forty in 1925, forty-one in 1929, and forty-one in 1933; anti-partitionists constituted twelve in 1921 and 1925 and eleven in 1929 and 1933.

Craig's aim, however, was to prevent any cracks in the Unionist monolith. He wanted to abolish proportional representation not to weaken Nationalist representation, but to discourage the growth of fissiparous Unionist parties, and of a Labour Party which might prove a more attractive and more constitutional opposition than the Nationalists. Craig's worry was that if the strength of the Unionist Party were dissipated, Northern Ireland's leverage *vis-à-vis* a Westminster Government seeking to negotiate with the Irish Free State over the heads of Northern Ireland would be weakened. Moreover, it was in his interest that the main opponent of the Unionists should not be the non-sectarian Labour Party, but the Nationalists who were condemned to a permanent minority position. The abolition of proportional representation did indeed lead to the over-representation of the Nationalists at the expense of Labour which was no longer able to benefit from the lower preferences of anti-government voters.

The effects of the abolition of proportional representation were therefore extremely unfortunate. Parties which could have bridged the sectarian chasm were denied effective representation. The Independent Unionists gradually disappeared, and the Northern

Ireland Labour Party, which might have succeeded in polarizing Northern Ireland's politics around issues of social and economic policy, also failed to acquire a foothold. Politics was to be dominated by the Ulster Unionist bloc and the Anti-Partitionists (Nationalists and Republicans). The sole issue henceforth on the agenda of Northern Ireland politics was the border.

Under proportional representation the Roman Catholic minority had secured some representation in every part of the province except for Belfast City. With the introduction of the first-past-the-post system, however, election results came to be a foregone conclusion, and there was a considerable increase in the number of uncontested seats, from none in the Stormont elections of 1923, to eight in 1925, twenty-two in 1929 after the abolition of proportional representation; and seventy per cent of the total of fifty-two in 1933. In this way, the change in the electoral system led to 'the stagnation of political life in Northern Ireland'.[16] Most important of all perhaps were the psychological implications of the change. To the Roman Catholic minority, unwilling to come to terms with the reality of exclusion from the Free State, it seemed a confirmation of their status as second class citizens in the province. 'Even if there had been no accompanying injustices of any kind this action revealed a complete lack of sympathy with the minority outlook. At the worst, it was a party manoeuvre; at the best a psychological mistake.'[17]

The abolition of proportional representation, therefore, helped to perpetuate the sectarian politics of the province. It reinforced the siege mentality of the Unionists of which it was itself an expression, and also the conviction of the minority that the Northern Ireland Government sought to deny them political legitimacy. To the Roman Catholic population it was symptomatic of the gross insensitivity of the Unionists. Nor did the Northern Ireland Government follow the U.K. Government in assimilating the parliamentary and local government franchise in 1948; it maintained a restrictive local government franchise which denied to one-quarter of parliamentary electors the right to vote in local elections, and, so it was held, disfranchised Roman Catholic voters.

The Northern Ireland Government was vulnerable also to accusations that it gerrymandered local government boundaries in the Unionist interest. But Westminster was unwilling to assert its supremacy by insisting upon an equitable franchise and fair constituency boundaries. For in 1923 the Speaker at Westminster had given a ruling that parliamentary questions could not be asked on matters for which responsibility was transferred to Northern Ireland.[18] The Speaker argued that no U.K. minister could be held responsible for such matters, and that the proper remedy for grievances was to be found in the courts.

The Speaker's ruling had the effect of stultifying discussion of alleged injustices in Northern Ireland. In July 1964, Mr. Henry Brooke, the U.K. Home Secretary, argued that matters connected with religious discrimination could not be the subject of debate at Westminster since in his view 'the reserve powers in the Government of Ireland Act do not enable the United Kingdom Government to intervene in matters which under Section 4 are the sole responsibility of the Northern Ireland Parliament and Government';[19]although Section 75 of the Act seemed to imply that no issues were the *sole* responsibility of the Northern Ireland Parliament and Government.

In 1965 when Mr. Crawshaw attempted to raise the issue of the property vote in local government elections in Northern Ireland, the Deputy Speaker ruled him out of order, saying 'We are now going into the details of local government in Northern Ireland, which is a matter for Northern Ireland . . . . he must show what the House of Commons can do about it and what some responsible Minister can do about it.'[20] In a later debate, the Deputy Speaker semed to imply that it was out of order for the House to discuss religious discrimination in Northern Ireland; '. . . discrimination in housing in Northern Ireland is not a matter for the United Kingdom Government; it is a matter for the Northern Ireland Government. . . . Any question of religious discrimination in Northern Ireland is not a matter for the United Kingdom Government . . . .' 'Boundaries for local government and Parliament in Ireland are matters for Stormont.'[21]

The U.K. Government thus found it difficult to ensure that the institutional framework in Northern Ireland conformed to common U.K. standards. During 1968–9 when the civil rights issue first began to make a serious impact upon the U.K. Government, she discovered that she could not exert influence upon the Northern Ireland Government except by threatening to repeal the 1920 Act and suspend Stormont. Mr. Callaghan, who was Home Secretary at the time, has described how, in order to exert influence upon Northern Ireland, he had to appoint a civil servant whose task it was 'to sit in a room next to Chichester-Clark's at Stormont Castle and . . . to explain British policy to Chichester-Clark and warn him where he was likely to get into difficulties with us. He would also be able to tell us what was going on.'[22] Westminster's supremacy therefore could not be practically vindicated except in a pathological political situation, and even then only with difficulty.

The constitutional problems of the Westminster/Stormont relationship thus proved very different from those the Lloyd George Cabinet had expected. For the 1920 Act had been drawn up in the expectation that the main problems would arise over the division of legislative powers and the attempt of *Southern* Ireland to circumvent it. The North, however, sought not to circumvent the constitution but to use it to secure the maximum autonomy for herself, while preserving the link with Britain and (as we shall see) the same standard of social services as that prevailing in the rest of the country.

III

Paradoxically, however, the Northern Ireland Government proved rather less effective in using her autonomy to develop a different pattern of public services from that prevailing in the rest of the United Kingdom. This was not because of U.K. intervention in the running of these services, but because Northern Ireland lacked the financial independence to support provincial autonomy.

The financial arrangements embodied in the Act of 1920 were based upon two complementary principles. The first was that Northern Ireland's autonomy could be secured by a division of the taxing power between transferred and reserved taxation. This was possible, in the government's view, since the imposition of war taxation had led to there being a surplus on the Irish account since 1915–16; and therefore the second principle, which had been established by Gladstone's Bill of 1886, viz. that Northern Ireland was to pay to Westminster an Imperial Contribution to cover the cost of services which remained with Westminster, could be brought into play.

The Act did not, however, give Northern Ireland financial autonomy; for it was framed with Southern Ireland in mind, and British politicians sought to retain tax-raising powers to ensure that Dublin did not withhold the Imperial Contribution. Expenditure on devolved services would be financed from Northern Ireland's revenue, either from transferred taxation, i.e. taxation imposed by the Northern Ireland Parliament, or reserved taxation, i.e. taxation imposed by Westminster. This meant of course that some estimate would have to be made of the share of total U.K. revenue which was properly attributable to Northern Ireland as her share of reserved revenue. Thus Northern Ireland would be treated as a separate financial region from the point of view of expenditure, in that revenue attributable to Northern Ireland could not be spent in any other part of the U.K.: but as a part of the United Kingdom from the point of view of reserved taxation, comprising income tax, customs and excise, and profits tax, and constituting the bulk of her revenue. The Imperial Contribution was to be determined by a Joint Exchequer Board, an impartial body removed from the political arena.

From the beginning, however, these arrangements proved unworkable, and Northern Ireland found it impossible to finance, from her revenue, a level of transferred services equal to that in the rest of the U.K. As early as June 1922, the Chancellor of the Exchequer was complaining that 'We have already gone far beyond what was contemplated in the Act . . .'[23] since Northern Ireland had been unable to make her accounts balance in the year 1921–2. Reserved revenue in the depression of the 1920s fell so far that it reached only one half of the anticipated level, whereas expenses proved far greater than foreseen, because of the high level of unemployment benefit and the cost of policing the province against the I.R.A. This meant that if the Imperial Contribution were to remain a first charge upon the revenue of Northern Ireland, the standard of public services there would be very low. Was it reasonable to expect her citizens, who paid common taxes with other citizens of the U.K., to endure lower standards in the social services? 'It would be a very sad day for us', argued Craig, 'if at any time it became known that it is better to live in Norfolk, or Suffolk, or Essex, or in any other county in England, than in the Province of Ulster.'[24] So after 'long and irritating controversies'[25] between the

Northern Ireland Ministry of Finance and the Treasury, the Colwyn Committee—the Northern Ireland Special Arbitration Committee was set up. It proposed in its final report in 1925 a drastic modification to the initial settlement, arguing that *per capita* spending on Northern Ireland services ought to increase at the same rate as *per capita* expenditure on services in the rest of the United Kingdom, and the sum required to secure such a rate of increase should constitute her necessary expenditure. The Imperial Contribution should not be paid until this necessary expenditure had been financed from the Northern Ireland budget. The result of the Committee's recommendations was to make it unnecessary for the Northern Ireland Government to raise the level of her own transferred taxes, for this would simply mean that the sum paid to the U.K. in the form of the Imperial Contribution would increase; it would not finance a higher standard of services. The Colwyn formula thus offered to Northern Ireland a guarantee that if her levels of both reserved and transferred taxation were equal to those in the rest of the United Kingdom, then her services would be improved at the same rate.

The Colwyn formula of equal expenditure *per capita* did not of course imply that social services in Northern Ireland would be of the same standard as in the rest of the U.K. since Northern Ireland had a disproportionately large number of claimants for these services. There was, in particular, a drain on Northern Ireland's finances, because of the high level of payments for unemployment insurance. The Colwyn formula was therefore supplemented by an Unemployment Insurance Agreement in 1926, the first of a number of agreements by which U.K. funds were transferred to Northern Ireland for specific purposes, thus further subverting the financial arrangements of the 1920 Act. The Agreement provided that if in any year the payment by the Northern Ireland Exchequer to the Unemployment Fund per head of population exceeded the corresponding payment by the U.K. Government to the fund in Great Britain, then the U.K. Government would meet three-quarters of the difference.

These measures did not, however, succeed in resolving Northern Ireland's financial problems. Indeed, by 1931 Northern Ireland was receiving more under the Unemployment Insurance Agreement than she was paying through the Imperial Contribution. The prospect arose of the Imperial Contribution being a negative amount, i.e. of Northern Ireland being unable to finance even her transferred services to an acceptable level from her total revenue. In 1932, therefore, the Colwyn formula was abandoned.

It was becoming clear (and it is difficult to understand how the framers of the 1920 Act failed to appreciate it) that Northern Ireland, like many other regions of the U.K., could not hope to finance herself as a self-sufficient revenue unit and provide services at a level equivalent to those in the rest of the United Kingdom. If, therefore, the alternative of a drastically reduced standard of living for Ulstermen was excluded, the U.K. government would have to offer further help to Northern Ireland.

This help came in the form of the Simon Declaration in 1938 when Sir John Simon, the Chancellor of the Exchequer, established the principle of parity which was to govern the future financial relations between the governments of the United Kingdom and Northern Ireland. According to this principle, in the event of 'a deficit on the Northern Ireland Budget which was not the result of a standard of social expenditure higher than that of Great Britain nor the result of a standard of taxation lower than that of Great Britain', the U.K. Government would 'make good this deficit in such a way as to ensure that Northern Ireland should be in a financial position to continue to enjoy the same social services and have the same standards as Britain.'[26] The U.K. Government also agreed to bear the cost of agricultural subsidies in Northern Ireland, although agriculture was a transferred service. In 1954, the parity agreement was augmented by arrangements designed to ensure that Northern Ireland received sufficient aid to make up the leeway which existed between her own services and those of Great Britain.

These arrangements were supplemented by further agreements whereby the U.K. Government assisted Northern Ireland with the cost of specific services such as National Insurance, industrial injuries, the agricultural support system in 1948, the regional employment premium in 1966, and in 1971 family allowances, supplementary benefits, and the new family income supplement.

Thus the settlement of 1920 was transformed out of all recognition. Northern Ireland's finances were now determined not by her revenue, but by her needs; the financial arrangements had become expenditure-based, rather than revenue-based. Perusal of a sample budget for Northern Ireland shows that the Imperial Contribution had become merely a book-keeping item (see Table below). The crucial element in the Northern Ireland budget was the determination of the size of the funds which could be transferred to Northern Ireland from the Treasury; and this, since 1946, was decided by negotiations between the Northern Ireland Ministry of Finance and the Treasury. After the breakdown of the arrangements proposed in the 1920 Act and the introduction of the Colwyn formula, it was imperative to secure agreement on how much Northern Ireland could spend on her own transferred services. This could be achieved in one of three ways. The first would have been by the use of a block grant given to Northern Ireland by Westminster, to spend as she pleased; the second was the method actually adopted, the principle of parity; the third method would have involved increasing the share of her revenue which Northern Ireland could finance out of her own taxation, i.e. increasing the share of transferred taxation.

Northern Ireland Budget 1971/2

Revenue		£m.
Share of United Kingdom Reserved Taxes		269
Less: Imperial contribution	1	
Cost of reserved services in Northern Ireland	4	
		5
Residuary share of reserved taxes		264
Revenue from transferred taxes		45
Total revenue accruing to Northern Ireland under the Government of Ireland Act 1920		309
Receipts from the United Kingdom Government:		
Health Service Agreement	20	
Social Services Payments	37	
Remoteness grant payable under Agriculture Act 1957	2	
Additional Selective Employment Premiums payable under Finance Act 1967	11	
		70
Other revenue (mainly interest from local authorities)		39
		418

In addition, Northern Ireland received £30m. from the United Kingdom Government to pay for agricultural subsidies in Northern Ireland, and £15m. for the Northern Ireland National Insurance Fund. The total amount she received from the U.K. was therefore £70m. (the sum transferred for specific services) + £30m. +£15m. = £115m., as well as the true value of the Imperial Contribution. Expenditure, in the form of the cost of Northern Ireland Services, was £418m.

Source: Report of Royal Commission on the Constitution, para. 1295.

If the path of parity was taken, this meant that there would have to be a working arrangement to ensure that Ireland was not taking advantage of U.K. generosity to provide superior services for herself. It was in this way that powers transferred to Northern Ireland, which would have allowed her to determine the standard of her public services, were to a considerable extent exercised by London. The financial autonomy of the Government of Northern Ireland was thus severely limited and, in particular, her powers to vary transferred taxes came to be worth little since if taxes were reduced parity was lost, while to raise transferred taxes except by a very considerable amount would produce little extra revenue, since they produced so small a proportion of Northern Ireland's total revenue.

The financing of devolution had thus been transformed from a revenue-based system in which Northern Ireland's level of taxation was dependent primarily upon the revenue raised, to an expenditure-based system where it depended upon the parity requirement. But what was parity? According to the Royal Commission on the Constitution, 'It is tempting to conclude that "parity" was simply what could be secured by negotiation.' (Para 1304.) That the system worked so smoothly however was not only because it was 'a monument to British pragmatism' (Para 1307.) but because the parties to the arrangement were predisposed from the start to reach agreement. This might not have been the case if the Treasury had been negotiating either with an Irish Nationalist Parliament in Dublin or a Scottish Nationalist one in Edinburgh.

Even so, there were serious weaknesses in the financial arrangements from the standpoints of both efficiency and democracy. They violated one of the canons of good government, that the spending power and the taxing power ought, as far as possible, to be in the same hands, for since spending is generally popular and taxing unpopular, it is only right that government should have to balance expenditure at the margin with taxation at the margin. The Northern Ireland Government, however, was responsible for ninety per cent of public expenditure in Northern Ireland while transferred revenue by 1972 equalled only fifteen per cent of total Northern Ireland revenue. The settlement with Northern Ireland thus dissociated the spending power, which remained at Belfast, from the taxing power which lay primarily in London. There was therefore little connection between the amount raised by the Northern Ireland Government and the amount spent there.

The 1920 Act had tried to establish a formula through which the Northern Ireland Minister of Finance could know what his revenue was likely to be in advance, so that he could plan a realistic spending programme. The revised arrangements, however, made him totally dependent upon the decisions of the U.K. Chancellor on Budget Day. But the particular problems of Northern Ireland would be unlikely to bulk large in the Chancellor's calculations. Modern financial planning requires expenditure to be planned in advance, preferably over a five-year period, but this was impossible for Northern Ireland.

our problem is that . . . we find it very difficult to plan our expenditure a long time in advance because we are at the mercy of the economic policy of the U.K. The Chancellor may change taxation, which could drastically reduce our revenue.

I think it is important in any regional set-up to be able to plan, to see something for at least five years ahead. We have been doing it on a yearly basis: this is wrong.[27]

The financial arrangements were, therefore, 'coming to the end of the road'. They were certainly inimical to modern conceptions of economic management.

From the point of view of accountability also, the arrangements were open to criticism: when it came to the main decision of internal politics in Northern Ireland—the size of her budget, and the shape of her expenditure—the government was responsible not to the legislature, but to the United Kingdom Treasury. In fact, neither Westminster nor Stormont was able to scrutinize the financial arrangements. The Northern Ireland budget was agreed each year in private negotiations.

Parliament has effectively ceded power to the executive; the outcome is that neither Parliament exercises sufficient scrutiny over the financial relations between the two governments. Westminster exercises no oversight on the Treasury's role in the negotiations to fix each year's Ulster budget; the Ulster Parliament, faced in recent years with generosity from the Treasury, is glad to take what it can get without stirring up questions of principle.[28]

The result was that 'financial questions of great public interest and importance were shrouded in secrecy.... it is apparently taken for granted, that the public have no right to know, except in purely general terms, how Ulster's revenue and permissible expenditure are fixed.'[29]

It is clear that the financial arrangements between Britain and Northern Ireland were hardly conducive to efficient, democratic government, and one would not wish to see them repeated in any future exercises in devolution. The issue, then, is whether one can frame a more constructive set of financial proposals which can reconcile the autonomy of the provincial unit with a rough equality of standards of service and successful management of the economy. If this cannot be done we should be compelled to agree that 'the grave financial problems . . . must surely drive a purely impartial observer to the conclusion that devolution is necessarily impracticable if not in fact impossible.'[30]

IV

What scope, then, was left for autonomy in Northern Ireland? Parity did not entirely inhibit the development of different policies, for a good deal of legislation did not involve finance, but related to issues concerning public mores. Thus Northern Ireland did not follow Great Britain in modifying her divorce, abortion, or homosexuality laws in the 1960s; nor did she abolish capital punishment or adopt the Conservative Government's Industrial Relations Act of 1971.

The Northern Ireland Government produced for the Royal Commission on the Constitution figures showing the proportion of Northern Ireland's legislation and statutory orders governed by the parity requirement. It turned out to be surprisingly small.

Acts of Parliament	1965	1966	1967	1968	1969
A. Parity legislation	6	13	5	3	9
B. Legislation falling between categories A and C	8	11	15	14	12
C. Legislation peculiar to Northern Ireland	8	17	16	14	15
Technical Acts	3	3	4	3	3
Totals	25	44	40	34	39

Statutory Rules and Orders	*1965*	*1966*	*1967*	*1968*	*1969*
A.	65	88	92	70	85
B.	110	98	109	94	138
C.	102	124	143	115	129
Miscellaneous	12	9	5	5	9
Totals	289	319	349	284	361

The Northern Ireland government further commented,

It is estimated that, if legislation is divided into two categories only— parity and non-parity matters—about two-thirds of both administrative and legislative time is spent on purely Northern Ireland matters. This is, however, a rough estimate only and the proportions vary from department to department; in the Ministry of Health and Social Security, for example, the proportion of time spent on parity matters would be much higher.[31]

This comment draws attention to the fact that devolution made much less sense in health and social security than in some other areas of government. The framers of the 1920 Act did not consider how the development of the Welfare State might affect devolution, and devolved functions which would probably now be retained at the centre. In the health service, uniform professional standards had to be maintained so as to facilitate mobility of staff, and not to handicap doctors and nurses working in Northern Ireland; and in the cash social services, 'Once the policy decision had been taken for uniformity throughout the U.K. and the necessary financial backing had been secured, the arguments for a separate system of legislation and administration had less validity.'[32] Where the proportion of time spent on parity matters was very high, it would probably have been better if responsibility for the service in question had been transferred to London. For where there was little scope for divergence of policy, devolution made little sense.

In some areas of government, however, the advantages of devolved government were manifest. Notable successes were achieved, for example, in agriculture and industrial development where the problems faced by Northern Ireland were very different from those in the rest of the United Kingdom.

V

The administration of both agriculture and industrial policy underwent an evolution characteristic of many federal states, whereby functions came to be shared between the provincial unit and the centre. Agriculture was a transferred subject under the 1920 Act, except as regards exports; but the U.K. system of agricultural support could not be sustained from Northern Ireland's own resources, and the U.K. government believed, as a matter of policy, that the support system ought to be uniform across the whole country. In the administration of this system, therefore, the Northern Ireland Ministry of Agriculture acted as an agent for the Ministry of Agriculture, Fisheries, and Food. There was also joint action on agricultural marketing.

Other aspects of agricultural development remained the responsibility of the Northern Ireland Government. This gave her greater freedom of variation and adaptation than Scotland which had only administrative devolution, since 'if legislation is required to do something, we can have it passed within a matter of months whereas Scotland have often made the point that when they want to do something it may take them some two or three years before time can be found for legislation at Westminster.'[33] Northern Ireland faced particular problems in agriculture because of the high proportion of her produce which was 'exported' to Great Britain. The British market would require a clear guarantee of the quality of produce from Northern Ireland before it would be genuinely competitive. The Government of Northern Ireland, therefore, took early steps to regulate the quality of eggs, fruit, potatoes, dairy produce, and meat by introducing a system of compulsory grading for eggs in the Marketing of Eggs Act 1924, and extending it to other produce. Such a system was not introduced into Great Britain until some years afterwards, and when it was introduced, the grading was entirely voluntary. This legislation would, therefore, probably not have been enacted had there not been a local parliament in Northern Ireland: as it was, however, the Assistant Secretary to the Northern Ireland Ministry of Agriculture was able to speak of the quality-conscious produce of Northern Ireland, and to claim that 'we have led the field in this respect'.[34]

In industrial policy, also, power came to be divided between Stormont and London. With the increase in government intervention in the economy, Westminster began to assume responsibility for regional policy, and sought, through the use of industrial development certificates, to hold a balance of power between the depressed regions of the United Kingdom. Moreover, Northern Ireland was bound to be affected by the macro-economic policies adopted by the U.K. government. Thus the line between reserved and transferred powers became blurred, and the clear-cut division of powers of the 1920 Act was undermined. This raised difficult problems of political accountability for economic policy in Northern Ireland.

Northern Ireland remained responsible for industrial development and regional planning: and the record of the Northern Ireland Government on aid to industry was imaginative. She can claim to have been a pioneer of regional policy in the United Kingdom, and many of the measures adopted by Northern Ireland in the immediate post-war period were later to be used in Great Britain by the 1964 Labour Government.

Northern Ireland confronted a similar problem to that faced by the other depressed areas in the United Kingdom—an outdated industrial structure and heavy regional unemployment. She also faced the special problem of a cost disadvantage for her goods which were in competition with other goods in U.K. markets, but was compelled to pay the transport costs of the voyage across the Irish Sea. To deal with these problems, therefore, the Government of Northern Ireland established a generous system of capital grants to industry, and pioneered the building of factories for rent or sale. The Government also offered grants towards the operating costs of factories situated in areas of high unemployment. To deal with the unfavourable differential in transport costs, the government offered a cost subsidy on fuels, and used her powers to vary road taxes to assist industry by reducing the cost of the licence for heavy vehicles.[35] She even opened an industrial development office in the United States two years before the United Kingdom did so.

The Government of Northern Ireland also adopted her own manpower policy geared to her own special requirements. She pioneered a manpower survey, unique in the U.K., to identify the particular needs of industry and develop training facilities in accordance with these needs. She encouraged the diversification of industry, building upon the particular skills of her labour force. In textiles, for example, she succeeded in attracting synthetic textile firms to help replace declining textile industries. Her success in this field can be quantified, for in the years 1961–7, the value of the net output of 'miscellaneous textiles'—a category including synthetic textiles—increased almost sevenfold from £4m. to £27m., and the share of 'miscellaneous textiles' in Northern Ireland's total output of textiles increased from fourteen per cent to forty-seven per cent.[36]

These developments probably owed most to the 'immense intangible advantage of regional government—accessibility of the decision-makers and consequent speed of decision. Red tape tends to be a result of sheer scale.'[37] The close relationships which firms could build up with the administration were clearly of great importance in eliminating delay. In its evidence to the Royal Commission on the Constitution, the Northern Ireland Council of the C.B.I. gave as its view

that such steps as have been taken are greater than would have been the case had we depended solely on the activity of a central legislature. The problems of Northern Ireland are pertinent, real and close to an indigenous government, but would be less urgent and pressing if merely those of one of a number of similar areas.

The Council was therefore 'convinced that the existence of the Parliament at Stormont has been, over the years, a major factor in the economic development of the Province.'[38]

Even more striking was the evidence of the Northern Ireland Labour Party, politically opposed to the Unionist administration, but nevertheless admitting that 'the machinery of regional autonomy, even under a Unionist Government, can be a means of readjusting of regional differences . . . The result . . . has been a better economic performance than the other regions of the United Kingdom which had basically similar economic problems—remoteness, and decline of the major traditional industries.'[39] It presented the following index of the growth of personal incomes in different regions of the U.K. to prove its point.

	1964/5 (1954/5: 100)
Northern Region	174
North West	182
South West	204
Wales	188
Scotland	182
Northern Ireland	204
United Kingdom as a whole	194

It must, of course, be admitted that these gains might not have been so great if the U.K. as a whole was divided up into regional units, and it would be undesirable for different regions to compete with each other to attract industry. 'Young man you must never again make a suggestion like that', Terence O'Neill was told when he advocated regional authorities in Britain with the powers of Stormont, 'we do not want any more provincial calves pulling at the one cow.' Nevertheless, the advantages to be secured from the accessibility of a regional level of administration are surely conducive to more effective government; and the experience of Northern Ireland shows that it is possible to devolve industrial development powers without undermining the overall responsibilities of the U.K. government in the management of the economy, provided that there is a careful co-ordination of responsibilities between the two governments, and a recognition of the fact that they have complementary and not conflicting roles to play in the process of economic development.

VI

A corollary to the intimacy of regional administration in Northern Ireland was the weaker role of local government in the province. Since Northern Ireland covered a relatively small geographical area, ministries were not compelled to delegate to the same extent as Whitehall departments. A number of services such as the fire service and the police which in Great Britain are the responsibility of local authorities were in Northern Ireland the responsibility of the government. Given that Britain was committed to parity in the provision of public services in Northern Ireland, it was of course to the advantage of Northern Ireland ratepayers to be able to transfer responsibility for these services to the British taxpayer. Moreover in housing and education the role of local government was severely reduced, since it had proved itself to be weak and unimaginative; and widespread discrimination against Catholics in the allocation of housing was alleged.

The poor house-building record in Northern Ireland between the wars led to the establishment of the Northern Ireland Housing Trust in 1945 to supplement the efforts of local authorities. This body gained 'a world-wide reputation for the provision of well

planned and competently administered housing estates'[40] and
Northern Ireland was the only part of the U.K. to enjoy subsidies
for private house building. But it was inevitably a first step towards
a housing authority completely centralized in Belfast, and in
October 1969, the governments of the United Kingdom and
Northern Ireland issued a joint communiqué saying that they had

reluctantly decided that local authorities are not geared—and cannot be
geared—to handle such a task and that the best hope of success lies in the
creation of a single-purpose, efficient and streamlined central housing
authority . . . to tackle this most urgent problem.[41]

The Northern Ireland Housing Trust thus proved to be the first
step in the setting up of a central housing department in the
province.

In education, also, powers which in Great Britain were exercised
by local authorities, gravitated to the centre. The salaries of teachers
in schools and colleges of further education under the control of the
local education authority, except for those in voluntary grammar
schools, were paid centrally. But as the Exchequer limited the
amount of its liability under this head, the remainder of the finance
had to be raised through a levy exacted from local authorities in
proportion to rateable values. This levy could prove to be much
greater than the cost of a particular authority's local education
services. In Downpatrick Urban District, for example, the education rate in 1967 was ten shillings and tenpence, of which
eight shillings and fivepence went towards the levy. This was a
crippling disincentive to economy on the part of local education
authorities who found that they had little effective control over
their spending, and were faced with a levy which would increase
rapidly with increasing numbers and rising salaries of teachers. In
County Down, the levy increased no less than 100 times between
1947 when it was £13,000 and 1965/6 when it reached the sum of
£1.3m. There was thus little scope for practical initiative on the
part of local education authorities, and therefore a strong case for a
central education authority in Northern Ireland.[42] This case was
strengthened by the sectarian attitudes of some authorities which
sought to discover the denomination of candidates applying for
teaching posts, thus arousing the suspicion that Roman Catholic
candidates were discriminated against in appointments to state
schools.

Local authorities in Northern Ireland were weakened yet further by the restrictive financial arrangements established by Stormont. The share of local authority finance falling on the Exchequer was greater in Northern Ireland than in England, and it was met to a larger extent than in England from percentage or specific grants rather than the block grant introduced in Britain in 1958. By 1969–70, grants to local authorities totalled £54,757,000 of which £41,374,000 was in the form of specific grants.[43] This led inevitably to close scrutiny of local authority projects. Since local authorities had to contribute to the fire service, and the police force which was run from Belfast, and to pay the education levy, the connection between local spending and local taxation was seriously under-mined. Certainly in Northern Ireland devolution tended to restrict local financial autonomy. Whether that is a necessary feature of devolution is a question which we shall have to consider in some detail later on.

VII

The strongest criticism made of the government of Northern Ireland concerns her use of the Civil Authorities (Special Powers Act) of 1922, in existence throughout the period of rule from Stormont. Section 1(1) of this Act gave the 'civil authority' powers 'to take all such steps and issue all such orders as may be necessary for preserving the peace and maintaining order . . .' Section 2(4) allowed a person to be punished for any threat to peace or the maintenance of order whether or not specifically provided for in the regulations under the Act, and the framing of regulations was left entirely to the executive 'with the result that the function of the court can be very clearly circumscribed.'[44] The regulations them-selves provided *inter alia*, for detention and internment without trial. After the immediate period of the 'troubles', however, they were little used; and there were no prosecutions at all in seven of the eleven years 1945 to 1956.

Nevertheless, even allowing for the serious difficulties faced by Northern Ireland from terrorists, not enough was done to assuage the fear of the Catholic minority that special powers were being used to buttress Unionist rule and this led to 'Widespread resent-ment among Catholics in particular.'[45] The regulations therefore contributed considerably to the alienation of the minority from government.

VIII

Lord Kilbrandon has argued that

The tragedy of Northern Ireland had nothing to do with the form of government under which she existed for half-a-century—that government was in many respects beneficial, and in any other place which was not torn by the impossible political and sectarian stresses with which we are familiar, could well permanently succeed.[46]

But this view cannot be wholly accepted. British standards in the field of civil rights might probably have been attained more rapidly if Northern Ireland had been governed from Westminster, although one should not exaggerate the likely gains: discrimination was more a matter of social attitudes than a result of action by public bodies. But one of its causes was the fear by Protestants that the Catholic population owed its primary allegiance to the Republic and not to the U.K.

If Northern Ireland had been governed from Westminster, however, the issue of the Border would have ceased to be the only vital concern of Northern Ireland politics, and there might have been an evolution of party politics along British lines. This would have allowed the voters of Northern Ireland to choose between competing social philosophies, and to consider which would be more suited to the needs of the province. The issues in Northern Ireland politics would not be partition or union with the Republic, but Conservatism or Social Democracy.

Moreover the smooth progress of Stormont/Westminster relationships was secured precisely because Home Rule was given, not as a concession to national or regional feeling, but as a by-product of an attempted solution to the Irish problem. This meant that the U.K. government was always willing to treat Northern Ireland generously, and to ensure that her services reached a level equivalent to those in the rest of the country; and the Ulster Unionists would never use their transferred powers so as to provoke a clash with the U.K. government. Had they been determined to retain sole control of transferred matters, or attempted to improve social conditions more rapidly than they were allowed to do by the U.K., clashes would undoubtedly have occurred, for if the U.K. Government refused to finance such developments, Ulstermen would have been tempted to blame London for her meanness.

For this reason Northern Ireland has been said to have 'evaded rather than refuted the Unionist thesis that Home Rule is impracticable. That thesis rested on the natural assumption that a regional legislature would insist on making full use of its powers.'[47]

Our purpose, however, is not to come to a final judgment concerning the unique circumstances of devolution in Northern Ireland, for we were intending to use Northern Ireland as a case-study in order to draw some general conclusions as to the value of devolution. We have already seen that, during the period of what might be called 'normal' working of devolution until 1968, Northern Ireland's position was very much akin to that of a unit in a federal state. The supervisory powers retained by the U.K. government proved to be worth little, since they could not be used to overrule an elected responsible government representing an area with considerable local patriotism. Stormont could not be persuaded or compelled to accept U.K. priorities, except to a limited extent in matters involving public expenditure where London held the purse-strings.

Secondly, therefore, the Northern Ireland example shows the vital importance of the financial element. If it is desired to secure provincial autonomy, there must be the financial independence with which to back it up. Otherwise powers which have been transferred will gravitate back to the centre, and priorities will be dictated by the Treasury.

The division of powers made in the 1920 Act left much to be desired. Matters concerning the franchise and electoral law ought not to have been devolved; and a strong case could be made for saying that powers connected with internal security should have been retained by Westminster. It is significant that these powers were not devolved to Northern Ireland in the 1973 Northern Ireland Constitution Act, the second, but short-lived attempt to create a workable devolved administration in Northern Ireland.

Some powers which were transferred, for example, powers over the cash social services, represented areas of government where serious divergencies between different parts of a country are hardly desirable; and in practice the benefits paid in Northern Ireland were the same as those in the rest of the United Kingdom. Here, also, devolution made little sense.

In other areas, such as industry and agriculture, the development of more sophisticated tools of economic management made Northern Ireland more dependent upon the policies adopted by the U.K. government than had been foreseen by the framers of the 1920 Act. A sharing rather than a division of power came to be necessary, therefore, in the administration of industrial and agricultural policy, and this sharing came about through a pragmatic basis of co-operation between the two governments. There was scope for devolution in these fields, but rather less than had been imagined in 1920, although more than the government was prepared to allow Scotland or Wales in 1978.

Despite these deficiencies of the Act of 1920, the advantages of devolution for Northern Ireland were clear. In many areas, Northern Ireland was able to pass legislation dealing with her own special problems; and, although Westminster could have done the same, it would have been unlikely to do so, since Northern Ireland was such a small and unfamiliar part of the United Kingdom. Indeed, the Northern Ireland Government frequently found it difficult to secure special attention to its interests, even when there was pressure from the government and from leading civil servants. How much more difficult it would have been if Northern Ireland had been compelled to depend upon Westminster for all of her legislation!

The gains for Northern Ireland in having a devolved assembly were in securing speedy attention to her needs, meaningful consultation with local interests affected by legislation, and the adaptation of United Kingdom legislation to her own special requirements. In some areas, indeed, the United Kingdom as a whole benefited from Northern Ireland's legislative innovations since, if they were successful in Northern Ireland, they could be adopted in Great Britain. This was particularly true in the case of regional policy where the policy instruments first used by Northern Ireland came to be adopted by the U.K. government in the 1960s.

It is a remarkable tribute to the success of devolution in Northern Ireland that, despite all the blemishes upon the record of the government, there was widespread support for devolved government in the province. The Northern Ireland Labour Party 'referred to advantages in the economic field and the benefits of closer Parliamentary accountability.' The Ulster Liberals told the Royal Commission on the Constitution 'that within the limits imposed by the deep political and religious divisions in the community, the experiment in devolution had worked remarkably well.' Sir Edmund Compton, the Ombudsman for Northern Ireland, maintained that

the individual citizen frequently gets a better service from a Northern Ireland Ministry than he would get from a United Kingdom Department in similar circumstances, owing to the easier access to central government that is both feasible and customary in a territory the size of Northern Ireland.

And the Commission itself concluded that

We have no doubt at all that home rule was of considerable advantage to Northern Ireland. Particularly in the large areas of government which were unaffected or at least were not dominated, by the community problem, conspicuous progress was made under it.[48]

The Northern Ireland Constitutional Convention chosen in 1975 by direct election, and representing all the main streams of political opinion in the province, argued in its Report with 'almost complete unanimity . . . in favour of some form of devolved administration and legislature within the United Kingdom . . . This unanimity . . . arose principally from a strong feeling among Members that Northern Ireland's problems could be best tackled by a regional government answerable to a local parliament or assembly.'[49]

If the ultimate test of the success of any governmental arrangements is the attitude to them of those whose lives they regulate, then devolution in Northern Ireland must be judged a success. Other areas of the United Kingdom might be able to enjoy the advantages which Northern Ireland gained from devolution, while avoiding the disadvantages which flowed from the uniquely sectarian nature of politics in the province. Devolution in Northern Ireland was an experiment which deserved not to fail.

4 Scotland

When we had a king and a chancellor and parliament—men o' our ain, we could aye peeble them wi' stones when they werena guid bairns. But naebody's nails can reach the length o' Lunnon.

Scott: *Heart of Midlothian*

I

Scotland and England were first united when James VI of Scotland became King of England in 1603: but for over a hundred years they remained, in most other repects, separate countries retaining separate Parliaments. Not until 1707 did the English and Scottish Parliaments agree to merge their two kingdoms indissolubly and establish a common parliament, for the new kingdom of Great Britain.

The precise constitutional status and significance of the Acts of Union have been the subject of much dispute. For Scottish Nationalists, the Scottish Parliament was abolished against the wishes of the Scottish people, and the vote for Union secured through bribery and the promise of high office in the new state. For the thorough-going Unionist, on the other hand, the new Parliament of Great Britain was but the English Parliament writ large. The new state was to be a unitary one and Scotland's position in it no different from that of Cornwall or Yorkshire.

Both of these interpretations—the Nationalist and the Unionist—serve, however, only to obscure the reality of what happened in 1707. The Nationalist interpretation is not accepted by serious historians, and it entirely ignores the concrete arguments which finally persuaded the Scottish negotiators to accede to Westminster's demands for Union; yet, contrary to the Unionist view, the Scots by no means intended Scotland's status to be that of a mere province or region of Britain. The Scottish negotiators believed that Union was desirable because they were political realists; but they needed to be convinced that Union could safeguard vital Scottish interests.

The treaty itself was a logical corollary of the restoration of constitutional government in England in 1689. The Union of Crowns of 1603 had been a purely personal union. It could work as long as the king remained the true source of authority in both kingdoms. In 1688, however, William III became responsible to the English Parliament. How could the Union of Crowns survive a limited monarchy? The king could not be responsible to two different parliaments, following different policies; and since it was the English ministry which determined policy and could exclude Scotland from English markets, the issue was, 'whether Scotland should continue subject to an English ministry without trade, or be subject to an English Parliament with trade.'[1] If the Scots were not prepared to be governed by an English ministry, 'either the monarchies must be separated or the parliaments must unite.'[2]

From a parliamentary union, Scotland would gain access to the expanding markets of England and her colonies: she would have a better chance of preserving Presbyterianism and avoiding the threat of a Stuart and Catholic restoration. Above all, she would ensure peace with her southern neighbour. For in the words of Lord Roxburgh, one of the nobles who held the balance of power in the Scots Parliament, 'if Union fail, War will never be avoided; and for my part the more I think of Union, the more I like it, seeing no security anywhere else.'[3]

To the Scots, the loss of their parliament was not quite so high a price to pay for Union as it might seem today. For the Scottish Parliament did not, until 1690, assume the dominant position in Scottish life, which the English Parliament had long claimed. It was never, even after 1690, a sovereign parliament but 'only one of a number of rivals for the exercise of executive, and even of legislative authority';[4] and 'In 1707 . . . a free Scottish Parliament was not a time-hallowed institution but a novelty (though highly appreciated) of seventeen years' standing.'[5] Scottish nationality was secured not be her parliament, but by other national institutions—the legal system, the courts, and above all the Scottish Church, the Kirk. It seemed, therefore, that a settlement with England which preserved these institutions, would also preserve the symbols of Scottish nationhood, and that two nations might be able to co-exist within a unitary state under a common parliament.

The Scots sought the preservation of those national institutions which were so important to them, by establishing safeguards in the Treaty which formed the basis of the new state. They secured guarantees of the Scottish legal system and judiciary (Articles XVIII and XIX), and an accompanying Act for securing the Protestant religion in Scotland, and the Presbyterian form of Church Government: which 'represented a real concession by England'[6] and without which the Treaty would not have been signed.

Article XVIII of the Treaty guaranteed Scots private law. It distinguished between matters of 'public right' which were to be regulated by the new Parliament of Great Britain, and matters involving the law of 'private right' in Scotland which were to remain unaltered 'except for evident utility of the subjects within Scotland.' It has been held that if this clause had not been accepted by the English negotiators, then there would have been little hope for the Treaty of Union in Scotland. Article XIX laid down that the Scottish Court of Session would 'after the Union and notwithstanding thereof, remain in all time coming within Scotland as it is now constituted by the Laws of that Kingdom, and with the same Authority and Privileges as before the Union'. Other Scottish Courts were similarly guaranteed. No Scottish lawsuit was to be tried before an English judge; and English judges were explicitly debarred from 'recognizing, reviewing, or altering the acts or sentences of the judicature within Scotland, or stopping the execution of the same.' 'It is in these provisions that the federal desires of the Scottish Commissioners appear and survive. The protection of this system of courts was undoubtedly essential to the approval of the Union Agreement in the Parliament of Scotland . . .'.[7]

The accompanying Act for securing the Protestant religion and Presbyterian form of Church Government enacted that this form was to be 'held and observed in all time coming as a fundamental and essential condition of any Treaty of Union to be concluded between the two Kingdoms without any alteration thereof, or derogation thereto in any sort for ever.' 'The solemnity of words could go no further.'[8]

Article 24 of the Treaty provided that the Scottish state regalia— the crown, sceptre, and sword of state—should be 'kept as they are within that part of the United Kingdom now called Scotland, and that they shall remain in all time coming, notwithstanding the Union.' This can be interpreted as symbolic evidence that the Scots did not intend to sacrifice their nationality together with their Parliament. Indeed it has been argued that this Article 'is perhaps indicative of a sort of radical reversionary right of Scottish sovereignty in event of the Union breaking down.'[9]

The Scots sought, therefore, to ensure the preservation of their nationhood within the framework of a unitary state. The British Parliament was to incorporate the Scottish Parliament, but not the Scottish nation. A patriotic Scot could thus support the Union since it would give, in the long run, the best guarantee for the preservation of Scottish institutions. The alternatives were either a Stuart restoration or possible conquest by England, with at the very least a period of political instability and strained relations. Since the Jacobite cause remained attached to Catholicism, this would also involve suppression of Scotland's most cherished institution—the Kirk.

To the Scots, the Acts of Union symbolized Scotland's position as an unconquered nation. It was not a step towards assimilation, much less a recognition of subjugation by the English as the Irish Union of 1800 was to be. What happened in 1707 was seen as a constitutional settlement which would serve to guarantee and not to undermine Scotland's national institutions. Today, a solution to the problem posed in 1707—the problem of reconciling Scottish nationality with Union—might be sought through the device of a federal constitution; and, indeed, one authority on the Union has expressed 'regret that the Scots Parliament, largely as a result of its new-found vigour and vitality, had to be abolished, and that the federal solution was not tried.'[10] But this regret is anachronistic. For the first federal constitution was not established until 1787, eighty years after the Treaty of Union. When they called for a federal relationship with England, the Scottish negotiators did not propose a division of powers between a federal Parliament for Great Britain, and 'provincial' parliaments for England and Scotland. They were thinking in terms of the Dutch *confederation*, the United Provinces which was a league of states without any constitutional provisions for unity of action. But the 'association of two equally sovereign parliaments' would be subject to just those quarrels and disagreements which had bedevilled Anglo-Scottish relations in the period leading up to the Union.

The Scottish negotiators themselves regarded the federal proposal as, in the words of Sir John Clerk of Penicuik, 'ridiculous and impracticable' and it seems to have been 'no more than a gesture for the benefit of the Scottish public, something to show that at least an attempt had been made to save their Parliament.' For federation was 'not worth the paines . . . and will be a mother of future dangers and discords at some unhappy occasion.'[11]

But the absence of the federal idea from the constitutional debate in 1707 meant that there was a crucial weakness in the settlement from the Scottish point of view; for there was no machinery through which Scottish interests could be defended in the face of a permanent English majority. Constitutionally, both England and Scotland lost their Parliaments; for both were merged into the new Parliament of Great Britain. But politically, of course, England was well able to secure her interests in the new Parliament because of the numerical preponderance of English members. There was therefore some danger that the safeguards in the Treaty would be ignored by the English, for without appropriate constitutional machinery, the settlement rested on nothing more than goodwill.

The Treaty itself has undergone considerable modification since it was signed; nine of the articles have been wholly repealed, and five have been repealed in part. Admittedly, Parliament has not attempted to repeal any of the articles whose amendment was expressly forbidden by the Treaty; but there seems little doubt that Parliament could repeal them if it so wished even in the face of opposition from Scottish M.P.s and public opinion.

The Treaty, although it sought to preserve Scottish identity, thus made no provision for this identity to be displayed either politically or juridically. No provision was made for political machinery, such as a plebiscite or a convention of Scottish M.P.s, through which the will of Scottish people could be ascertained; and judicial review was, of course, a weapon unknown to the Scots in 1707.

Nevertheless, it could be argued that England, by signing the Treaty, morally bound herself to respect within the framework of Great Britain those claims which were specifically Scottish. That at least was the view of the constitutional lawyer, A. V. Dicey.

To Dicey, the Scots negotiating the Treaty had been trapped in a logical contradiction in attempting to bind 'an absolutely sovereign legislature' 'by unalterable laws'. Yet 'the enactment of laws which are described as unchangeable, immutable, or the like, is not necessarily futile' since it displayed the conviction of the Scots that certain provisions 'ought to be morally or constitutionally unchangeable, even by the British Parliament'. 'A sovereign Parliament, in short, though it cannot be logically bound to abstain from changing any given law, may, by the fact that an Act when it was passed had been declared to be unchangeable, receive a warning that it cannot be changed without grave danger to the Constitution of the country.'[12]

England thus took upon herself an obligation of honour—not a legal but a moral obligation—when she signed the Treaty. That obligation was to respect the institutions and practices which maintained for the Scots their sense of nationality. For only in this way could 'The permanent success' of the Union in creating a United Kingdom of Great Britain be ensured.[13]

The retention of a separate Scottish legal system and judiciary made possible by the Treaty has been a vital factor in ensuring that Scotland has retained her identity. For it has meant that, even during the years when Scotland seemed as 'North Britain' to be assimilated to English norms, Parliament, both in administering and legislating for Scotland, was compelled to take account of the existence of a wholly distinctive system of law. In this way the seeds of devolution were sown by the Scots who negotiated the Treaty.

Historians seem to agree that the Union was not at first popular in Scotland: if it had been put to referendum, it would almost certainly have been defeated: and dissatisfaction with the Union was compounded when in the years immediately after 1707 the British Parliament ignored some of its provisions. Nevertheless, after a period of initial unpopularity, the Union gradually came to be accepted by the Scots as a satisfactory settlement; and it was never regarded with the same antagonism as the Irish displayed towards their Union with Britain in 1800.

The spirit with which political negotiations are carried out is often as important as their substantive result, and the Scottish

Union, unlike the Irish was negotiated on a firm footing of equality. It had the character of a freely negotiated contract between two consenting parties, and it allowed the Scots to continue to regard themselves as an unconquered people freely participating in the affairs of a new state. Retaining her own institutions as objects of national reverence and attachment, Scotland's emotional response to Union was bound to be very different from that of the Irish who saw the connection with Britain as a mark of subjugation. Thus, there can be little doubt that the terms of the Union with Scotland contributed markedly to its success. For Scotland, unlike Ireland, retained her native church and her own legal system; and for most of the period since the Union, the executive acts of government in Scotland were carried out by Scotsmen, whereas the Irish Executive was composed of English ministers and civil servants. Therefore, in Gladstone's words, 'the mainspring of law in Scotland is felt by the people to be Scotch; but the mainspring of the law in Ireland is not felt by the people to be Irish . . .'[14].

II

Since 1885, the executive government in Scotland has come to be in the hands of the Scottish Office, headed since 1926 by the Secretary of State for Scotland who is, except in wartime, a member of the Cabinet. The Scottish Office has seen a continual increase in its functions as the scope of central government has expanded until, by the 1960s, the Secretary of State was expected to take an interest in all matters affecting Scotland, and to put the case for Scotland in the Cabinet. The Secretary of State is responsible not only for social and environmental policy in Scotland, but he also has economic powers: he is now 'recognized as responsible for taking the lead in the preparation of plans for economic development in Scotland, and for co-ordinating the execution of these plans.'[15]

In June 1973, the Scottish Office was reorganized into five departments; the Secretary of State's increasing responsibilities in the economic field were recognized by the creation of a Scottish Economic Planning Department, and he was given co-ordinate responsibility for oil development in Scotland; in 1975 statutory responsibility for the Scottish Development Agency, and for selective assistance to industry in Scotland were given to him. The Scottish Office is thus the real heart of executive government in Scotland, and there can be few governmental decisions affecting Scotland which do not involve it. There can be little doubt that the Scottish Office is one of the more successful of British government departments. The Balfour Commission laid down in 1954 two criteria in terms of which the effectiveness of government arrangements in Scotland could be assessed; the first was that 'the machinery of government should be designed to dispose of Scottish business in Scotland' and the second was that Scottish needs and the Scottish point of view should be borne in mind 'at all stages in the formulation and execution of policy'.[16]

The wide range of statutory powers conferred upon the Secretary of State undoubtedly meets the first criterion; indeed it is not easy to think of any specifically Scottish matter which has not been decentralized to the Scottish Office, and it seems likely therefore that the limits of administrative decentralization have been reached. The second requirement is met by the governmental arrangements which allow Scotland to be formally represented upon any policy-making committee whose decisions might affect Scotland, even where these decisions lie outside the Secretary of State's area of statutory responsibility.

In addition, the Scottish Office, administering a population of only five million, enjoys closer contacts with individuals and with local authorities than a U.K. department is able to achieve; and, although this has led to stronger central direction of local authorities in Scotland than in England, the accessibility of the Scottish Office is something that is very much welcomed by public opinion in Scotland. Civil servants working in the Scottish Office possess a remarkable *esprit de corps*, which gives the Office an entirely different flavour from a U.K. department. This *esprit de corps* derives from the strong identification with Scotland made by many civil servants working in the Scottish Office, and there is a strong determination to do what is best for Scotland, which undoubtedly makes for more effective administration.

There is some concrete evidence that the second criterion laid down by the Balfour Commission is also met through current governmental arrangements for Scotland. Over recent years, public expenditure per head in Scotland has been consistently higher than in England as a whole, or any of the English regions, including the North and the North West whose economic problems are comparable in seriousness to those in Scotland. A written answer on 2 December 1977 elicited the fact that if the block grant for services devolved to Scotland were based on the same expenditure per head of population as in England, then public expenditure per head in Scotland (excluding rates raised locally in Scotland) would be reduced with respect to the devolved services by between twenty-five and thirty per cent.[17] With regard to regional shares of public expenditure, the shares of the various regions have been elicited by the Northern Region Strategy Team (See Table below).[18] It would be reasonable to assume that some at least of this difference is due to the advantage which Scotland enjoys through having a minister of her own at Cabinet level to secure special recognition of Scotland's special needs.

Region	*Per Capita* Index 1969/70-1973/4 (G.B. = 100)
Northern Region	112.4
Yorkshire and Humberside	87.0
East Midlands	92.4
East Anglia	94.7
South East	102.8
South West	97.1
West Midlands	83.4
North West	98.0
Wales	110.5
Scotland	117.0

(N.B. These figures relate to public expenditure as a whole, including services which are not being devolved to Scotland.)

Yet the very effectiveness of Scottish administration brings into greater prominence the problems of accountability resulting from the Secretary of State being seen as 'Scotland's minister' while also being bound by the convention of collective Cabinet responsibility. For he is, of course, no more than one not very senior minister in a Cabinet of (say) twenty-four. He can therefore easily be over-ruled by the Cabinet, and will then have to support policies which both he and Scottish public opinion believe to be hostile to

Scotland's interests. Even where he is successful in securing gains for Scotland, the convention of collective responsibility will serve to hide this from the public, and prevent him from parading his successes. In 1975, for example, the Cabinet considered the possibility of allowing the closure of the Chrysler plant at Linwood near Glasgow; and a threat of resignation on the part of Mr. William Ross, then Secretary of State for Scotland, was widely believed to have been instrumental in persuading the government to change its mind. Yet Mr. Ross could only convey his success to Scottish public opinion by a series of winks and nods. The governmental policy-making process for Scotland lacks political visibility; the Royal Commission on the Constitution found that fifty-two per cent of those questioned did not know of the existence of the Scottish Office, and that the remaining forty-eight per cent were largely unaware of its responsibilities. That is a serious weakness at a time when not only the official Opposition, but also the S.N.P. are willing to suggest that their policies would have served Scotland better.

This lack of political visibility is accentuated by the sheer physical impossibility of the Secretary of State spending enough time in Scotland to satisfy his critics. When Parliament is sitting, he is unable to spend more than half of the week in Scotland, and he has to include in this period his constituency business and meetings with Scottish Office officials as well as the numerous pressure groups who demand an audience with him. An iron constitution is certainly one quality required of the Secretary of State, and it must be questionable whether it is in the interests of good government to allow a Cabinet minister to spend so much of his time shuttling between London and Edinburgh.

It is these difficulties of communication which make it peculiarly difficult for ministers at the Scottish Office to secure effective control over the department. It is frequently claimed that the Scottish Office suffers from an especial lack of accountability to elected representatives. But there is no evidence that there is a greater degree of delegation of decision-making in the Scottish Office than in other U.K. departments; nor that matters which in England are dealt with by ministers are dealt with by civil servants in Scotland. But the crucial difference is that, because the minister is 400 miles away from the department for much of his time, the degree of control that he can exert on the *implementation* of his decisions, is bound to be limited.

Moreover the wide range of responsibilities enjoyed by the Secretary of State, covering matters for which nine U.K. departments are responsible, leads to the over-loading of the executive in Scotland, and makes it difficult to ensure that sufficient attention is being given to each area of policy. To take one example, education which in England is the responsibility of five ministers is, in Scotland, the responsibility of the Secretary of State and a parliamentary under-secretary who also has to deal with social work, sport, and the arts.

In practice, then, a considerable amount of discretion is bound to remain with civil servants; and since the Commons also finds it difficult to hold the Scottish Office accountable, with Questions only once every three weeks to cover a wide range of functions, there can be little doubt that the arrangements for disposing of government business in Scotland are highly unsatisfactory.

A different kind of limitation upon the value of administrative decentralization in Scotland lies in the fact that expenditure on Scottish Office functions is limited by the need to ensure comparability with expenditure in England. Decisions upon expenditure are taken on a functional and not a geographical basis. The criterion on which they are judged is that of need, rather than geography. This is in order to ensure observance of the general principle that there should be common standards and criteria for the provision of services throughout Great Britain. Variation of expenditure between programmes requires Treasury approval. Even where this approval is given, however, there are practical limitations upon switching since 'By the time you know you are going to be underspent in a particular year or in a particular period on one particular programme, there is really in practice very little scope for switching, if the case arose, because it is too late to do much about it.'[19] This means that it is very difficult for the Scottish Office to determine its own priorities for Scottish expenditure.

'Let us say,' a Scottish M.P. enquired of the Permanent Under-Secretary of State in 1969, 'a U.K. decision was taken to spend a great deal more on housing than on roads and that the housing budget should expand faster than the road budget. You could not envisage a situation in which the machinery would allow Scotland under the Secretary of State for Scotland to take a separate decision and reverse that process?' The answer he received was 'No, not a decision that would be in a major way at odds with it.'[20] This means that expenditure priorities in Scotland cannot be determined, except at the margin, in accordance with Scottish needs, but must be compatible with conventions which ensure that major powers of decision are in practice retained at the centre. There are thus very serious limitations upon the extent to which the Scottish Office is able to shape policies suited to Scotland's needs.

III

Just as Parliament has long recognized that Scotland is a separate unit for administrative purposes, so also it has made special arrangements for the conduct of Scottish business in the House of Commons. The committee stage of Scottish business is taken in two Scottish standing committees, and dealt with very largely by Scottish M.P.s; and the Second Reading debate and Report stage of Scottish Bills can be taken in the Scottish Grand Committee, a committee composed of all the M.P.s sitting for Scottish constituencies, together with between ten and fifteen additional members when necessary to ensure a party balance. The Scottish Grand Committee also discusses the Scottish Estimates for six sittings in each session, and debates Scottish issues for two sittings in each session.

The value of these arrangements is also limited, however. For although all the stages of a Scottish bill except for the formal First Reading, the Second Reading vote, and the formal Third Reading, can be taken in Scottish committees, the Standing Orders of the House of Commons ensure that this procedure cannot be used unless there is already very wide agreement on the merits of a particular measure. It needs only ten M.P.s to object to prevent a Scottish Bill being sent to the Scottish Grand Committee, and, when a Bill returns for a Second Reading vote in the House, it requires only six M.P.s to sign an amendment for the Second Reading debate to take place again on the floor of the House. For the House of Commons is jealous of its authority, and unwilling to delegate it to committees. It therefore insists upon retaining the power to vote on purely Scottish issues. Indeed, Scottish M.P.s themselves might well resist a greater devolution of parliamentary authority to the Scottish Grand Committee, since they wish to remain full members of the Commons, and would resent being forced off the floor of the House.

Moreover the Grand Committee and the Standing Committees are unable to act as a political forum for Scotland, since they can undertake only legislative work. But 'if one is to provide a proper outlet for expression of opinion, a proper means of exerting influence upon governmental activity and policy-making, any Parliamentary assembly must have more than merely legislative powers. It must have an inquisitive function, a deliberative function.'[21]

For it to genuinely fulfil its function as a forum of Scottish opinion, a 'little Scottish House of Commons inside the House of Commons of the United Kingdom',[22] the Scottish Grand Committee would have to be empowered to question Scottish Office ministers, to scrutinize projections of public expenditure for Scotland and the activities of the wide range of nominated bodies in Scotland, such as the Highlands and Islands Development Board and the Scottish Development Agency. The Select Committee on Scottish Affairs was able to examine government policy for Scotland in some depth in two broad areas—economic development and land-use planning—during its short life from 1968 to 1971, but since its demise, there is no other parliamentary body able to perform a similar function.

Moreover, the Grand Committee does not escape the warfare between Government and Opposition. There may be an incentive for a government to send issues away from the floor of the House and into the Grand Committee, since it rarely votes and attracts little publicity; the more business that is sent to the Grand Committee the more time remains for other government business on the floor of the House. But, by the same token, the Opposition will be unwilling to allow the government of the day to save time, since lack of time remains almost the only hope the Opposition has of preventing government legislation. In the 1974–9 parliament, the Conservative Opposition was unwilling to allow even non-controversial items to go to the Scottish Grand Committee, so as to deny the government time on the floor of the House for more controversial measures.

The value of the Scottish Grand Committee, then, is severely limited. Its main consequence is to create a Scottish parliamentary sub-system within the House of Commons, whereby Scottish concerns are dealt with only by Scottish members. English M.P.s who dare to speak in the Scottish Grand Committee are met with 'a certain humorous resentment',[23] and the appointment of non-Scottish additional members to the Grand Committee, David Steel commented, 'is a threat which the Chief Whip holds over any laggard or recalcitrant English Member'. 'When a Tory face appeared there one wondered what he had done to incur the displeasure of his Whips.'[24]

On the floor of the House, also, suggestions are sometimes made that English members should not vote on purely Scottish matters. Both Labour and Conservative governments have been unwilling to allow English members to override the wishes of Scottish M.P.s on such 'non-political' issues as the reform of the Scottish divorce law, and the reform of the homosexuality laws was not extended immediately to Scotland, because of luke-warm support for reform amongst Scottish members. When Scottish local government was being reformed in 1973, a revolt in the Scottish Standing Committee led to the creation of the county of Fife as a region; but the Secretary of State for Scotland accepted this, saying 'The Government do not intend to take the initiative to reverse the decision unless we are pressed to do so by a majority of the Scottish Members of parliament.'[25] On the other hand, on more truly political matters, the government will generally insist on getting its own way, whatever the majority view of Scottish M.P.s.

Scottish M.P.s tend to devote their time and attention in Parliament to issues affecting Scottish material interests. They rarely take part in standing committees on bills relating only to England and Wales, and play a less important role than English members in committees concerned with foreign, commonwealth, or defence matters. 'Like representatives in a federal system, Scottish M.P.s are pursuing distinctive concerns at the Scottish level, while supporting their leaders at the national level.'[26]

It is clear, then, that the distinctiveness of Scotland as a political entity is recognized, both at the executive level in the development of the Scottish Office, and at the parliamentary level in the structure of the Scottish committees in the Commons. But the conventions of the U.K. political system are bound to limit the extent to which Scotland can be governed as a distinctive unit within the framework of the unitary state.

Collective Cabinet responsibility prevents the Secretary of State for Scotland from acting as a genuine Minister for Scotland; and the requirement that the Cabinet be a constitutional unity means that the Secretary of State may represent, as in 1970–4, a party which has only a minority of seats in Scotland. The growth in the functions of the Scottish Office has, paradoxically, led to less accountability over Scottish matters, since it has given greater power to the Secretary of State and to civil servants, without providing an effective democratic counterweight.

In the Commons, the traditions of Parliament, and in particular its unwillingness to lose control of its business to any sub-group within it, prevents effective parliamentary scrutiny of the Scottish Office, and restricts Scottish control over Scottish business to comparatively uncontroversial matters.

Since 1945, Scottish politicians, civil servants, and pressure groups have used these distinctively Scottish political institutions to further Scotland's interests. The Secretary of State, backed by public opinion in Scotland, has ensured that Scottish opinion is not ignored in the policy-making process; and he is helped by Scottish M.P.s using 'the leverage of Scottish representation to improve both U.K. economic policy in general and its impact on Scotland in particular.'[27] It is, as we have seen, difficult to evaluate the success of this tactic owing to its lack of political visibility; and for this very reason, even when it is successful, it cannot make a striking impact upon the electorate in Scotland; for if it did, there is always the danger that it would arouse an English backlash in regions not favoured by separate representation in the Cabinet or by separate regional arrangements in Parliament.

Moreover the success of the relationship between Scotland on the one hand, and Westminster and Whitehall on the other, presupposed a process of steady economic improvement in the U.K. as a whole, so that Scotland's gains would not appear to be made at the expense of other parts of the United Kingdom. But this consensus was breached by the economic difficulties of the late

1960s, since when many Scots have come to believe that economic policy-making is shaped too greatly by England's requirements, and that Scotland's problems receive insufficient attention. Given the secretive nature of the policy-making process, these accusations are difficult ones for Scotland's political representatives to refute. The economic decline of the U.K. thus casts doubt on the value of traditional Scottish Office tactics, and a new approach may be required if the economic benefits of the Union are to be effectively displayed.

The mainspring of the case for devolution to Scotland, then, has little to do with the alleged 'exploitation' of Scotland by England as many nationalists claim, but consists of the need to re-establish a relationship which has been seriously undermined. The prime need is to provide a more adequate structure of government for Scotland since the arrangements for handling Scottish business, both at the executive and at the parliamentary level, are now highly unsatisfactory, and likely, in the absence of devolution, to remain so.

The great increase in the centralization of government since 1945 makes these maladjusted governmental arrangements more difficult to bear, since government itself plays a so much larger role in the life of Scotland than it did a generation ago. When the scope of government was limited, it mattered less whether government was situated in London or in Edinburgh, since its decisions affected the individual less than the decisions of indigenous Scottish institutions. In the modern world, however, it is the decisions of governments which, for good or ill, affect individual lives, and so the institutions guaranteed by the Union—the legal system, the courts, and the Kirk—have been displaced from their position as guarantors of Scottish identity. It can be argued, therefore, that this identity can only be preserved if the government of Scotland is seen to reflect Scottish interests more adequately.

But if the real case for devolution has more to do with contemporary trends in government than with the wilder claims of the nationalists, it is nevertheless true that without the electoral successes of the S.N.P., devolution would never have assumed so prominent a place on the U.K. political agenda. It is to an explanation of the rise of nationalism, therefore, that we must now turn.

IV

The Union brought political stability and economic progress to Scotland, and this had helped to ensure its acceptance. Nevertheless, even during the period of the Union's greatest success, there remained in Scotland 'a persistent sense of loss, and a perennial sense of outrage at English condescension',[28] an instinctive and emotional nationalism most poignantly expressed by Burns and Scott, which did not immediately find political expression because it was outweighed by a rational calculation of the benefits of Union.

Assimilationist feeling in Scotland probably reached its peak during the period 1750 to 1850, the years of greatest economic advance for Scotland. Economic factors and the development of communications were beginning to make Britain a much more integrated economy, and Edinburgh, from being a centre of government and politics, was becoming but 'an inn or half-way house between London and the Highland Muirs'.[29] During the nineteenth century, indeed, Scotland was frequently referred to as North Britain, and it seemed on the way to losing its separate identity and becoming a mere province of England. That this did not happen was due to two factors: first Scotland's separate legal and administrative system which meant that institutions such as the poor law and the education system continued to be organized on a Scottish basis; and secondly, the influence of the Irish Home Rule agitation, which gave rise to a stirring of national feeling in Scotland and Wales.

But Scottish nationalism never displayed the emotional hostility to the British connection which animated the Parnellites. It has always been essentially moderate, and has adhered strictly to constitutional methods. The first distinctively modern political nationalist movement, the Scottish Home Rule Association, was set up in May 1886, one month after the first Irish Home Rule Bill was introduced into the Commons. It emphasized not the injustice of British rule after the fashion of the Parnellites, but 'the legislative neglect of Scotland', and the need to reform the licensing laws, and the land, game, and fishery laws.[30]

From 1890 to 1914, measures proposing Scottish Home Rule appeared thirteen times before the House of Commons, being accepted in principle by the House on eight occasions and securing the support of a majority of Scottish M.P.s on eleven occasions. But none of the Bills was successful in reaching the Committee stage, and this reflected the low priority attached to Scottish Home Rule even amongst M.P.s sympathetic to the cause.

For it would be wrong to suppose that the frequency of appearance of Scottish Home Rule Bills corresponded to any great popular feeling on the issue in Scotland. They seem rather to have been introduced as ritual gestures on the part of Liberal and Labour M.P.s who felt duty-bound to argue that Scotland had claims no less important than those of Ireland. There was no Parnell, nor even a Tom Ellis in Scotland, because Scottish grievances were not felt powerfully enough to form the major part of a political programme. Before 1914, Scottish nationalism had the character of an imitative and artificial movement.

V

The founder of modern political nationalism in Scotland was John MacCormick who, while a student of Glasgow University, left the Labour Party to form a university Nationalist Society. He was the first leader of the Scottish National Party (S.N.P.) which was born in 1934, but his aim was to secure a Scottish Parliament within the framework of the United Kingdom and not independence from England. During the War, however, MacCormick was ousted, and the S.N.P. became an explicitly separatist party committed to fighting elections against the other political parties. It succeeded in winning Motherwell in a by-election in April 1945 during the wartime electoral truce, but the seat was lost in the ensuing general election two months later, and when party politics were resumed, it was rapidly reduced to a picturesque party of cranks and faddists. From 1955, however, the S.N.P.'s electoral performance improved steadily if unspectacularly until, in the General Election of 1966, its twenty-three candidates secured five per cent of the Scottish vote, an average of 14.1 per cent per opposed candidate.

Election	Candidates	Total Votes	Percentage of Scottish total
1955	2	12,112	0.5
1959	5	21,738	0.8
1964	15	64,044	2.4
1966	23	128,474	5.0

Source: F. W. S. Craig: *British Electoral Facts: 1885–1975*, London, 1976, p. 89.

Then in March 1967 in a by-election at Glasgow, Pollok, the S.N.P. succeeded in breaking through the constraints of the British party system. In a marginal seat, won by the Conservatives from Labour, it succeeded in gaining 28.2 per cent of the vote. Pollok was followed by Mrs Ewing's victory at Hamilton in November 1967 in what had hitherto been a Labour stronghold: and in 1968 the momentum was continued with widespread gains in the municipal elections, the S.N.P. winning nearly 100 seats, and securing the balance of power in Glasgow, thus depriving Labour of overall control for the first time since 1952. But, unfortunately from the S.N.P.'s viewpoint, there were then no more parliamentary by-elections in Scotland until October 1969 when the Labour Government's popularity had recovered somewhat. Nevertheless fighting in Glasgow, Gorbals, the S.N.P. candidate secured one-quarter of the vote, even though Gorbals was particularly unfavourable ground for the S.N.P. because of the high proportion of Roman Catholics in the constituency; for a number of surveys have shown that Catholics are less likely than Protestants to switch from Labour to the S.N.P. There was to be only one further parliamentary by-election in Scotland in the 1966–70 Parliament—in South Ayrshire in March 1970 where the S.N.P. secured one-fifth of the vote. Overall, its average performance in the four by-elections of the parliament was 29.2 per cent.

In the general election of 1970, the S.N.P. fought on a broader front that it had ever previously done, contesting sixty-five out of the seventy-one Scottish seats. Its progress between 1970 and 1974 is shown below.

Election	Candidates	Seats	Total Votes	Percentage of Scottish total
1970	65	1	306,802	11.4
By elections 1970–4	4	1	(Average in the four seats)	31.4

Election	Candidates	Seats	Total Votes	Percentage of Scottish total
Feb. 1974	70	7	633,180	21.9
Oct. 1974	71	11	839,617	30.4

Source: See Table, p.92.

In February 1974, the S.N.P. gained six seats, four from the Conservatives and two from Labour, and in October a further four seats, all from the Conservatives. It became the second largest party in Scotland, overtaking the Conservatives, in terms of its percentage of the vote in Scotland. After October 1974, it had eleven seats, and was second in a further forty-two seats, including thirty-five of Labour's forty-one Scottish seats: a swing of five per cent to the S.N.P. from the sitting incumbent would have given it a further sixteen seats, and destroyed the Labour Party's electoral position in Scotland.

VI

What is the explanation of the spectacular growth of support for the S.N.P.? Its success not only caused serious problems for the three U.K. parties, it also posed a challenge to those who explained electoral behaviour, forcing them to readjust their preconceptions about electoral motivation. The conclusions of psephology had very much reflected the social democratic consensus of the immediate post-war period: and the social sciences had given little attention to those historical factors which made one part of the United Kingdom different from another. 'Class,' it was said, 'is the basis of British politics: all else is embellishment and detail.'[31] This made it difficult to explain the advances of the nationalists as being anything other than a 'protest vote' against the two-party system, a temporary and somewhat irrational departure from a stable political norm. Such a view received partial confirmation in the 1970 General Election, although the failure of the S.N.P. to win more than one seat masked a steady improvement in its vote spread as it was over a far larger number of constituencies than had ever been fought before.

The modicum of truth in the 'protest' explanation is that until the late 1960s the nationalist parties were able to do well only when disillusionment with government was strong enough for the Liberal

Party in England to do so also. According to William Miller, who has produced the most sophisticated explanation for the rise of the S.N.P., 'From its inception the S.N.P. did well at the polls only when other alternatives to Labour and Conservative did well throughout Britain.'[32]

From 1945 until 1959, the period when satisfaction with the two-party system was at its height, the S.N.P. never succeeded in securing more than 1.3 per cent of the Scottish vote in a general election. But in 1961 and 1962, during the time of the Liberal upsurge in England when the Liberals succeeded in winning Orpington, one of the safest Conservative seats in the country, the S.N.P. gained nearly a fifth of the vote in a by-election in Glasgow, Bridgeton, and nearly a quarter of the vote in a by-election at West Lothian, fought against Tam Dalyell. But when the Liberal tide receded, and the Labour Party came to be seen as the natural alternative to the Government, support for the S.N.P. lessened also. In three Scottish by-elections in 1963, the S.N.P. was able to secure no more than an average of eight per cent of the vote.

In the 1966–70 Parliament, disillusionment with government in England led not to support for the Liberals but to massive Labour abstentions and very large swings to the Conservatives. The Liberals were unable to attract Labour abstainers in England, but in Scotland and Wales, disillusioned Labour supporters had an alternative to abstention: they could vote for the S.N.P. or Plaid Cymru. In Scotland and Wales the nationalist parties were thus able to channel political protest which would otherwise have expressed itself in disillusionment or apathy.

In the 1970–4 Parliament the S.N.P. did not do well until after the Liberal breakthrough at Rochdale in October 1972. From then until the February 1974 General Election the Liberals gained five seats in England, four of them from the Conservatives and one from Labour. In addition, Mr. Taverne at Lincoln succeeded in holding his seat standing as a Democratic Labour candidate against official Labour opposition. During the same period, the S.N.P. scored 30 per cent of the vote in Dundee East, 42 per cent of the vote in Glasgow, Govan winning the seat from Labour; and 19 per cent of the vote in Edinburgh North. In February 1974, the S.N.P. secured 21.9 per cent of the vote in Scotland, as compared with the Liberals' 23.6 per cent average share of the vote per opposed candidate in the U.K. as a whole, and in October 1974 the S.N.P. made a further advance as its vote went up to 30.4 per cent, whereas the Liberal vote declined to 18.9 per cent per opposed candidate. The advance of the S.N.P. could no longer be explained by the mobilization of those who had previously not voted, since turn-out was 4.2 per cent lower than it had been in February. Nor could it be explained simply as a 'protest'.

The S.N.P. had succeeded in breaking the constraints of the two-party system in Scotland, something that the Liberals in England had often been on the verge of doing, but had never quite succeeded in achieving. What might perhaps have originally been a protest vote had solidified into something much deeper. For the notion of protest does not explain why support for the S.N.P. increased at a time when support for the other 'protest' parties— Plaid Cymru in Wales and the Liberals in England—remained stable or fell, so that the S.N.P. was able to establish itself as one party in a three-party system in Scotland, while the Liberals and Plaid Cymru (except in seats in North and West Wales) could not. To explain the new alignment in Scottish politics, we must understand the powerful sense of Scottish nationality, buttressed by a history of shared institutions, which gave to economic grievance a shape unmatched in other parts of Britain.

We have already seen that the preservation of the national institutions of Scotland ensured that Scottish identity would not be destroyed by the Union. This sense of identity provided the basis for the electoral success of the S.N.P. Indeed the potential for a nationalist revival in Scotland has probably existed for some time; and in 1965, before the S.N.P. upsurge, Budge and Urwin felt that

One awkward question has not been faced by our discussion: if Scottish feeling is so widespread through all groups and both classes, why have the Conservatives and Labour parties not lost more ground to the S.N.P. and the Liberals who have promised to implement Home Rule?[33]

The answer seems to be that, until the late 1960s, nationalism was not given a sufficiently high priority by the electorate. Part of the reason for this must be simple inertia, but a more important reason was that hitherto the Labour and Conservative Parties had seemed able to secure Scotland's interests. When the Conservatives were in power during the inter-war period and the 1950s, Labour could be relied upon to 'speak for Scotland'; and the post-war Attlee Government, although it possessed a centralizing ethos, brought considerable economic and social benefits to Scotland.

In office in the late 1960s, Labour again showed little interest in Scotland's national claims, but this might not have mattered if London government had been accompanied, as in the 1940s, by economic progress. For centralization had been defended as a process by which Scotland, through her Secretary of State, could secure important economic advantages. The combination of centralized government and economic failure led, however, to disillusion with Labour, but voters in seats such as Hamilton found it difficult to cross class barriers and support the Conservatives. Instead, if they were sympathetic to self-government, they could support the S.N.P. which was not perceived as a class party. Later, in the 1970s, disillusionment with the Heath Government persuaded Conservative voters sympathetic to self-government to support the S.N.P.

Nation-wide economic grievances thus acted to break up traditional party allegiances. But the sense of nationality in Scotland meant that the reaction to economic failure when it came would take a different form from that in England. The S.N.P. gained support not so much as the party of independence or separatism, but as the party of Scottish identity, the party that 'speaks for Scotland'.

Moreover, support for the S.N.P. had a self-reinforcing effect, when it was shown that the very successes of the party could secure benefits for Scotland, as the Labour and Conservative Parties rushed to counter its appeal. Voters came to see that the S.N.P. could act as a powerful pressure group for Scottish demands, so that even those who did not wish to see an independent Scotland, could appreciate that supporting the S.N.P. was one way of ensuring that Scotland received economic benefits.

In its October 1974 Scottish General Election manifesto the Labour Government proclaimed how much it had done for Scotland in its seven months of office. It had doubled the Regional Employment Premium, bringing Scotland an extra £40m. a year; it had given Edinburgh and Leith development area status, bringing in a further £8m. a year; it had moved the Offshore Supplies Office to Glasgow; it had agreed to establish the British National Oil

Corporation in Scotland; it had promised to move 7,000 civil service jobs to Scotland by the early 1980s, and had tightened the limit for industrial development certificates so as to increase Scotland's chances of attracting new industry. There were also a large number of promises—to establish a Scottish Development Agency, and a Centre for Oil Drilling Technology in Scotland, to halt rail closures in Scotland, and to modernize the Glasgow underground at a cost of £11.8m., as well as the promise to establish a directly elected legislative assembly. One would not have to be very cynical to ask how many of these reforms and promises would have been made in so short a time without the electoral threat posed by the S.N.P. It is little wonder that when asked by the British Election Study survey whether they felt that on balance, S.N.P. successes had been 'good for Scotland', only 14 per cent said that they had not, while 76 per cent (including 70 per cent of Labour voters, and 68 per cent of Conservative voters) thought that they had.

During the early 1970s, two things happened which increased the credibility of the S.N.P., and shifted significantly the balance of argument in favour of Scottish independence. The first, of course, was the discovery and commercial exploitation of oil in the North Sea. This seemed to overturn the central argument of Unionists that the Union with England was a pre-condition of Scotland's economic health. The choice could now be presented as one between rich Scotland and poor England. It could now be argued that the Union placed Scotland under an economic handicap. Scots could claim that it was in their interests to secure a slower rate of extraction of North Sea oil than the U.K. government demanded, so as not to exhaust her resources too rapidly, while the government's priority was simply to pay off its debts as quickly as possible. Moreover, a rapid rate of extraction of the oil might have serious effects upon the environment in the North East of Scotland, and it could be argued that the priorities of the Department of Energy as between Britain's energy needs and Scotland's environment, were not necessarily the right ones.

This argument over the rate of extraction is by no means an invulnerable one. It tends to slide over the point that a slower rate of extraction might lessen the benefits of North Sea oil and also lessen the improvement in employment. Nevertheless, whatever the weaknesses in the argument, it is easy to see that it would appeal to many in Scotland.

A further problem to which the discovery of North Sea Oil gave rise was the use to which the oil revenues should be put. For the real benefits of the oil lie in the gain to the Balance of Payments and the revenues accruing to government, and not in the immediate effects upon employment and incomes, which are likely to be small. An independent Scotland might,if her legal right to ownership of the oil fields was conceded, be able to enjoy the benefits of the oil revenues, while as part of the U.K., unless the government made a positive attempt to use the revenues to revive Scotland's industrial structure, the real benefits of the oil might escape her entirely. When we come to deal with the Scotland Act, we shall see how some M.P.s attempted to ensure that the Scottish Assembly would be given royalties from the oil revenues, and this reflected a view that the discovery of oil would require Unionist politicians to pay a higher price if they wished to retain Scotland in the Union.

Nevertheless, it would be wrong to place too great a stress upon the discovery of oil as an explanation of the rise of Scottish nationalism. For the rise of the S.N.P. in the late 1960s pre-dated the discovery of oil, and numerous surveys have shown that support for Scottish independence has remained at twenty per cent since 1968 until recently with no dramatic increase in support when the commercial exploitation of the oil began.

The S.N.P.'s 1973 campaign 'It's Scotland's Oil' was not a success, and a survey carried out for the British Election Study shows that the desire to keep the oil revenues in Scotland was likely to persuade voters to support the S.N.P. only if they were already strong supporters of devolution or separation. According to Miller, 'Attitude to self-government was clearly much more influential than attitude to oil revenues', for 'Oil and, by extension, the feeling that Scotland could "go it alone economically" cannot be seen as more than a constraint breaking influence that reduced the perceived costs of an already desirable objective.'[34] If there had not already been a considerable reservoir of support and goodwill for the S.N.P., therefore, it is doubtful whether the discovery of oil by itself would have led to new political alignments. Oil reinforced the electoral support of the S.N.P. rather than causing it.

The second factor which altered the nature of the argument

about Scottish independence was Britain's entry into the Common Market. This altered the whole context of the Scottish debate, since it emphasized the disadvantages of remote government for Scotland, and lessened the benefits to be obtained from membership of the United Kingdom. If important layers of decision-making came to be removed from London to Brussels, it could be argued that Edinburgh would become even more remote from the centre of power. If Scotland was already part of the U.K. periphery, and not central to the consciousness of most English politicians, how much more peripheral it would become from the point of view of Brussels.

Economically, also, Scotland would become more peripheral. She would remain at some distance from the major European markets situated in the 'Golden Triangle' centred on the Ruhr. High transport costs would make it more difficult for industry located in Scotland to penetrate European markets, and Scotland would also find it difficult to attract a skilled supply of labour upon which economic growth in good part depends. For all these reasons, Britain's entry into the E.E.C. was likely to accentuate even further the great advantages of the South East, and operate to the detriment of Scotland.

But if Scotland secured her independence, all this might be changed. For if, as an independent country, she was able to secure entry into the E.E.C., she would retain access to a duty-free British market. In that way she could avoid what had hitherto been seen as the main disadvantage of independence, namely that England would be able to ruin Scottish industry by imposing a tariff on Scottish goods. Such a policy would now be forbidden by the rules of the E.E.C. The E.E.C. would therefore give Scotland many of the economic advantages of Union without requiring the political union to be retained. Moreover an independent Scotland would, through its representation in the central institutions of the E.E.C., be able to lobby powerfully for its interests, and thus secure more favourable terms for Scotland than the U.K. government would be able to do.

These arguments weighed powerfully with some Scottish socialists who, led by Mr. Jim Sillars, decided that the European dimension not only made possible but required Scottish self-government. Mr. Sillars, together with another Labour M.P., were

to break away from the Labour Party and found the Scottish
Labour Party to promote an independent socialist Scotland within
the E.E.C. In a draft discussion paper on Scottish Government,
the Scottish Labour Party claimed:

The framework of the European Community permits us to consider and
achieve a full-blown independent Scottish presence at the top levels of
Community decision-making without having to endure agonies of doubt
over the trading and economic consequences of old-fashioned pre-Europe
ideas of independence.

When the U.K. was a 'separate' country outside the E.E.C., Scottish
independence held many dangers which in turn held many people back
from embracing that objective. Now that we are within the Community
there are limits placed upon independence, but those very limits also
ensure that disruption of trade and loss of markets are no longer real
threats. The European dimension changes all. Within the Community
interdependence and shared sovereignty have clipped the wings of
independence for all the countries and nations involved. But even that
diluted independence when compared with the powers Scotland has today,
or does not have today, would be an enormous leap forward in terms of
self-government.[35]

Even though the Scottish Labour Party may prove to be a short-
lived creation, its central argument on the relevance of the European
dimension is one that is likely to grow in strength as the power and
authority of the E.E.C.'s central institutions are increased. Like
the oil issue, the European dimension will force the British government to pay a higher price to avoid the break-up of the Union.
Britain's entry into the E.E.C., therefore, offers the S.N.P., which
opposed entry except on Scotland's terms, a powerful weapon
which it will not hesitate to use.

Thus what had begun as a part of a nation-wide revolt against
bad government came to be anchored to a party which offered a
clearly understood remedy for bad government. The S.N.P. has
turned out to be the prime vehicle for the politics of locality which
may gradually come to replace the politics of class, not only in
Britain, but in countries as diverse as France and Canada. If this is
so, the nationalist parties, as well as being pressure groups for their
nations, will also act as transmission belts for new ideas in politics,
which the traditional parties fail to articulate.

For it would be mistaken to imagine that the nationalist parties
represent nothing more than a desire to refight the battle of
Bannockburn, or retreat behind Offa's Dyke. These elements are

present, but they have also brought to the fore of British politics issues of centralization and community, which have been on the whole ignored by politicians. The nationalist parties represent, therefore, a feeling wider than separatism. They symbolize a discontent with government which may also be felt by those in England who lack the opportunity to vote for nationalist candidates. A wise polity would have attempted to isolate the sources of this discontent, rather than initially dismissing the phenomenon as beneath its notice.

VII

Politicians, then, found themselves confronted by a new political movement with a rapidly growing momentum. How would they react to it? Their attitudes would reflect a complex mixture of tactical consideration and principled commitment, with conceptions of material interest jostling with ideologies inherited from long ago. Labour's philosophy of social democracy meant that devolution could not be allowed to undermine the centralized allocation of economic resources, to be decided upon grounds of need rather than regional or national pressures. The Conservatives were hampered in dealing with Scottish devolution by a need to exorcise the traumas of Irish Home Rule, and by the fact that they had become increasingly an English party, and therefore more suscep-tible to the prejudices of their English members.

The Liberals would seem to have been in the most favourable position to take the Nationalist tide at the flood. For devolution had long been a Liberal policy, supported not only by Gladstone but also by his opponent Joseph Chamberlain who in his 'Unauthorised Programme' of 1885 had advocated a considerable measure of decentralization from Westminster.

More recently, the Liberals have retained an entirely consistent support for devolution, having advocated the establishment of Parliaments in Scotland and Wales in every general election since 1950: and since surveys of Scottish opinion have regularly shown that the majority of Scottish voters prefer devolution or federalism to the separatism of the S.N.P. or the *status quo*, the Liberals would seem to have been well-placed to capitalize upon the politics of locality as the basis for a new Liberal breakthrough.

But the Liberal Party's reiteration of support for Scottish and Welsh Home Rule had, by the late 1960s, become little more than ritualistic. For Liberals were on the whole unwilling to give the claims of Scotland the kind of priority that supporters of the S.N.P. demanded, since this would mean alienating the English electorate. Besides, there was a conflict between the autonomous Scottish Liberal Party which saw a federal system for Britain as one involving an English Parliament with the same powers as a Scottish one, and English Liberals who sought regional assemblies with the same powers as a Scottish Parliament. The Scottish Liberals' proposal would do nothing to cure remote government in England: and the English conception involved giving Scotland the powers of an English region, rather than those appropriate to a nation.

During Mr. Jo Grimond's period of leadership—from 1956 to 1967—the main aim of the Liberal Party had been to seek the support of the 'new middle class' and the affluent worker, in the hope that these groups might be willing to support a radical, non-socialist alternative to Conservatism. So although the Liberals were trying to break up the two-party system in British politics, they still relied upon the traditional assumption that class was the central motivating factor in voting behaviour. For the new middle class would, so it was suggested, be resentful of the class-conflict type of politics which the Labour party personified, and yet unable to identify socially with the Conservatives.

This policy, apart from isolated successes such as the Orpington by-election in 1962, was a total failure, and such support as the Liberals were able to gain from new social groupings remained only temporary; for, even if these new groupings possessed common interests, they were unable to identify specific Liberal policies which could promote these interests. If a focus for the resentment of voters was required, Enoch Powell and later the National Front might be able to supply it far more effectively, since they fastened upon a clear and concrete, if distorted, sense of grievance amongst voters.

There was, however, according to John Vincent in a perceptive article written for *New Society*, 26 January 1967, room in Britain 'for a party which puts locality before party conflict', a party which focused the resentments of provincial England, Scotland, and Wales against the metropolis. Where the Liberals could most easily have secured a new electoral base was in the peripheral areas of Britain, areas reacting against excessive centralization. In 1964, they had gained three seats in the Scottish Highlands—Caithness and Sutherland, Ross and Cromarty, and Inverness; and in a by-election in 1965, they gained Roxburgh, Selkirk, and Peebles, a Border constituency in what is 'to some extent a second Scottish periphery'[36] suffering as it does from some of the same pressures of remoteness, poor communications, migration, and disruption of traditional community values as the Highlands. By 1966, of the twelve Liberal seats, five were in Scotland, one in Wales, two in Cornwall, and one in Devon—nine in the 'Celtic fringe', leaving only three seats in English suburbia. As Vincent commented, the Liberals had 'set their cap at the London commuter, and ended up with the Ross and Cromarty crofter'.

In Scotland, the Liberal Party faced the tactical problem of how to secure a breakthrough; should it attempt for the price of a few deposits to destroy the S.N.P. before it became a serious threat, and then put itself forward as the party of self-government; or should it follow the precedent of the 1938 Liberal/S.N.P. agreement and ally itself with the S.N.P. on a self-government platform. Liberals followed neither course consistently, and in the end their support disappeared to the S.N.P.

Three times in the 1960s the Liberals had the option of an alliance with the S.N.P. placed before them. The first occasion when the dilemma was posed was in March 1964 by William Wolfe, the future chairman of the S.N.P. But the reply of the Scottish Liberals was that for them self-government ranks 'in priority with defence, co-partnership, and other major Liberal policies. . . . The Scottish Liberal Party, although autonomous, was part of the Great Britain Liberal Movement and would not contemplate any unilateral action for Scottish self-government.'[37] Nevertheless, in the General Election of 1964, the Liberals and S.N.P. fought against each other in only four out of the seventy-one Scottish seats.

Then in 1966 Ludovic Kennedy put forward a motion to the Conference of the Scottish Liberal Party at Perth demanding that Scottish Home Rule should now be 'the principal aim and object of our policy', and that in domestic matters 'all other issues should be considered in relationship to it'. 'To my great astonishment', according to his own account in the *Spectator* 10 November 1967, 'this resolution was carried unanimously, and thereafter, and equally unanimously ignored.'[65] The Liberal candidate in the Glasgow, Pollok, by-election devoted ten out of the 150 lines of his election address to the subject. He secured only 735 votes, and was humiliatingly bottom of the poll. The S.N.P. candidate gained nearly 11,000 votes.

After the Pollok by-election, Ludovic Kennedy, together with Michael Starforth, then treasurer of the Scottish Liberal Party, attempted to commit Scottish Liberals at their 1967 Conference to an alliance with the S.N.P. They were pre-empted, however, by a motion from James Davidson, the Liberal M.P. for West Aberdeenshire declaring

This Conference would welcome any indication from the leaders of the Scottish National Party that they are willing, in recognition of the need for both Parties to place the national interests of Scotland, before short-term Party interests, to co-operate with the Scottish Liberal Party to achieve a Scottish Parliament.

Such a motion, requesting the S.N.P. to make the first move in seeking an electoral alliance, was hardly appropriate in the light of the respective performances of the S.N.P. and Liberal candidates in the Pollok by-election; and the S.N.P. which was on a rising electoral curve, can be forgiven for not taking it seriously. Ludovic Kennedy then resigned from the Scottish Liberals to speak for Winifred Ewing at the Hamilton by-election, and Michael Starforth left the Liberals for the S.N.P.

After this by-election, the Scottish Liberals, led by Jo Grimond and David Steel, tried again to secure a pact with the S.N.P., but this would have involved putting Scottish Home Rule as the first item on the Liberal programme, and subordinating the aims of English Liberals to the overriding aim of Home Rule for Scotland. The new Liberal leader Jeremy Thorpe was, however, unwilling to surrender the chance of winning votes in England from those disillusioned with the Labour government, and no pact was possible. In 1968 a joint Conference of English and Scottish Liberals declared that Scotland should be given a Parliament with the same powers as an English regional assembly, and this symbolized the Liberal position that Scottish Home Rule was for Liberals, merely a part of a wider policy of reforming the machinery of government.

It was not the most important item in the Liberal programme and Liberals would not make it a priority. Indeed, if they were able to secure a powerful enough bargaining position to press their claims, most Liberals would probably have fought to implement proportional representation rather than Scottish Home Rule. Thus any Scot who felt that Home Rule was a matter of urgency would have been well advised to vote S.N.P. rather than Liberal: for Liberal successes would not be 'unequivocal pointers to a demand for home rule, as those of the National Party are.'[38]

The results of the Liberal Party's vacillation and indecision could be seen in the 1970 General Election when the Liberals lost Ross and Cromarty (Caithness and Sutherland had been lost in 1966) and Aberdeenshire West, while the S.N.P. won the Western Isles, and broke through for the first time in the northern seats 'mainly in the eleven county constituences from Angus and Argyll northwards' together with Galloway, 'a socially similar constituency in the south-west corner of Scotland.'[39] Its average vote in the twelve seats in the region was 21.2 per cent, although it had only fought one seat in the area in 1966—E. Aberdeenshire where it had pushed up its percentage of the vote from 8.6 to 29.8 per cent— and only one other seat in the area, the Western Isles, since the war. Argyll was to fall to the S.N.P. in February 1974, and Galloway on the retirement of the sitting Conservative member in October.

Thus the General Election of 1970 (in which the Liberal vote fell by 1.3 per cent in Scotland while the S.N.P. vote rose by 6.4 per cent) destroyed any chance the Liberals might have had of making an electoral breakthrough by championing the peripheral areas as they had done in the nineteenth century; and although their percentage of the vote rose in the two elections of 1974 by 2.5 per cent and 0.3 per cent respectively, this rise was minuscule compared with the increase in the S.N.P. vote of 10.5 per cent and 8.5 per cent; and far smaller than the rise in the Liberal share of the vote in England. The Liberal Party in Scotland with 8.3 per cent of the vote in the October 1974 General Election lay a derisory fourth, well behind Labour, the S.N.P., and the Conservatives.

VIII

Neither of the other two U.K. parties would seem to have been as well-equipped as the Liberals to meet the Nationalist challenge. For neither the Labour nor the Conservative party in Scotland enjoyed the very real autonomy of their Liberal counterpart. The Scottish Conservatives' role in policy-making was entirely subordinate to that of the leader of the Party as a whole; while the Labour Party's Scottish Council was merely a regional branch of the British Labour Party, possessing little more power than, for example, the East Midlands branch. The Labour Party in Scotland was dominated by elderly councillors and lack-lustre trade unionists. It was an intellectually unimaginative party, with a penchant for mouthing Left-wing slogans whose relationship to reality remained obscure. By the late 1960s the Labour organization in Scotland was also moribund, reflecting a situation in which Labour's role was not to debate political issues, but to secure economic benefits for Scotland through manoeuvring in Whitehall. This task was carried out, on the whole successfully, by the Labour Secretary of State for Scotland, Mr. William Ross, who 'pushed the modern government system to its limits. No threat or ploy or precedent was neglected to screw more money out of the Exchequer.'[40] It was natural then for the leaders of Scottish Labour to be hostile to devolution, until they realized that the threat of separatism could not be contained without making judicious concessions.

The Scottish Conservatives seemed to suffer from equally serious handicaps when it came to understanding the new forces in Scottish politics. They represented a socially narrow base, and many of their M.P.s and constituency leaders were almost entirely anglicized, and seemed to lack any appreciation of the need for a Scottish dimension to U.K. politics. Christopher Harvie has suggested that, during the period of the Macmillan government, the appearances of the Prime Minister north of the border 'suggested that the Tories still viewed Scotland as a huge sporting estate, and were doing their best to keep it that way'. Their 'perception of Scottish politics seemed to be that of the custodians of the picturesque political museum whose exhibits—Clydeside reds and grousemoor lairds alike—were to be cherished rather than challenged.'[41]

It therefore seemed that, of the two major parties, the Conservatives would have been the least likely to sympathize with Scottish claims. Indeed, the Scottish Conservative Party had called itself the Unionist party between 1912 and 1965, thus seeming to indicate its hostility to any measure of devolution. Yet there were also the remnants of a 'Jacobite' Conservative tradition in Scotland in the Scott tradition, which sought to ensure that Scotland was able to retain her national identity within the framework of the U.K.; and the Conservative Party had a respectable record of encouraging administrative decentralization to the Scottish Office—both the Gilmour and Balfour Committees were set up by Conservative governments; and Winston Churchill had attempted to use nationalist resentment against the centralization of the post-war Labour government in the interests of the Conservative cause.

By the late 1960s, however, the Conservatives in Scotland were a sharply declining electoral force. In 1955, they had secured both a majority of the Scottish seats and a majority of the Scottish vote—the only time that this result has been achieved by either major party since the war. By 1966, however, the Conservatives had only twenty seats in Scotland, and their vote in Scotland was down to 37.7 per cent. Within eleven years they had lost sixteen seats, and one-eighth of their vote. The traditionalist attitude of the party was proving deeply unattractive to an electorate becoming increasingly worried at the economic difficulties facing Scotland. The Scottish Conservatives were therefore eager to inject some element of Scottish awareness into their policies, and in the summer of 1967 they set up a committee under the chairmanship of Sir William McEwan Younger to consider how the structure of government could be made more responsive to Scottish needs. At the same time, a parallel investigation into Scottish government was being carried out by a new Conservative 'ginger group' called the Thistle Group, which was to become identified as a pro-devolution pressure group.

Both of these investigations were begun some time before the Hamilton by-election and were motivated more by a concern for Scottish government and for the waning fortunes of the Scottish Conservatives than by fear of the S.N.P. The two groups came to strikingly similar conclusions, and agreed that the existing structure of government in Scotland was inefficient, because the range of functions for which the Scottish Office was responsible was too wide to be scrutinized properly either by Parliament or by ministers, and the system therefore allowed too much power to rest in the hands of civil servants.

Mr. Heath, the party leader, was not unresponsive to the argument for devolution in Scotland. He was himself, of course, concerned to combat the decline of the Party in Scotland; and devolution would offer him the chance to present a distinctive policy which contrasted the Conservative Party with the centralizing socialists and the separatist S.N.P. But there seems to have been more to Mr. Heath's support for devolution than tactical manoeuvring, for in his Diaries (Vol.2, p.550-1) Crossman reports him as saying a week before the Hamilton by-election that 'nationalism is the biggest single factor in our politics today'.

Mr. Heath's speech at the Conference of the Scottish Conservatives at Perth in 1968, where he proposed the creation of a directly elected Scottish Assembly, explicitly recognized the need for devolution as a counterweight to the centralizing tendencies of the E.E.C., and displayed a far-sightedness which, in different circumstances, might have done much to pre-empt the later successes of the S.N.P. He emphasized the contrast between the Conservative Party's stand for diversity and the 'world of mass industrialization, mass communications, and increasingly complex organization' in which the strongest influences were those of 'uniformity and centralization'. These pressures had led many individuals to feel that they were losing control over the shaping of their lives and there was, as a result, frustration and resentment with government. The Labour Party, being the party of state control, was unable to understand this new source of discontent: the S.N.P. understood the cause, but proposed a wholly inappropriate remedy which involved sacrificing the gains of centralized economic management together with the losses. 'The art of government', however, 'was to reconcile these divergent needs. The need to modernize our institutions so as to cope with our complex changing society. And the need to give each citizen a greater opportunity to participate in the decisions that affect him, his family, and the community in which he lives'. The reconciliation of these needs involved finding a balance between two divergent principles—the one being the unity of the United Kingdom, and the other being 'our belief in the devolution of power'. He concluded appropriately with a quotation from Quintin Hogg's *Case for Conservatism*, 'Political liberty is nothing else but the diffusion of power. If power is not to be abused, it must be spread as widely as possible throughout the community.'

A committee was then set up, chaired by Sir Alec Douglas-Home, whose function was to consider whether, while preserving 'the essential principle of the sovereignty of Parliament'[42], it was possible to meet the 'very reasonable desire of the majority of the people of Scotland to have a greater say in the conduct of their own affairs'.[43] This Committee reported in March 1970, and advocated that a directly elected Scottish Assembly be established, to deal with the Second Reading, Committee, and Report stages of Scottish Bills, leaving only the Third Reading and House of Lords stages to Westminster. It would thus take over much of the work done by the Scottish Grand Committee and by the Scottish Standing Committees.

The great advantage of this scheme was that it could be presented as 'a natural evolution and extension of Parliamentary practice as we know it'.[44] It did not make too great a breach with existing constitutional practice, since the proposed Scottish Assembly, or Convention as it was to be known, would take its place as a part of the Westminster machinery. Awkward questions, such as the future of Scottish representation at Westminster after devolution, simply would not arise under this scheme since legislative power was not being devolved. The Douglas-Home proposals in fact offered the maximum degree of devolution possible within the continuing framework of the unitary state.

It was not difficult of course for critics to find weaknesses in the Douglas-Home Report. The proposed Convention, they claimed, would do little to make the Scottish Office more accountable since the Scottish Office would still be responsible to Parliament and not to the Convention. Moreover, Scotland's viewpoint as expressed in the Convention could still be overturned at Westminster, and conflict would be bound to arise whenever the majority in the Convention was of a different political colour from the Westminster government. The Committee denied that the setting-up of the Convention would increase conflict, since it would discuss only Scottish legislation which 'In the main consists of legislation which is not unduly controversial.' But in that case it was not clear whether the Convention would have broad enough powers to deal with the grievances most strongly felt in Scotland. Was the proposal of the Douglas-Home Committee sufficient to deal with the serious weaknesses in Scottish government which the Committee itself had diagnosed? For example, the Committee had deplored the slow pace of decision-making on Scottish industrial matters. 'Long delays in deciding on matters which seriously affect the level of Scottish employment and generally influence the Scottish standard of living cannot be tolerated.' And the Committee found itself 'particularly impressed by the working of the Northern Ireland Ministry of Commerce—and especially by the speed of its decision-making.'[45] Yet of course what was proposed fell far short of the Stormont model, and the Convention, since it would have no executive powers, would be able to do nothing to speed up the process of administration.

Nevertheless, it could be argued that these criticisms were, in a sense, beside the point. For the setting-up of the Convention would appear to the Scottish electorate as a signal that Westminster would henceforth take more notice of the Scottish point of view. It would provide explicit recognition of Scotland's right to a political forum in which her problems could be discussed. Even if it did not provide the final answer, therefore, to the problems of Scottish government, it might serve as a practical point of departure for further evolutionary development.

The Douglas-Home Report was accepted by the Conservative leadership and the Conservative election manifesto of 1970 promised that its recommendations including the 'Scottish Convention sitting in Edinburgh will form a basis for the proposals we will place before Parliament, taking account of the impending re-organization of local government'. The Queen's Speech in July 1970 also promised that measures would be produced 'for giving the Scottish people a greater say in their own affairs'. Nevertheless, Mr. Heath's government made no move to establish a Scottish assembly.

Two explanations have been given for this omission. The first is that the government did not want to legislate in advance of the Report of the Commission on the Constitution, which did not appear until October 1973, and by that time Britain was in the grip of the rise in oil prices which followed the Yom Kippur war.

Had the Conservatives simply gone ahead with devolution, the members of the Commission would have resigned, and this would have caused considerable political embarrassment. Possibly the Government could have pressed the Commission to issue an interim Report, as a basis for rapid action, but it did not do so.

The second explanation is that the Conservatives decided, while waiting for the Royal Commission's Report, to proceed with Scottish local government reform, and that was hardly compatible with a commitment to devolution. Mr. Heath when in government argued that devolution was a less important priority than local government reform. He wrote to John Mackintosh in May 1973.

We for our part have always held that reform of local government is a matter of importance and urgency for the people of Scotland and that there should be no avoidable delay in putting in hand the complex arrangements needed to implement it. The question of devolution, while clearly a related matter, has always seemed to us one which should be pursued separately, and *later,* in a U.K. context . . . (My italics.)[46]

Reorganization created a two-tier government structure in Scotland, the upper tier of which consisted of regions, with the largest region—Strathclyde—containing over half of the population of Scotland. This meant that if ever a Scottish assembly was set up, local government would have to be reorganized again, since the Assembly would not easily be able to co-exist with Strathclyde. As Mr. Malcolm Rifkind, a Conservative spokesman on Scottish affairs, claimed in October 1975, 'We find it inconceivable that Strathclyde could long survive the Assembly. It cannot be desirable that the Assembly should operate alongside a local authority that covers a massive geographical area and over half the population of Scotland.' The Conservatives had promised in their manifesto, moreover, to establish an Assembly, '*taking account of* the impending reorganization of local government', and the most natural procedure would have been to establish the Assembly and allow it, as the representative body of Scotland, to put forward its own proposals for local government reform. The future shape of government in Scotland should have been decided first, and the new local government system should have taken its place within that framework. For devolution was not, as Mr. Heath suggested in his letter to Mackintosh, an issue 'which could be pursued separately', and the Conservative Government can be accused of making a serious misjudgement through not considering the inter-relationships between the two issues.

The probability is that devolution had ceased to be an important priority for Mr. Heath after 1970. The nationalist threat seemed, until 1973, to have disappeared, and the energies of the government were devoted to other issues, industrial relations legislation, incomes policy, and the E.E.C. It would have been difficult to pilot two major measures of constitutional reform through one Parliament, and so, while the formal commitment to devolution remained, nothing was done about it.

In the two elections of 1974, the Conservatives lost a further eight Scottish seats, all of them to the S.N.P., and thirteen per cent of their vote. In twenty years they had lost no less than twenty seats in Scotland and a quarter of their vote. The Scottish Conservatives reiterated their commitment to devolution, but the election of Mrs. Thatcher to the leadership of the party replaced a supporter of devolution by someone whose instincts were on the whole hostile. In December 1976 the Shadow Cabinet decided, despite the advice of the majority of Scottish Conservative M.P.s, to issue a three-line whip opposing the Labour Government's Scotland and Wales Bill; and in May 1977, the party's spokesman on devolution, Mr. Francis Pym, announced that the party's commitment to a directly elected Scottish Assembly was now 'inoperative'. The Conservatives had become the party of the Union again.

The history of Conservative attitudes to devolution does not seem to show the Party as being motivated by any particular steadiness or consistency of purpose. The Party seems to have found it difficult to take up any clear attitude towards the successes of the S.N.P. In particular it did not seek to enquire whether increasing support for the Scottish nationalists might not be an expression of a deep-seated political attitude whose validity is worth considering; an attitude favourable to the diffusion of power from Westminster and Whitehall and therefore consistent with Conservative aims. After the resignation of the pro-devolutionist Alick Buchanan-Smith from his position as Shadow Secretary for Scotland in December 1976, Sir Ian Gilmour was the only member of the Shadow Cabinet who perceived this connection. Speaking to the Oxford University Conservative Association in May 1976, he argued that the desire of most Scots to have a greater say in the running of their affairs is wholly natural and fully conservative. We are one of the most over-centralized countries in the world and there is nothing unconservative in the diffusion of power. It is after all not Conservative doctrine that the man in Whitehall always knows best. But it is very much Conservative doctrine that the diversity within the state is to be encouraged and that centralization should be diminished.

This view was, however, ignored by most English M.P.s who, after all, represented all but twenty-four of the 276 Conservatives returned in October 1974, and who almost overwhelmingly believed that genuine devolution would undermine national unity. These instincts may give rise to difficulties for a future Conservative Government, since it is difficult to see how a Unionist stance can provide the springboard for a permanent electoral revival in Scotland; and the widespread demand for devolution in Scotland will make it more difficult for a Unionist party representing a minority in Scotland to govern her successfully than at any time since 1707.

X

It was the Labour Party that seemed in the most immediate danger from the nationalists in the late 1960s. For the S.N.P. advance threatened its strongholds in central Scotland—a decayed mining area such as Hamilton seemed symbolic in this respect—and in 1968 Labour's majority on Glasgow council was destroyed for the first time in sixteen years by the S.N.P. Moreover, the Labour Party had only succeeded twice in its history—in 1945 and 1966— in securing a majority of English seats. Therefore separatism in Scotland or Wales, or even a reduction in the number of Scottish or Welsh M.P.s following devolution, foreshadowed the possibility of Labour becoming a permanent minority at Westminster.

It has been said of the Independent Labour Party, forerunner of the Labour Party, that it was 'in many respects a rebellion of the provinces and intrinsically regional in character';[47] and the Scottish Labour Party, founded in 1888, influenced by men such as Keir Hardie and Cunninghame Graham, inherited the Liberal mantle of Scottish Home Rule. At Scottish Labour Party Conferences between 1916 and 1923, Home Rule for Scotland was regularly passed without dissent; and the Scottish Party helped to draft a Home Rule Bill in 1924. By 1922, Labour was already the leading party in Scotland. Why, then, should it wait for the rest of the U.K. to be converted to socialism: could not Scottish Labour establish a socialist state of its own in an independent Scotland? Such were the thoughts of a number of Scottish socialists, amongst whom John Maclean was the most prominent, in the early 1920s.

With the onset of mass unemployment, however, socialists came to believe that only centralized planning could secure economic stability; and the search in the 1930s was for measures of state control which could cure the slump. Tom Johnston, by no means unsympathetic to Home Rule, warned that a Scottish Parliament might have nothing to administer but 'an emigration system, a glorified Poor Law and a graveyard',[48] and the trade union wing of the movement came to be hostile to Home Rule since it sought national wage-bargaining to maintain wage levels in Scotland. Indeed, even as they claimed to support Home Rule, the Scottish trade unions pressed for national bargaining, prompting J. H. Thomas to remark that 'Scotsmen are far-reaching people. They want Home Rule in everything that does not cost anything.'[49]

During the period immediately following the Second World War, Scotland benefited from the government's regional policy and the Labour movement was unwilling to put its gains at risk through Home Rule. In 1945 the Scottish Council of the Labour Party defeated by 113 votes to five a motion by the nationalist Douglas Young calling on the party immediately to implement Home Rule; and Arthur Woodburn, a future Secretary of State for Scotland, argued that agitation for a Scottish Parliament would scare English industrialists away from Scotland. The policy of Home Rule suffered a further setback in the Labour Party when it came to be used by the Conservatives in their campaign against the 1945–51 government. 'London Government' became a euphemism for the Labour Government.

These centralist reactions received little critical scrutiny in the late 1960s and, whereas in the Conservative Party grass roots pressure in Scotland had created a favourable climate for devolution proposals, pressure in the Labour Party came from the top.

The reaction of the Scottish Council to the rise of nationalism was that it was a product of economic setbacks, and that with recovery it would disappear. Devolution would threaten the position of the Secretary of State and the over-representation of Scotland in the Commons, both of which enabled Scotland to gain advantages when it came to the allocation of public expenditure. In 1968, therefore, the Scottish Labour Party Conference rejected devolution by a large majority, and in its evidence to the Commission on the Constitution, the Scottish Council declared, 'We think that legislative devolution would damage Scotland's economic development. Labour's record in this respect . . . is something we cannot afford to lose.' And Mr. W. Marshall, Scottish Secretary to the Labour Party, insisted that 'There is . . . no such thing as a separate political will for Scotland.'[50]

These attitudes were reinforced by Mr. William Ross, the Secretary of State for Scotland, who was adamantly opposed to devolution and, according to Richard Crossman, was 'determined to treat nationalism as a mere emotional attitude which can be cured by economic policies alone'.[51] Ross seems to have converted Harold Wilson to this view, and the Wilson administration of the late 1960s proved unsympathetic to demands for devolution.

After the General Election of February 1974 however, when the S.N.P. won six seats, two of them from Labour, devolution was once more on the political agenda, especially since the minority Labour government would have to go the country again in a short time. At Westminster, therefore, Labour M.P.s became reluctant devolutionists: and at its Conference in March 1974, the Scottish Council reluctantly supported a directly elected Assembly; but in June the executive of the Scottish Council—meeting with one-third of their members absent watching a World Cup football match—turned devolution down by six votes to five as 'irrelevant to the real needs of the people of Scotland', since

The essential strategy for the Labour Party is to bring about a fundamental and irreversible shift in the balance of power and wealth in favour of working people. Public ownership and control of North Sea oil is a vital element . . . constitutional tinkering does not make a meaningful contribution towards achieving our socialist objectives.

This decision caused considerable embarrassment to the Labour Party's National Executive in London which was involved in preparing a programme for the next election, and was convinced that unless Labour committed itself to devolution it would suffer further losses to the S.N.P. Indeed a poll sponsored by the National Executive showed that Labour would lose thirteen seats if it did not alter its policy on devolution.

The Scottish organizer of the Labour Party was therefore summoned to London, and various pressures were put on constituency parties and unions in Scotland to call a special conference to reverse the decision of the Scottish Executive. At this special conference on 16 September, two days before the announcement of the election, 'The devolutionists got their way by arm-twisting',[52] with the assistance of the union block vote offered to the government as part of the Social Contract. Mr. Tam Dalyell, an opponent of devolution wondered how one union leader 'believing what he does about the Assembly, will be able to look at himself in his shaving mirror.'[53] In the October general election, therefore, Labour was able to appear as a party supporting devolution, and for the first time it produced a separate manifesto for Scotland, although 'There were complaints, nonetheless, that the Scottish Manifesto had been written in London and shown to the Scottish Executive only when it was too late to make any major changes.'[54]

The members of the Labour Party in Scotland, then, were devolutionists at the eleventh hour. In March 1975, a narrow majority was gained at its annual conference for devolution providing that economic power remained centralized; but in 1976, Scottish Labour for the first time adopted a maximalist position urging that a Scottish Assembly should be given trade, industry, and revenue-raising powers.

Thus, while the Conservative Party, under pressure from English back-benchers, had become the party of the Union, Labour, under pressure from its English leadership, became the party of devolution. The conversion, of course, came too late to carry conviction, appearing to be, as Mr. Willie Hamilton put it at the 1976 Scottish Conference, an act 'of blatant political appeasement'. An attempt by the Scottish Council to campaign against the S.N.P. on the slogan 'Devolution not separation' fizzled out badly, since the Scottish party was too divided and unsure of itself to carry much conviction. The Labour Party was therefore unable to isolate the S.N.P. by attracting to itself all those groups in Scotland who sought devolution but rejected separatism; and the prospect of a referendum, although welcomed by the opponents of devolution, was feared by the party organization since it would again expose Labour's divisions publicly.

It is nevertheless a paradox that the Labour Party's dominant electoral position in Scotland makes it the strongest force in Scotland for the maintenance of the Union. For in many parts of Scotland the Labour Party is the only political party capable of holding off the S.N.P. challenge, and Labour's recovery in Scotland in 1978 seemed to show that the advance of the S.N.P. was not irresistible. Labour's policy of devolution, therefore, adopted unwillingly and haltingly defended, may yet offer the best chance of ensuring that Scotland remains a part of the United Kingdom.

5 Wales

Britain is the creation of the state, Wales the creation of providence.
Gwynfor Evans: *Wales Can Win*

I

The sense of nationality in Ireland, Scotland, and Wales manifests itself in very different ways in accordance with the history of their relationships with England. We have already seen that, while Irish nationalism acquired its motive force primarily from hostility to Britain and a desire to break the British connection, Scottish nationalism has been concerned more with securing a governmental framework to guarantee her distinctive institutions.

Welsh nationalism differs from both of these, for it is primarily a defensive movement whose aim is to preserve a threatened culture and way of life, within the framework of an incorporating union which originally recognized no place for distinctive Welsh institutions.

The Acts of 1536 and 1543 which united Wales to England were, unlike the Acts of Union of 1707, integrationist both in purpose and in result. The Tudors who fashioned the settlement offered Wales 'a providential chance of release at long last from the sense of national subjection'.[1] They aimed to remove the legal disabilities of the Welsh, and to give Wales fair representation in Parliament. But they wanted also to eliminate competing sovereignties, and to construct a powerful and unified administrative system in the interests of national security. It was for this reason, and not out of a deliberate intent to suppress the Welsh language, that they insisted that English, and not Welsh, be the official language of Wales:

all Justices . . . shall proclayme and kepe . . . all . . . courts in the Englisshe tonge . . . no personne or personnes that use the Welshe speche or langage shall have . . . any maner office . . . Within the Realme of Englande, Wales or other Kinge's Dominion . . . onles he or they use and exercise the speche or langage of Englisshe.

But in 1563, Elizabeth ordered the translation of the Bible and prayerbook into Welsh to secure Welsh allegiance to the state Protestant religion which she was establishing; and this had a profound impact on Welsh life, since it ensured the survival of the language.

Politically, however, Welsh identity was not recognized, and Wales was administered as a part of England. Indeed, in 1746 it was explicitly stated that 'in all cases where the Kingdom of England, or that part of Great Britain called England, hath been or shall be mentioned in any Act of Parliament, the same has been and shall from henceforth be deemed and taken to comprehend and include the Dominion of Wales'.[3] 'The distinction between England and Wales', Gladstone was to claim, '. . . is totally unknown to our constitution'.[4] Wales was thus unable to preserve, as Scotland had done, those independent institutions which not only ensured separate treatment, but, more crucially, preserved the memory of independent statehood. Scotland, being administered after the Union mainly by Scotsmen, and surrounded by the institutions of nationhood, could preserve the characteristics which distinguished her from England.

In Wales, however, nationalism lacked such an institutional focus, and therefore had to be built around less concrete factors—language, religion, and culture. It was left to writers, poets, and preachers to create 'the cultural form, the tracery of a nation where no State had existed'.[5] In this task, the Welsh faced the same uphill task as the Corsicans and the Bretons—they were attempting to create a national movement on the basis of symbols, language and religion, whose importance was declining in the modern world. Indeed, the only example of complete success to inspire the Welsh is that of the Jews, who succeeded, through the tenacious retention of cultural and religious symbols, in restoring a state which had not existed for 2000 years, and resuscitating a language which was, for almost every Jew, his second language.

These differences between Wales and Scotland are summed up by Marxists in terms of the distinction between a 'historic' nation and a 'non-historic' nation, between a nation which has succeeded in retaining the institutions of statehood, and one which has not. For the latter, indeed, Engels had little sympathy. They were merely remnant people, left over from an earlier population, forced back and subjugated by the nation which later became the repository of historical development. These remnants of a nation, mercilessly crushed, as Hegel said, by the course of history, this *national refuse*, is always the fanatical representative of the counter-revolution and remains so until it is completely exterminated or de-nationalised, as its whole existence is in itself a protest against a great historical revolution.[6]

II

Wales, however, has always been very far from being a 'fanatical representative of the counter-revolution'. Indeed it is characterized by its remarkable record of support for the British Left, first for the Liberals and then for Labour. Before the First World War, Wales was the most anti-Conservative of any of the regions of Britain; during the years 1885–1914, there were only two Welsh constituencies where the average Conservative vote was higher than the average Liberal vote, and the Conservatives performed appreciably worse than the Liberals in rural constituencies, 'at a time when in Britain as a whole the Conservatives were regarded as the party representing most effectively the interests of both landlord and farmer.'[7] The Conservative Party in Wales was the political representative of the alien Anglican Church and the landowner, influences which seemed hostile to the national as well as to the social aspirations of Wales. 'A Welsh nonconformist who is a Conservative in politics is considered by his co-religionists a traitor to his sect, and almost a traitor to his country.'[8]

The Liberal ascendancy began with the general election of 1857, and it coincided with a remarkable re-awakening of Welsh national consciousness. The Liberals sought to have the special characteristics of Wales recognized, and they achieved their first success in 1881 when the Welsh Sunday Closing Act was passed—the first time that a legislative principle was applied to Wales as a separate entity from England.

The demands made by Welsh Liberals were national demands, and for many radicalism and nationalism were indistinguishable. Tom Ellis, the inspiration behind the nationalist *Cymru Fydd* (Wales of the Future) movement, declared in his election address at Merioneth in 1886, 'I solicit your suffrages as a WELSH

NATIONALIST'; and Lloyd George characterized himself in Dod's Parliamentary Companion until 1923 as a Radical and Welsh Nationalist. But this nationalism did not entail separatism, for it was

recognized, not only that union with England is inevitable, but that it provides the best opportunity that Wales could have to deliver her mission . . . to the world. The closer the connection the better it will be for the purposes of *Cymru Fydd*; for it is by influencing England that Wales can influence the world. The one condition which is insisted upon is that the connection shall not be closer at the expense of Welsh nationality or at the sacrifice of some national qualities. The voices of England and of Wales should be joined, not in unison, but in harmony.[9]

Nor, lacking the institutions of incipient statehood, was Home Rule central to the Welsh claim. Indeed it was, as we shall see, a divisive issue in Wales; and for Tom Ellis '. . . it was the nonconformity of Wales that created the unity of Wales, rather than any spontaneous demand for Home Rule'.[10]

The issue of Irish Home Rule gave an impetus to the sentiment of nationality in Wales as it did in Scotland, but there were a number of reasons why Home Rule did not play as central a role in Welsh politics as it did in Ireland. Wales, it is true, shared with Ireland an agrarian problem and resentment at English domination: but their experience of English rule was very different, and there was no equivalent in Welsh history to the Irish famine and forced emigration which had so embittered Irish attitudes.

In Wales, unlike Ireland, the land problem was not complicated by the existence of an alien and absentee landlord class belonging to the dominant nation. However much the landlords had become anglicized, they were still either Welsh or linked in marriage to the native Welsh, and many of them were Welsh-speaking. It was impossible to feel towards them the deep-seated antagonism which the Irish peasant felt for his English landlord.

Furthermore, the effects of the gradual democratization of Welsh life were more tangible than in Ireland. In the first elections to the Welsh county councils in 1889, 'the Welsh national feeling' was 'very strongly brought out', and the Liberals succeeded in winning every county except Brecknock. Yet, precisely because these new local authorities succeeded so completely in undermining the rule of the landowner and the gentry, it was shown that reform in Wales did not depend upon Home Rule. Indeed, the results of the elections 'created a social transformation more striking even than the extension of democracy at the national level', and in Wales, there was no doubt that Home Rule could be killed by kindness.

Home Rule, moreover, was a divisive issue in Wales and schemes for establishing Welsh national institutions were continually to founder 'on the same rock, the balance of representation between Glamorgan and Monmouth and the rest of the country'.[11] In 1892, for example, a proposal for a Welsh national body to take over the powers of the Local Government Board, the Board of Guardians, Commissioners for Works, and the Charity Commissioners for Wales, was discussed. But there was no agreement on the basis of representation in the new body. Glamorgan favoured representation on a population basis under which it would secure twenty-five of the fifty-nine seats while Merioneth and Radnor would secure only two each: Radnor therefore sought representation by county on the lines of the American Senate. Lloyd George attempted to secure control of the nationalist *Cymru Fydd* movement as a territorial basis for his own political ambitions, but the more power that he acquired, the more South Wales came to oppose him. *Cymru Fydd* collapsed in 1896, when Lloyd George's proposal to create one national *Cymru Fydd* federation was defeated; and Alderman Bird of Cardiff, an English-speaking Liberal, insisted that 'a cosmopolitan population from Swansea to Newport' would 'never bow to the domination of Welsh ideas'.[12]

The development of industrialism in South Wales served further to weaken the pressure for Home Rule. It did so in two ways. First, it helped to relieve the growing pressure on the land, and thus provided an alternative to migration of a kind not available to Irish Catholics. Secondly, industrialization introduced a new divisive element into Wales, threatening not only the Liberal Party, but the radical nonconformist nationalism which had first triumphed in 1868. For class conflict cut across the old Liberal/Conservative and Welsh/English divisions, and the Welsh nonconformist industrialist such as D. A. Thomas (Lord Rhondda), who was on the progressive side of politics in the late nineteenth century, now found himself branded as a class enemy. Moreover, industrialism, by tying the economy of South Wales closer to the English economy, made nationalism appear not only sociologically irrelevant but economically foolish also.

III

In Wales, then, the sentiment of nationality was not powerful enough to sustain a strong Home Rule movement, and Welsh Liberals concentrated their efforts upon winning recognition of Welsh cultural aspirations and religious distinctiveness. Rather than a Welsh Parliament, they sought national educational institutions and the disestablishment of the Welsh Church. The first of these aims proved easier to achieve than the second, and in 1889 the Intermediate Education Act made Welsh county councils the first local education authorities in Britain. They were empowered to raise a halfpenny rate for secondary education, with a Treasury grant being made available to county councils equivalent to the sum raised, the system later adopted in England in Balfour's Education Act of 1902. In 1893, a charter was granted to the University of Wales; and in 1896, a Central Welsh Board was established to administer examinations. The Welsh educational system was thus to become 'a national system, the first and most striking expression in institutional terms of the reawakened consciousness of nationhood'.[13]

Above all, Welsh Liberals demanded disestablishment of the Welsh Church, a church representing only a minority in Wales to which no Welsh-speaking bishop had been appointed between 1715 and 1870, and yet a church to which Welsh tenant-farmers were compelled to pay tithes. The 'tithe war', under which tithes were withheld, linked together the issues of land and church, class and religion so that allegiance to Welsh Liberalism was powerfully strengthened, and in Wales, it was disestablishment, rather than Home Rule, which served to unify Welsh nonconformist opinion.

But Welsh disestablishment was a highly contentious issue in British politics, and when Gladstone embarked upon his Home Rule crusade it had to take second place to the Irish demand. As a result, it proved impossible, during Gladstone's final ministry between 1892 and 1894, to secure priority for disestablishment. A Bill was, it is true, introduced in 1894, and given its First Reading without a division, but it never received a Second Reading; and in April 1895 another Bill passed its Second Reading, but the government was to fall before it could proceed further.

This put Welsh Liberals in a cruel dilemma; for if they remained tied to the Gladstonian Liberal Party, they had no guarantee that Welsh interests would ever be given sufficient recognition. Even if Home Rule was achieved, Liberals would not want a new 'Welsh Question' to further block the path of social reform. It seemed, therefore, that Wales could achieve advancement only in those areas where English and Welsh interests coincided, for the more far-sighted Liberals were beginning to appreciate that the Party could not survive merely as a vehicle for Celtic claims. Thus Welsh Liberals could either subordinate specifically Welsh demands in a wider Liberal programme, or they could form an independent party on the Parnellite model, threatening to withhold support from any government which did not meet their wishes. Welsh Liberals were in no doubt as to how the dilemma should be resolved. They decided to give Liberalism priority over Nationalism, because they sought not separation, but recognition. 'The ideal of Wales was to be recognised as a part of the British political and social structure: the ideal of Ireland was to be severed from it. The object of the one was equality: the aim of the other was exclusion.'[14]

But if Welsh Liberalism was a political instrument fashioned to secure this recognition, it was less successful in meeting the challenge of industrialism, for too many of its policies assumed a social homogeneity that was rapidly disappearing in Wales. Welsh liberalism and nationalism became increasingly tied to symbols— the land, religion, and the language—whose importance in Welsh life was diminishing. In 1895, the *Cymru Fydd* programme had placed 'labour and industrial' questions seventh, well behind such nostrums as Home Rule for Wales, temperance reform, and security for the tenant farmer. Lloyd George himself 'remained an Old Liberal in Wales, although a "New Liberal" in England',[15] and for Wales he argued that 'the land question, the temperance question and the question of disestablishment were equally matters of interest to labourers as was an Eight Hours Bill'. National claims had been focused upon the limited aim of disestablishment, and when that was achieved in 1920 the movement faded, and Welsh Liberalism lost its vitality.

In 1918, Welsh Liberals allied themselves with Lloyd George in the 'coupon election', and this was fatal to the claim of Liberals to be the radical party in Wales. Already, by 1922, Labour had replaced the Liberals as the dominant party in Wales, and by 1951 there were only three Liberal M.P.s left in Wales, and they held their seats through Conservative support. In 1959, the Liberals could field only eight candidates to Plaid Cymru's twenty. They were no longer either a radical or a national party in Wales.

IV

The Labour Party has always held an ambivalent attitude to Welsh national claims. In part, it inherited the mantle of Liberalism as the party of the provinces and the periphery, but it was also one wing of a national movement which saw class rather than community as the basis of political action. The trade unions, the industrial wing of the Labour movement, regarded themselves as national bodies, and feared that, if they were divided by geographical boundaries, this would provide an excuse for employers to cut wages in the less prosperous parts of the country. They even protested when, as a concession to national sentiment, Lloyd George agreed in 1911 to set up separate administrations for National Health Insurance in Scotland and Wales as well as in Ireland.

During its early years, however, Labour in Wales provided a unifying force in politics. Like the Liberals, Labour offered a broad cultural appeal, based less upon class consciousness than upon the chapel and the Sunday School. The Labour Party, in the words of Tom Jones, was 'not bound by a narrow economic doctrine; our approach was ethical or rather we were striving to bring the economic and religious factors into a right relation . . . we wanted a classless society but not a class war'.[16] This cultural dimension implied recognition of ethnic diversity as a vital repository of energy in the state. For, in the view of socialist pioneers such as Keir Hardie, men were moved as much by spiritual as by economic forces. Labour, therefore, willingly inherited the Liberal commitment to 'Home Rule All Round', and to a Welsh Parliament.

But we have already seen that the issues of Home Rule and the redress of nonconformist grievances were becoming less and less central to Welsh politics once disestablishment was conceded by Westminster. There was after the First World War a brief flurry of interest in regionalism and nationalism, but this was followed by an almost total lack of concern. A conference on devolution in

Wales held at Shrewsbury in 1922 failed disastrously, the industrial counties of Glamorgan and Monmouth not even bothering to send representatives.

During the inter-war period, faced with mass unemployment and migration from South Wales to the West Midlands and London, it would have been frivolous to argue that nationalism had anything to offer to the Welsh working class. Politics was dominated by class feeling, and the unemployed looked 'fixedly, if resentfully, to the government in London, apparently seeing no prospect of salvation under a separate system of government in Wales'.[17] The solution to the problems of Wales was to be found in centralized economic planning and not in the establishment of a Welsh Parliament.

In office after 1945, Labour's main concerns lay in the fields of economic policy and social reform, and this tended to reinforce its centralist outlook, an outlook epitomized in Aneurin Bevan's comment made in 1944: 'My colleagues, all of them members of the Miners' Federation of Great Britain, have no special solution for the Welsh coal industry which is not a solution for the whole of the mining industry of Great Britain. There is no Welsh problem.'[18]

As the Labour Party seemed to become, in the late 1960s, the governing party of Britain, it appeared to be wholly dominated by the problems of economic management, and concerned itself less with 'striving to bring the economic and religious factors into a right relation'.

Yet Labour was still electorally dependent upon the peripheries, and without its support from Wales, would not often be able to form a government. It is not surprising, then, that Labour's relationship to Wales should be an ambivalent one, its centralist philosophy clashing with its traditional role as the party of peripheral protest, and with its electoral self-interest.

V

The Welsh Nationalist Party, Plaid Cymru, was born in an atmosphere of disillusion and depression in 1925. As with the founding of the S.N.P., so the birth of Plaid Cymru was a sign not of the strength of Celtic Nationalism, but of its weakness. For both movements were founded on a recognition that neither national self-government nor even devolution were to be obtained from the

United Kingdom parties. The policy adopted by Nationalists of 'burrowing from within' the Liberal and Labour Parties had clearly failed, for the Liberals were no longer in a position to offer Home Rule, and Labour seemed uninterested in doing so.

The problems faced by Plaid Cymru were, however, far more daunting than those of the S.N.P. For in Scotland nationalism was a unifying force, and the institutions of nationhood elicited feelings of sympathy amongst almost all Scots. In Wales, on the other hand, the symbols of nationality—the land, religion, and the language—were products of a dying culture, and the language, the most obvious badge of Welsh identity, was a deeply divisive force, tending to confine Plaid Cymru to 'Welsh' Wales, the North and the West, as opposed to the industrial South East. It is this, as much as the discovery of oil in the North Sea, which accounts for the greater electoral success of the S.N.P.

In the twentieth century, the language has been in steady retreat, until in 1971 only 21 per cent of Welsh people spoke Welsh. Thus, if language was the criterion of Welshness, nearly 80 per cent of the inhabitants of Wales are not truly Welsh, and would hardly vote for a party whose main platform was the promotion of Welsh. If, on the other hand, Plaid Cymru underplayed the language issue, it might lose its central core of support from those who saw, as the main purpose of self-government, the preservation of the language.

Plaid Cymru's dilemma is highlighted in its statement of aims published in 1973. For it seeks, as well as self-government for Wales and a seat for Wales at the United Nations, to 'promote the culture, language and tradition, and the economic life of Wales'. That the promotion of the Welsh language may conflict with the aim of self-government has become painfully clear to Welsh Nationalists, but the conflict has not been resolved.

Plaid Cymru began as a movement to preserve the language, and it was originally almost a 'cultural conservationist society', [19] rather than a political party. Saunders Lewis, its President from 1926 to 1939, proclaimed in a radio broadcast as late as 1962 that the language 'is the only political question deserving of a Welshman's attention at the present time'. The language was

more important than self-government . . . if we were to have any sort of self-government for Wales before the Welsh language is recognised and used as an official language in all the administration of State and local authority in the Welsh areas of our country, it would never attain official status, and the doom of the language would come more quickly than it will come under English government.[20]

Saunders Lewis hoped that Welsh would become the sole official language of Wales as English was the sole official language of England. The intransigence of Saunders Lewis and the Welsh Language Society has given Plaid Cymru a highly unfavourable 'image' amongst non-Welsh speakers, which is difficult to shake off. But a later generation, under the leadership of Gwynfor Evans, Plaid Cymru's President since 1945, has adopted a more moderate stance on the language issue. In his book *Plaid Cymru and Wales*, published in 1974, Mr. Evans insisted that

since common membership of the Welsh community rather than language or descent is the test of nationality in Wales, nationalists are proud to know them [i.e. English-speaking Welshmen] as fellow-Welshmen. Wales has no finer patriots than some who have no knowledge of the national tongue . . .[21]

The party has tried hard to dissociate itself from the extremists of the Welsh Language Society, which Dr. Phil Williams has accused of 'alienating increasing numbers of the population' and creating 'hostility to the Welsh language'.[22] But Plaid Cymru did not adopt a policy of bilingualism until 1968, and then somewhat reluctantly.

In its early years, Plaid Cymru was so preoccupied with the language question that it gave little thought to the economic changes which were visibly altering the face of Wales. Much of its history over the past twenty years can be understood in terms of 'a campaign of attrition by a growing band of Modernists to bring the party into the world of modern Wales, to drag the movement, however reluctantly, away from total preoccupation with the cultural strongholds of the North and West'.[23] During the 1960s, study groups were established to consider the problems of the Welsh economy. The Plaid's specific proposals are, however, frequently naïve and woolly-minded, and they lack the sophistication and worldliness of the S.N.P.'s approach.

Plaid Cymru has, nevertheless, made some contribution to practical political thought by asking new questions which throw a shaft of light 'on the conventional wisdom as to the range of alternatives available to the future direction of the industrial state'.[24] Its ideological position is based to a considerable extent upon the work of the 'Small is Beautiful' school of E. F. Schumacher and Leopold Kohr, a Professor at Aberystwyth, and its central aim is to establish a basis for the identification of the individual with his ethnic community.

For Gwynfor Evans in his book *Wales Can Win* (1973), the motives of action are not economic or material, but cultural in origin. Men progress when they see the possibility of identifying their achievements with their community, their history, and their language. Moral energy is itself at least as much of a prerequisite for economic advancement as economic incentives, and so 'Those who think that a nation's culture is something quite separate from the social and economic order make a grave mistake.' The failure of Labour in Wales, and the failure of socialism to solve the economic problems of Wales, derive from the fact that it has become a centralizing and materialistic creed, which has lost its cultural roots.

The Rhondda was unique in that the leading spirits of the new barbarism were school-teachers, Labour to a man: to be Labour was one condition of promotion. Barbarism is not too strong a word to describe the policies which brought a rich culture . . . so near to ruin; and so it will be seen by the next generation.

To combat this barbarism, Gwynfor Evans believes individuals must actively seek identification with their communities. They must re-establish the link between the present and the past.

Adaptation requires a hold of the past, of traditional life. The past lives in the tradition of the national community; if it is destroyed no adaptation is possible. Therefore, although they are a radical party which seeks fundamental changes in Wales, nationalists have been conscious of the necessity for roots and continuity in human society and of the importance of identity and community in human life.[25]

Such a philosophy, hopelessly idealistic though it may appear, has close connections with the mainstream of British conservative thought as represented by, for example, Burke, Scott, and Disraeli. It seeks to answer fundamental political questions—what is the relationship between communal identity and economic progress, how far do cultural and economic factors interact in the process of social development. It puts forward a view of man 'far broader in scope than the dominant view of the citizen as economic man or woman, or as consumer . . .'.[26] A wise polity would surely have benefited by seeking to discriminate between what was valuable in such a philosophy and what was not, rather than rejecting the whole of it with patronizing contempt.

VI

Like the S.N.P., Plaid Cymru's first electoral forays brought little success, and the party made an impact only during the political truce in the Second World War, in the University of Wales seat which was abolished in 1948, and in by-elections in Ogmore and Aberdare in 1946, when it scored 29.4 per cent and 20 per cent of the vote respectively. From 1950 to 1956, Plaid Cymru joined in an abortive all-party campaign to press for a Welsh Parliament. A petition was drawn up which received a quarter of a million signatures, equal to 14 per cent of the Welsh electorate, but it was ignored by both government and opposition, and the Labour M.P.s who were associated with the campaign—including Cledwyn Hughes, a future Secretary of State for Wales—were carpeted by Labour's National Executive Committee for defying official Labour policy on the issue.

Until 1959, Plaid Cymru concentrated its electoral battles in the Welsh-speaking areas. As late as 1969, seven seats in Glamorgan and Monmouth had never seen a Plaid Cymru candidate. Yet, ironically, Plaid Cymru's breakthrough, when it came, occurred not in the rural Welsh-speaking areas of Merioneth or Anglesey, but in the areas of industrial decline at the head of the valleys—Rhondda and Caerphilly—and in Carmarthen, where in July 1966, Gwynfor Evans overturned a 9,233 Labour majority to win the seat. Even more remarkable was the by-election in Rhondda West, one of the safest Labour seats in the country, where in March 1967, Plaid Cymru all but won the seat slashing a Labour majority of 16,888 to 2,306. And in the third and last by-election in Wales in the 1966–70 Parliament, at Caerphilly in July 1968, Plaid Cymru was also a close second. 'In the Midlands', commented David McKie in the *Guardian* on 20 July, 'the slump in the Labour vote looked merely like the collapse of a habit: in South Wales, it looks like the death of a religion.'

In the two general elections of 1974, however, Plaid Cymru failed to emulate the S.N.P. and its percentage of the vote remained static at 10.7 per cent, while 26 of its 36 candidates lost their deposits. Although Plaid Cymru succeeded in winning three seats in 1974, there were only five seats where its vote exceeded 20 per cent, and it saved only four deposits outside the six predominantly Welsh-speaking constituencies. It did not, therefore, pose as serious a threat to Labour as the S.N.P. did in Scotland. In contrast to Scotland, where the S.N.P. all but eclipsed the Liberals, the demand for a third force in Welsh politics found its outlet not in Plaid Cymru but in the Liberal Party, whose share of the vote increased from 6.8 per cent in 1970 to 15.5 per cent in October 1974.

But, as we have seen, Welsh national identity is far too pervasive a phenomenon to be equated with support for Plaid Cymru; and it is possible that in Wales the Labour party has succeeded in resisting nationalism rather more effectively than its Scottish counterparts precisely because it has appreciated better the need to act as a vehicle of national self-expression.

VII

Just as Wales in the late nineteenth century secured recognition of her distinctiveness in the field of legislation, so also the machinery of administration in Wales has come to assume a distinctive nature. Indeed, over the past seventy years, the process of administrative decentralization in Wales has underlined the notion of a Welsh nationality by adding flesh and blood to the skeletal framework created by nineteenth-century radicals.

The causes, however, of separate administrative treatment for Wales lay as often in the needs of central government as in the Welsh claim for separate treatment. In 1907, the first Welsh Department of a ministry, the Welsh Department of the Board of Education, was set up to meet not a national demand but an administrative difficulty caused by the confusion of accountability for education in Wales between the newly established Board of Education and the Central Welsh Board.

This reform was the first recognition by any government department that separate treatment was necessary for Wales, and its significance lay in 'the recognition thereby accorded to the fact of the separate and distinct entity of Wales. This recognition is big with meaning and with future consequences.'[27]

It was also an administrative innovation which was to show the advantages of devolution in education; for the Welsh Department was able to ensure 'a unified approach to the educational problems of each individual authority so that, at any one time, officials of the Welsh Department were able to see the whole range of educational services provided in a particular area'. The Department was in a stronger position than the Board to decide whether, for example, primary or secondary education was more in need of funds, for the Board was organized in branches based upon the stages of education, and it was difficult to shift money intended for primary education to the secondary schools; whereas the Department was able to look at the needs of Welsh education as a whole, and it had the added advantage that 'it was possible for the officers of the local authorities to establish a close personal relationship with the Department's officials'.[28] The Department was also given 'a very free hand'[29] in encouraging the Welsh language, and indeed the outstanding feature of the Board's work in its first two years had been 'the definite recognition of the Welsh language and Welsh literature in the curriculum of the Schools and Training Colleges of Wales',[30] and since that time teachers in Wales have always been a powerful pressure group for the promotion of the Welsh language.

The next instalment of administrative decentralization in Wales occurred in 1911 when, under Lloyd George's National Insurance Act, Commissioners were being established. Once it had been decided to establish a separate administration for Ireland, Scotland and Wales demanded a similar concession, and Lloyd George, who had originally hoped for a unified system of administration, was compelled to give way, since 'you have got to defer to sentiment'.[31] The Welsh commissioners exercised 'an influence and authority which nobody sitting in and operating from London could have hoped to exercise'.[32] It was therefore 'not only a necessary but a very successful experiment in applied home rule'.[33]

The third area of administrative decentralization was in agriculture where in 1912, a year after the Scottish Board of Agriculture had been set up, the office of Agricultural Commissioner for Wales was established, together with an advisory Agricultural Council for Wales. The Report of the Welsh Land Enquiry Commission in 1914 was 'convinced that the problem of land in its varied features is so vast and complicated that it is impossible to deal effectively with Wales by a department located in Whitehall and staffed by men out of touch, and more often than not, out of sympathy with the special needs of Wales',[34] and in 1919 a Welsh office of the Board of Agriculture and Fisheries was set up.

Although the principle of administrative decentralization with respect to Wales had been recognized in three different areas of administration, this did not reflect any overall plan of devolution. For the process of decentralization was a piecemeal and pragmatic one, differing as it did from department to department. There was no obvious reason, for example, why the Welsh Board of Health, the successor to the Insurance Commissioners, came to be given far more autonomy than the Welsh Department of the Ministry of Agriculture, so that by 1950 it was responsible for exercising the major powers of the Ministry of Health in Wales. Decentralization came about as a result of changes in departmental machinery, and not because of a positive belief in the dispersal of power. Nevertheless, by the 1950s, 'there were no fewer than seventeen departments which had established administrative units in Wales'.[35]

The scope of decentralization was, however, inevitably limited by the conventions of British government. In particular, ministerial responsibility implied that ministers were answerable to Parliament for policy and expenditure in Wales. Any divergence in policy might create unwelcome precedents in England, and so there were limits to the discretion which civil servants could exercise.

If there were a minister whose responsibility it was to concern himself specifically with Wales, then, it could be argued, policy would be shaped more readily to meet Welsh needs. Therefore the logical next step to follow administrative decentralization was the demand for a separate Minister for Wales. This demand was rejected by Neville Chamberlain, and by Attlee, but in 1951 Winston Churchill appointed his Home Secretary, Sir David Maxwell-Fyfe, Minister for Welsh Affairs. Sir David was to be answerable to the Commons for the general effect of government policy in Wales, for the annual White Paper on government action in Wales, and he was also to lead in Welsh Day debates; but he was given no executive powers, and lacking a departmental machine, his effectiveness was bound to depend upon the degree of influence which he enjoyed over his Cabinet colleagues. There was perhaps always the danger that, like other ministers with roving commissions, the Minister would come to be seen by his colleagues as a nuisance, so that his advice was regarded as interference and politely ignored.

In January 1957, Harold Macmillan announced that the Minister of Housing and Local Government would in future be the Minister for Welsh Affairs, since the Minister, unlike the Home Secretary, had executive responsibility for a wide range of matters affecting Wales. He would therefore be in a position to 'take the initiative and give a lead by the use of his own departmental powers'.

In the same month, however, the Council for Wales and Monmouthshire, an advisory council composed of nominated members and established in 1948 as a sop to demands for further autonomy, produced its Third Memorandum on the subject of the machinery of government administration in Wales, and recommended the establishment of a Secretary of State for Wales. The Council came to this conclusion after a thorough investigation of government in Wales which had taken two years, on the ground that only a Secretary of State could effectively co-ordinate the Welsh departments of Whitehall ministries, so as to produce a policy which reflected the distinctive needs of Wales. The Government did not reply to this Memorandum until December 1957, when Mr. Macmillan rejected its central recommendation, but proposed instead the appointment of an Under-Secretary in the Welsh Office of the Minister of Housing and Local Government to be known as the Minister of State for Welsh Affairs: this was widely regarded in Wales as insufficient and the Chairman of the Council resigned in protest.

From this point, the initiative in the process of administrative decentralization to Wales passed to the Labour Party, which had advocated a full-time Minister for Welsh Affairs in 1954. The election of James Griffiths, M.P. for Llanelli, as Deputy Leader of the Labour Party in 1955 led to Welsh interests being given a greater prominence in Labour's policy-making, and in the 1959 and 1964 election manifestos the Party promised to create a Secretary of State for Wales. James Griffiths duly became the first Secretary of State for Wales when this commitment was carried out in October 1964.

His powers were, however, rather more limited than had originally been promised in Labour's 1963 policy document

Signposts for the Sixties; for he was given executive authority only over the functions of the Ministry of Housing and Local Government in Wales, and responsibility for roads; the policy document, however, had promised that he would be given responsibility for education, health, and agriculture also. The Secretary of State, therefore, had been given only transport in addition to the executive functions which the Minister of Housing and Local Government had possessed as Minister for Welsh Affairs. Gradually, however, his responsibilites were extended, and in 1968 he was given powers over health functions in Wales, and in 1970, powers with respect to primary and secondary education. In 1978, agriculture, further education, and higher education (excluding the universities) were transferred to the Welsh Office, so that its responsibilities were nearly as great as those of the Scottish Office.

In addition to his executive powers the Secretary of State was given, in 1964, powers to participate in the process of policy formulation of the economic plan for Wales in conjunction with the newly established Department for Economic Affairs, which retained ministerial responsibility for the Plan. He was also given powers of 'oversight within Wales of the execution of national policy' by other domestic departments in Wales, which in Harold Wilson's view would enable him 'to express the voice of Wales'.[36]

VIII

There can be no doubt that the setting up of the Welsh Office gave to Wales advantages not enjoyed by the regions of England: for not only does Wales have a representative at Cabinet level, but she is also represented at the crucial inter-departmental committees involved in policy formation. It is, however, difficult to measure the precise degree of influence exerted by the Welsh Office, because of course the role of individual ministers in the process of policy formation is discreetly veiled from the public eye.

The main limitations upon the influence of the Secretary of State for Wales are likely to be two-fold. The first is the restriction imposed upon spending plans for Wales by the process of public expenditure determination; and the second the restriction imposed by the constitutional conventions of British government.

Decisions on both the allocation of public expenditure between England and Wales, and the allocation between different services within Wales, are made not in Cardiff, but in Whitehall. These decisions are taken, therefore, not on a geographical, but on a functional basis, with given amounts being put aside for each service. This means that expenditure on public services in Wales cannot be expected to differ significantly in terms of its functional composition from expenditure on public services in other parts of Britain.

In its written submission to the Commission on the Constitution, the Welsh Office made it plain that its roads programme was determined 'in consultation with the Treasury', that U.K. ministers determined the total housing expenditure in the country as a whole, and that the ceiling on capital expenditure on the environmental and health services was determined in the annual Public Expenditure Survey Committee review; moreover, the Welsh Office's powers in economic planning amounted to no more than working 'in close touch with the headquarters of the Department of Economic Affairs in order to ensure that planning in Wales fits into the Government's overall strategies for development . . .'.[37] They did not give the Welsh Office powers to draw up its own economic plan for Wales.

Questioning of Welsh Office officials by Dr. Norman Hunt (now Lord Crowther-Hunt) revealed very sharply the limitations upon the powers of the department. Speaking of the P.E.S.C. exercise, Dr. Hunt asked whether it was true that it was conducted on a functional basis as a rolling programme for a five-year period:

Dr. Hunt: 'It is expressed in terms of education, transport and other services not in terms of a block amount for Wales to cover all of them'—
W. Brenig Jones (Welsh Office): 'That is true.'

Dr. Hunt: 'When the thing has been decided you do not have powers—in the Welsh Office—correct me if I am wrong—to say "Well we have got £X million for Wales, and in point of fact we are not going to spend this on roads but we are going to spend less on roads and more on education".'

J. W. M. Siberry (Welsh Office): '. . . just a bit round the margin perhaps'.

Dr. Hunt: 'The exercise is on a functional basis and not a geographical basis?'

Mr. Siberry: 'Yes, there is a functional approach within the Welsh Office's own figuring.'[38]

So in this way the degree of autonomy of the Welsh Secretary is limited not only by the constraints of Cabinet and party government, but also by the centralizing influences created by the processes through which public resources are allocated.

But this should not be taken to mean that there is no discretion at all in the allocation of public expenditure in Wales. For, even though he receives his budget in the form of earmarked revenues rather than a block grant, the Welsh Secretary has some power to seek a modification of the proposed expenditure, so as to secure a different expenditure mix for Wales. One area where this power has been successfully used is in the roads programme for Wales, since the Welsh Office has put a high priority upon expenditure on roads, to compensate for the poor communications network which it inherited. Moreover, the Welsh Office is able to secure a transfer of funds, even after P.E.S.C. programmes have been agreed, in a way that is impossible for an English region. In the year 1976–7, for example, the Welsh Office underspent by £28.3m. on housing in Wales.[39] The Cabinet agreed, following a request by the Welsh Secretary, to allow £6,300,000 of this amount to be spent on roads and transport instead.[40]

There is, therefore, in Wales what has been called 'a grey area where expenditure is in line with nationally established policy, yet altered to meet special Welsh circumstances as the Welsh Office perceives them'.[41] It is difficult to delimit precisely the boundaries of this grey area, except in general terms, for obviously it will depend to a considerable extent upon the political weight of the personalitites involved; but it is fair to say that the Welsh Secretary even if he 'doesn't really originate general policy . . . does put the Welsh nuance into U.K. policies'.[42]

In broader areas of policy-making, also, the Secretary of State has probably exerted some influence. According to Edward Rowlands, a former junior minister at the Welsh Office, the Welsh Secretary was instrumental in the transfer of the Royal Mint to Wales, and he was successful in persuading the 1966–70 Labour government not to build a reservoir in the Dulas valley, and to keep open the Llanelli-Shrewsbury railway line, which serves central Wales. In none of these areas did the Secretary of State have executive functions, and so they are all examples of the influence of his 'oversight' powers. On the central economic issues affecting

Wales, such as pit closures or investment in the steel industry, however, the Welsh Office seems to have been able to exert less influence. Indeed, according to Rowlands, the Welsh Office does not seem to have exercised its policy-making powers in a very imaginative way. 'The emphasis has been upon continuity and conformity with Whitehall . . . In evidence before parliamentary committees, officials have made few claims of originality.'[43] It may well be, of course, that this caution is the natural response of a new Department gradually feeling its way. In time, perhaps, as the Welsh Office comes to be accepted in Whitehall, it could acquire as much influence as the Scottish Office has done.

Yet it would be wrong to believe that current governmental arrangements in Wales offer a satisfactory solution to the problem of adjusting national policies to Welsh needs. For the conventions of British government are bound to limit the autonomy of the Secretary of State, even if to a lesser extent than was the case with the Welsh departments of U.K. ministries. The Welsh Secretary is bound by the policies of his party even if these do not coincide with the desires of the majority of Welsh voters, a situation particularly likely to arise when the Conservatives are in government; and the traditions of the civil service remain hostile to excessive experimentation in one part of the country, lest it create an undesirable precedent for other areas.

Moreover, the Welsh Secretary is unlikely to be a powerful figure in Cabinet. The post is not one that is likely to be offered to a politician of the front rank, and promotion to one of the leading offices of state is unlikely to result from competence in the office. Indeed, the Welsh Secretary, now that this office is a separate one, is far junior in Cabinet rank to his predecessors, the Home Secretary and the Minister for Housing and Local Government, when they exercised responsibility for Wales. Sir Keith Joseph, in opposing the setting up of the Welsh Office, argued that 'a Minister who speaks for a large Department has slightly more of a chance of getting his case put or heard, than a Minister who speaks for a smaller Department'.[44] Paradoxically the one factor that may have increased the influence of the Scottish and Welsh Secretaries in recent years has been the rise of the nationalist parties. Without such pressures, governments might well, to take one example, have done less to improve communications in Wales, so that proposed rail closures would have been implemented, and less would have been spent on roads.

The convention of Cabinet secrecy makes it difficult for voters in Wales to attribute clear responsibility for policy decisions affecting Wales. The Secretary of State may often have to defend policies with which he disagrees, and he will be unable to parade his triumphs except surreptitiously. He is also in a peculiarly anomalous position, in that he is popularly regarded as the 'Minister for Wales' even though he is statutorily responsible for only a limited range of government policy in Wales. Where he fails to prevent pit or rail closures he may be blamed by Welsh public opinion, even though these matters do not fall within his statutory competence.

A further difficulty of the Secretary of State's position is that the more responsibilities he accumulates, the more danger there is that, in the words of Sir Goronwy Daniel (the first administrative head of the Welsh Office) to the Commission on the Constitution, Wales would come to be governed 'by an élite civil service'. There were, according to Sir Goronwy, two ways in which this might happen: 'One might be that if accountability is only to Westminster, the amount of parliamentary time which can be made available is limited. The other factor would be that as the functions of the Secretary of State grow it becomes more necessary to delegate more and more work to officials.'[45]

The distinctive parliamentary arrangements adopted for Wales are hardly designed to overcome these dangers. Welsh Questions last for a little over an hour every three weeks, and the Welsh Grand Committee, established in 1960, is an even weaker body than its Scottish counterpart, since there is so little legislation which relates exclusively to Wales. It cannot hold Second Reading debates on the Welsh aspects of legislation, nor can it discuss Welsh Estimates. It therefore 'has some value in providing a talking shop for Welsh members and a forum for the discussion of Welsh affairs. It is less certain that it achieves the other purpose for which it was set up, namely to provide scrutiny of Government policy in Wales.'[46] There are also occasional Welsh Day debates on the floor of the House.

As the Welsh Office comes to be entrusted with greater responsibilities, therefore, it will become less accountable, and it will become subject to the same criticisms as the Scottish Office. The Welsh Office will be responsible for a wide range of policy-making in

Wales, but will be subject to no effective scrutiny by Parliament. After his retirement from the civil service, Sir Goronwy Daniel, in his first major speech as Principal of the University College of Wales, Aberystwyth, insisted that the structure of central government in Wales did not secure effective accountability. He added:

now that the principle has been adopted of having a separate Minister with responsibility for Wales alone, the question is naturally asked whether it is right that accountability should still be wholly to Parliament in Westminster and not to some form of assembly representative of the particular population which these Ministers are serving.[47]

IX

Because the Labour Party has been the dominant party in Wales for so long, the recent history of the devolution debate in Wales is very largely the history of an internal Labour Party debate. But the debate has a very different flavour from that in Scotland. In contrast to the Scottish Labour Party's gradual yet grudging concessions on devolution, the Welsh Labour Party committed itself to an Assembly in the mid-1960s, but it has had to fight hard to maintain this commitment against increasingly recalcitrant M.P.s and constituency parties, especially in the South East of Wales.

The initial response of Labour in Wales was so much more enthusiastic than in Scotland for two reasons. The first was that the control of *ad hoc* nominated bodies such as the Welsh Hospitals Board was, in Labour's view, a means through which Conservatives, who had never been the majority party in Wales, were able to retain a hold on Welsh life. It was therefore vital to make these bodies accountable to a directly elected all-Wales body. The more important reason, however, was that in Wales, unlike Scotland, devolution could be linked to the issue of local government reform, and the case for an Assembly was first presented in the mid-1960s, as part of a broader argument for a two-tier reform of Welsh local government. So, whereas in Scotland local government reform and devolution were conflicting priorities, in Wales they seemed to be complementary. Indeed, as originally conceived, the all-Wales body would not have been a devolved administration at all, since its powers would have been those of a local authority, and it would not have assumed any of the functions of central government in

Wales. It would be likely, however, that an all-Wales body would seek to control Welsh nominated bodies, and its political weight would be such that it would soon demand the right to exercise Welsh Office powers in Wales. Indeed, when debating the Report of the Royal Commission on the Constitution, the Welsh Council of Labour argued that a Welsh Assembly should be 'integrated with the reorganization of local government, and thus be part of a general reorganization of the machinery of government'.[48]

But, if the Labour Party in Wales was more sympathetic to devolution than its Scottish counterpart, it was nevertheless desperately anxious that its proposals should avoid the taint of separatism. M.P.s who might be perfectly prepared to vote for a new local government structure were quite unwilling to support what they saw as a concession to separatism. So the rise of Plaid Cymru in the late 1960s undermined Welsh Labour's commitment to devolution, whereas in Scotland, where the Union seemed in real danger, the S.N.P. acted as a spur to it. In Wales, the fear of making any concession to nationalism gave the Labour Cabinet in the late 1960s an unanswerable argument against an all-Wales body; although, ironically, the inadequacies of local government reform in Wales when it did come were to yield a further argument for devolution.

The Executive Committee of the Welsh Council of Labour first proposed an elected council for Wales in 1965, as a top tier of a reformed local government structure; and at the same time, an inter-departmental working party set up by the Welsh Office to advise the Secretary of State on local government reform made a similar proposal. One of the members of this working party was Ivor Gowan, Professor of Politics at Aberystwyth, and he gave further publicity to its findings by advocating an all-Wales body in his inaugural lecture *Government in Wales*, delivered in 1966, although he was hostile to devolution.

Thus the idea of an all-Wales body was not at first linked directly to devolution, and it was put forward before Plaid Cymru appeared to be a threat to Labour. It is perhaps best understood, together with the rise of Plaid Cymru, as an illustration of the reassertion of Welsh identity in the late 1960s.

The first two Secretaries of State for Wales, James Griffiths and Cledwyn Hughes, were sympathetic to an elected Welsh Council, and they had an ally in the Labour Cabinet of the late 1960s in the person of Richard Crossman who asked: 'Why not accept this local government reorganization as a political necessity and then go for a really ambitious plan for a Welsh Council or Parliament?'[49] When, however, the proposal for an elected council reached the Cabinet, it met the determined opposition of William Ross, the Secretary of State for Scotland, who feared that it would become impossible to resist the demand for a Scottish Assembly if an all-Wales body was set up; and ironically, in view of later events, of James Callaghan, who feared that the Welsh Council would provide a powerful forum for Plaid Cymru, and whose electoral base was in Cardiff where local Labour parties were bitterly hostile to any reorganization of local government. The proposal was thus watered down in Cabinet, so that the Welsh Council became a nominated body with purely advisory and promotional powers. This prompted the *Western Mail* to make the tart comment that Cledwyn Hughes 'had been placed in charge of a Government department which though set up to deal with Wales's unique problems is forbidden to propose uniquely Welsh solutions, because of the repercussions in England and in Scotland'.[50]

The advocates of an all-Wales body were placed in an even more uncomfortable position when, in January 1968, Cledwyn Hughes was replaced as Secretary of State for Wales by George Thomas 'who regards Cledwyn's views as sheer treason'.[51] Thomas and his Minister of State, Mrs. Eirene White, dedicated themselves to winning the next battle against Labour's Welsh devolutionists, and preventing the Welsh Council of Labour from advocating a directly elected Assembly in its submission to the Commission on the Constitution. They succeeded, however, only in modifying the position of the Welsh Council, which offered a compromise by abandoning its claim that the Assembly be given legislative powers. The Welsh Council's evidence to the Commission on the Constitution, therefore, contains the germ of the notion of executive devolution, which was finally to emerge as the Labour Government's policy after 1974.

In retrospect, however, it is clear that an excellent chance to secure an all-Wales body was lost in the 1960s. Also lost was the opportunity for a specifically Welsh reform of local government, for after the Cabinet battle over the powers of the proposed Welsh

Council, the Labour government gradually retreated from the policy of a separate Welsh reorganization.

The Conservative Government which came to power in 1970 did succeed in reorganizing local government in Wales, but it did so in an Act which applied to both England and Wales. Reorganization in Wales was determined, therefore, by the same principles as reorganization in England, and a two-tier structure was set up. In Wales, the top tier consisted not of an all-Wales body, but of eight county authorities, and this meant that devolution would become more difficult, since an elected council for Wales established after local government reform would, in the Welsh Council of Labour's view, be 'like a jellyfish on a bed of nails'.[52] 'No responsible government', claimed Dr. Phil Williams of Plaid Cymru, 'would totally reorganise local government in Wales without first deciding the pattern of devolution. Unfortunately we underestimated the total irresponsibility of the Heath Government.'[53] The central consideration operating in the mind of the Heath Government was perhaps less that of refusing to give openings to nationalism, than an argument of administrative uniformity; and Peter Thomas, the Secretary of State for Wales at the time, almost certainly lacked the political weight to counter this argument.

The Labour Opposition moved an amendment to the 1972 Local Government Bill, calling for an elected Welsh Council, and this amendment was moved by George Thomas who had undergone what a Conservative Member called 'the fastest conversion in Wales since the Forward Movement, and faster than recent conversions to North Sea Gas'. According to George Thomas, the Opposition were '100 per cent in support of this Motion which I am proposing to the Committee this morning—that there shall be established from 1 April 1976 an elected Council for Wales'.[54]

This claim of 100 per cent support proved to be rather optimistic, for, since 1974, the anti-devolutionists in the Welsh Labour Party have been conducting a powerful rearguard action against the Labour Party's commitment to devolution in Wales. They have been helped by the very successes of Plaid Cymru and the Liberals in West and North Wales which have tilted the balance against the devolutionists by depriving them of such staunch advocates as Goronwy Roberts and Elystan Morgan.

The anti-devolutionists in Wales did not mount a frontal attack against the commitment to a Welsh Assembly, but contented themselves with demanding a referendum, a proposal hotly resisted by the Welsh Council of Labour, which argued, not very plausibly in the light of the 1975 referendum on membership of the E.E.C., that 'The introduction of government by referendum would be a complete reversal of our whole system of Government . . .'.[55]

The government, however, was forced to concede a referendum in December 1976, in order to secure a Second Reading for the Scotland and Wales Bill; and, after the withdrawal of this Bill, the government thought it prudent to make a further political concession to opponents of devolution in Wales, by requiring the Welsh Assembly, in the revised Wales Bill, to review the structure of local government in Wales and report upon its findings to the Secretary of State for Wales. In this way the government hoped to harness the unpopularity of local government to support for an Assembly as the best way of securing a more satisfactory local government structure.

These concessions were not, however, sufficient to end the internal debate in the Labour Party and it entered the referendum campaign unhappy and divided, threatened by the pro-devolutionist Liberals and Plaid Cymru in the West and North, and by the anti-devolutionist Conservatives in the South East where hostility to devolution seems greatest.

The political climate in Wales has also changed from the optimistic years of the 1960s when institutional reform was seen as the remedy for so many ills, to a more sceptical approach. It is for this reason that Wales might reject devolution. But even if she does, it will be necessary for the institutions of government to take special account of Welsh national feeling. The sense of Welsh nationality is subtle and elusive, but there can be no doubt that it exists; and this makes it doubtful whether Wales will, in the long run, remain content without a political forum of the kind granted to Scotland. To fashion a structure of government shaped to the distinctive needs of Wales poses as much of a challenge to contemporary governments as it did to Gladstone and Lloyd George when modern Wales was born.

6   The government's response

England is not governed by logic but by Parliament.

Disraeli

I

From the time of the secession of Southern Ireland in 1921 to the
rise of the nationalist parties in the late 1960s, devolution was not
an issue in British politics. The most important reason for this is
that the seeming interest in devolution between 1885 and 1921 was
in reality a search for an equitable way of disposing of the Irish
problem. Concern about improving government through decentralization was subordinate to that. As soon as Lloyd George
made the decision to deal separately with the Irish problem, the
impetus behind the movement for devolution collapsed.

After the Lloyd George coalition was overthrown, the downfall
of the Liberal Party served to remove devolution from the agenda
of politics, and it corresponded with an important change in the
basis of political alignments. For before the First World War,
political opinion was based as much upon locality as it was upon
class.

The politics of locality had most force where the grievances of
peripheral regions of the country could be linked with a national
cause. This was most obviously the case with Ireland where, over
much of the country, the Liberal/Conservative battle had no meaning
at all; but it was true also in Scotland and Wales, whose percentage
of support for Conservatives was the lowest in the country. Henry
Pelling, in his study of electoral patterns before 1914, has shown
convincingly that 'nationalism contributed something to political
feeling which went beyond the mere sense of economic grievance'.[1]

After the First World War, however, the democratization of the
franchise and the growth of class feeling turned national and
regional resentments into class politics, and the Liberal Party, the

party of the periphery and the provinces against the metropolis, was eclipsed by Labour, the party of class. The transition is symbolized by the transfer of the mine owners in South Wales, some of whom were Welsh-speaking nonconformists, from the progressive side of politics as members of an alien church, to the reactionary side as members of an alien class.

Labour, as well as representing the politics of class, also retained the support of the periphery and articulated the old radical grievances against the centre. That is why it inherited Liberal strength in rural Wales, and in Scottish constituencies such as the Western Isles. But, whereas the pre-1914 Liberal programme had emphasized the dispersal of power, the Labour Party, through its programmes of nationalization and economic planning, was essentially an agent of centralization. Thus Labour in office might well disappoint the hopes of those who supported it as a party of locality. In the late 1940s there was, as we have seen, a mild nationalist revolt in Scotland; but it never gained much credence, since Labour's policies offered such an improvement over the inter-war economy with its mass unemployment and poverty. In the late 1960s, however, the centralization of power under Labour governments was combined not with economic success but with economic failure, and the politics of class came again to be complemented by the politics of locality. Labour was, therefore, ideologically ill-equipped to deal with nationalism.

Hugh Seton-Watson has argued that 'European socialists inherited the tradition, deriving from Louis XIV but reinforced by the French Revolution and Napoleon, that large centralized states were progressive and small regional autonomies reactionary'.[2] The Labour Party is no exception to this generalization, for it came to see indigenous nationalism as a force splitting the working-class movement. It was reinforced in this view by the attitudes of the trade unions who, even when they supported Home Rule, demanded national wage bargaining and were, understandably, fearful lest decentralized bargaining allowed employers to lower wages in the less prosperous areas of the country.

Labour came to believe that economic efficiency required centralization. The unemployment of the inter-war period could be cured only by the state assuming powerful new weapons of economic management. To devolve economic functions would threaten planning and was incompatible with Keynesian demand management. To devolve the administration of social policy would raise the possibility of different standards of social welfare in different parts of the country, and weaken the Welfare State. Devolution would therefore undermine the twin pillars of Labour's programme, full employment and the Welfare State. During the inter-war period and immediate post-war years, socialists in Scotland and Wales shared this view. Like their counterparts in the North of England, they demanded not more autonomy but a government which took more notice of their grievances. They sought to increase the strength of London government, not to reduce it.

II

It was natural, therefore, for the Labour government to adopt a cautious response to the rise of nationalism in the late 1960s. For not only might concessions to nationalism weaken the government's chance of solving Britain's economic problems, and its commitment to equality, but, as we have seen, Labour had the most to lose from any reform which threatened the position of Scottish or Welsh M.P.s or of the Secretaries of State for Scotland and Wales.

On the other hand, the government did not wish to dismiss the claims of Scotland or Wales out of hand, for this would further alienate disillusioned supporters, who were coming to believe that Labour was insensitive to their problems. The government therefore resorted to a favourite expedient of a harassed administration: a Royal Commission, chaired first by Lord Crowther and, after his death, by Lord Kilbrandon. In this way, the demand for immediate concessions to meet the nationalist threat could be contained, and by the time the Kilbrandon Commission reported the S.N.P. and Plaid Cymru might no longer be so credible politically, in which case its findings could be quietly pigeon-holed. It seemed that nothing would be lost by playing for time. In retrospect, however, it can be argued that the establishment of the Commission wasted valuable time which might have been used to pre-empt the Nationalist challenge. The decision to set up the Commission was taken in the autumn of 1968, but its members were not appointed until April 1969, and did not report until October 1973; so there was a period of five years between the inception of the Commission and the publication of its Report. During that time, governments could conveniently use the Commission's existence as an excuse for dismissing devolution from their minds.

The Commission itself was beset by difficulties. Its first Chairman and another member died, and three other members resigned while it was deliberating. The Report was not unanimous, and it was accompanied by a Memorandum of Dissent by Lord Crowther-Hunt, a Labour peer and Fellow of Exeter College, Oxford, and A. T. Peacock, then Professor of Economics at the University of York, and a supporter in general of the free market school of economics.

The Report and the Memorandum of Dissent differed not so much on specific proposals as on the interpretation of the very wide-ranging terms of reference given to the Commission which required it to 'examine the present functions of the central legislature and government in relation to the several countries, nations, and regions of the United Kingdom', and to consider 'having regard . . . to the interests of the prosperity of Our people under the Crown whether any changes are desirable in those functions or otherwise in present constitutional and economic relationships'. This, as the Memorandum of Dissent pointed out, meant 'that virtually every aspect of the central legislature and government is subject to our scrutiny . . . Indeed, only if we recommend the abolition of the Monarchy would we be in conflict with our terms of reference.'[3] The signatories of the main Report, however, took the view that 'the main intention behind our appointment was that we should investigate the case for transferring or devolving responsibility for the exercise of government functions from Parliament and the central government to new institutions of government in the various countries and regions of the United Kingdom'.[4] The Report, therefore, might be more accurately described as a Report on Devolution, rather than on the Constitution, and the Commissioners who signed it were perhaps guilty of assuming that devolution was the only plausible response to the dissatisfaction with government which they found.

The Memorandum of Dissent, on the other hand, interpreted the terms of reference more widely, and produced a far-reaching scheme of constitutional reform, involving not only devolution, but also reform of Parliament and the structure of the political parties.

Broadly, it recommended that Britain adopt the West German model of federal government, but there were various nuances of West German government which tended to escape the signatories of the Memorandum of Dissent, and they did not devote sufficient attention to the problems involved in transposing a system of government which worked well in one country into another with wholly different traditions of law-making.

The ill-defined terms of reference offered to the Commission were but a symptom of the levity with which the government had approached the problem of nationalism. Another example of the lack of interest displayed by the government was its failure to seek to co-ordinate the work of the Commission on the Constitution with that of the Redcliffe-Maud Commission on Local Government in England and the Wheatley Commission on Local Government in Scotland. Indeed, according to Richard Crossman, Harold Wilson only told Lord Wheatley of the signifiance of the Constitutional Commission after it had been set up, 'without of course even asking John Wheatley's advice'.[5] Yet, if the Committee on the Constitution was to consider devolution seriously, its proposals would be bound to have an important impact on local government reform. Unfortunately, after setting up the Commission, the government seems to have forgotten about it, as the nationalist threat seemed to recede after 1968.

III

It has been said that Royal Commissions are not suitable bodies to consider proposals for change, since they are likely to be composed of representatives of different outlook who are generally unwilling to alter their views. The result in such circumstances will be a Report which is 'vague, general, ambiguous, or perhaps even expresses conflicting views in different corners'.[6] That is certainly true of the Report of the Royal Commission on the Constitution, a diffuse and long-winded document in which it is difficult to disentangle the essential arguments. Indeed on the issue of devolution itself, the division between the signatories of the Report and the Memorandum of Dissent is itself misleading and does not expose the true divergence of opinion. In fact, three different streams of thought can be discerned. The first may be labelled nationalist, not in the sense that its supporters were in favour of independence for Scotland and Wales, but because they believed that Scotland and Wales deserved special treatment on grounds of nationhood. They therefore recommended legislative devolution for Scotland and Wales, but were opposed to directly elected regional assemblies for England. This group included all the members on the Commission from Scotland, Wales, and Northern Ireland (including the Chairman, Lord Kilbrandon), but only one member from England.

The second group consisted of what might be called regionalists. They believed that the causes of dissatisfaction with government were common to all parts of Britain, even if, in the absence of nationalist parties, they could not be so easily expressed in England as in Scotland and Wales. They also insisted that devolution be based upon a principle of equality of political rights for those living in all parts of the United Kingdom, since the claims by Scotland and Wales to separate nationality did not, in the view of the Memorandum of Dissent, 'entitle the people in Scotland and Wales to be better governed or to have more participation in the handling of their own affairs than is offered to the people of Yorkshire or Lancashire'. Indeed, for Professor Peacock, the principle of equality of rights was 'not only an important matter of principle, but also a reasonable prediction of what would be politically acceptable in the long run'. For, without equality of rights, 'there would no longer be any reality to the concept of the practical unity of the United Kingdom'.[7]

But the principle of equality of rights was supported not only by the two signatories of the dissenting Memorandum, but also by two who signed the Report, Lord Foot and Sir James Steel. Significantly, all of the four who upheld this principle had strong regional ties, and none of them hailed from London or the South East. Sir James Steel was an industrialist from the North East concerned lest Scotland gain advantages through devolution which would be denied to this area. Professor Peacock had spent much of his academic life at York, Lord Crowther-Hunt, although an Oxford academic, was born in the North, and Lord Foot came from the South West. Their concern for equality of rights led them to advocate a form of executive devolution for all parts of Britain, thus giving to Scotland and Wales nothing which was to be denied to England.

The third group, consisting of Mrs. Trenaman, Principal of St. Anne's College, Oxford, and a former civil servant, Sir David Renton, a Conservative M.P., and Harry Street, Professor of Law at Manchester University, might be described as sceptics. They were against devolution to England and Wales, but two of them—Mrs. Trenaman and Professor Street—thought that there was a case for legislative devolution to Scotland, although Mrs. Trenaman has since retracted that view.[8]

The Commission was unanimous only in rejecting separatism and federalism, in supporting a directly elected assembly for Scotland, and in recommending the single transferable vote system of proportional representation for elections to any devolved assembly.

IV

Faced with so wide a range of differing views whose significance was concealed rather than brought out by the form of the Report, it was natural for M.P.s to greet its appearance with some bafflement. Appearing immediately after the Yom Kippur War at a time when there was a serious threat to Britain's oil supplies, it seemed a totally irrelevant, if harmless, diversion from real political issues. The Report received a brief debate in the Commons in which Government and Opposition promised to consider it carefully, and it was then forgotten. Neither the Labour nor the Conservative election manifestos for the February 1974 election advocated devolution, although both promised to continue with their consideration of the Commission's findings.

Devolution, however, took on a new lease of life after the February 1974 election when the Scottish Nationalists gained six seats and Plaid Cymru two. Mr. Wilson took office as head of a minority government which could ill afford to alienate Nationalists or Liberals, both of whom would be sympathetic to devolution. In the Queen's Speech, therefore, it was announced that the government would 'initiate discussions in Scotland and Wales on the Report of the Royal Commission on the Constitution, and . . . bring forward proposals for consideration'. In answer to an interruption from Mrs. Ewing, Mr. Wilson said 'we shall publish a White Paper and a Bill'.

With another election in the offing, however, time was short. A consultative document, *Devolution within the United Kingdom: Some Alternatives for Discussion*, was published, laying out the various proposals made by the Royal Commission. The document invited comments from members of the public, but it was published on 3 June and the deadline for comments was 30 June. The summer months were spent in ensuring that the Labour Party in Scotland supported the government's commitment to devolution, and on 17 September 1974, a day before the election was announced and three weeks before polling day, the government took the decision in principle with the publication of a White Paper *Democracy and Devolution: Proposals for Scotland and Wales* (Cmnd. 5732).

This hurriedly produced document laid down the government's 'decisions of principle' (Para. 1) from which it was never to depart. These were that there would be directly elected assemblies for Scotland and Wales, with the Scottish Assembly having legislative powers while the Welsh Assembly would have executive powers. The Assemblies would be financed mainly through a block grant allocated by Parliament. There was to be no reduction in the number of Scottish or Welsh M.P.s, and the Secretaries of State for Scotland and Wales would continue to have places in the Cabinet. A decision on devolution in England was postponed for later consideration.

Because this White Paper had to be produced at such speed, and because the issue was so bound up with the Labour Party's election prospects, the party machinery at Transport House, together with the government's newly appointed constitutional adviser Lord Crowther-Hunt, appear to have secured more influence over the 'decision in principle' than the Cabinet and the civil service. It was believed that many senior Cabinet ministers, especially those connected with economic affairs, were sceptical as to whether devolution could be reconciled with the efficient management of the economy; and there were thought to be some doubts amongst civil servants as to whether the Government's 'decisions of principle' added up to a viable package at all. Unfortunately there was no time to explore these doubts, and the decisions announced in the

White Paper formed the basis upon which the devolution proposals were constructed.

These decisions were worked out in much greater detail in a further White Paper, *Our Changing Democracy: Devolution to Scotland and Wales* (Cmnd. 6348), published in November 1975. This White Paper put forward a minimalist conception of devolution circumscribing the proposed Assemblies with seemingly powerful restraints. The government proposed not to devolve economic and industrial powers, or matters related to energy or agriculture. It rejected any major devolution of revenue-raising powers. But the most noteworthy feature of the White Paper was the role which the Secretary of State for Scotland would assume after devolution. He would not only enjoy the constitutional functions of a monarch or Governor General in appointing the Chief Executive and the cabinet of the Scottish administration and in formally ratifying Scottish legislation; but he would, in addition, retain powerful political functions, through his substantial powers in the non-devolved areas of Scottish government and his right to veto Scottish legislation (even though *intra vires*) not only on the grounds of *ultra vires*, but also if a Bill was 'unacceptable on policy grounds' (Para. 58). This power of veto on policy grounds was not, in the government's view, to be subject to review by the courts. These provisions were attacked by the Faculty of Advocates in Scotland on the grounds that 'The concept of a legislative body dealing with matters affecting the life, liberty, and other interests of the individual being constitutionally subordinate to a member of the Executive is offensive to the principles established in both Kingdoms at the end of the seventeenth century.'[9]

The S.N.P., predictably perhaps, attacked the White Paper as 'An affront to Scotland', and one Scottish Nationalist member, Mr. George Reid, claimed that the Scots 'expected to be disappointed. They did not expect to be insulted.' But, even outside the S.N.P., the reaction to the White Paper was muted; it was a White Paper with few friends. The Government decided therefore to make concessions in yet another White Paper, *Devolution to Scotland and Wales: Supplementary Statement* (Cmnd. 6585), published in August 1976, when it removed the provision that the Secretary of State could overrule an Assembly Bill on policy grounds, giving him a more limited power of override which would be subject to parliamentary approval. Consideration of the *vires* of Assembly Bills was to be by the Judicial Committee of the Privy Council, and not the Secretary of State. It was in addition decided to devolve wider powers to Scotland in the field of Scots private law, and to devolve to Scotland and Wales responsibility for the operation of the recently established Scottish and Welsh Development Agencies.

After this 'White Paper chase', all was ready for the Scotland and Wales Bill, although there was some further delay before the Prime Minister, Mr. Callaghan, moved the Second Reading, on 13 December 1976, of a Bill which proposed constitutional changes which were 'the most fundamental of their kind in Great Britain for centuries'.[10] 'With all its defects, remarked one M.P., who sought a wider devolution of powers than the government was prepared to offer, 'the Bill marks a point of no return. Even if it were to be defeated on Thursday, it still marks a point of no return.'[11]

The Bill passed its Second Reading comfortably by 292 votes to 247, a government majority of 45. There was a considerable amount of cross-voting amongst the major parties. On the Labour side, ten M.P.s voted with the Opposition and thirty abstained. Five Conservatives voted with the government and twenty-eight abstained. Amongst the latter were Mr. Heath and Mr. Peter Walker; and amongst the former Mr. Buchanan-Smith, a former Shadow Secretary of State for Scotland.

The composition of the Government's Second Reading majority was a clear sign that the Bill would not have an easy passage through the House. For the government, if it was to succeed, would need to obtain a majority for a guillotine motion during the Committee stage of the Bill. Otherwise it would be filibustered to death. But on a guillotine motion the Conservative dissidents, having made the point that they were in favour of devolution in principle, would rejoin their Party, whilst the Labour dissidents were mainly irreconcileables whom it would be difficult to win back. Equally ominous was the attitude of the Liberals, upon whose support the Government was relying. For Mr. Steel, the Liberal leader, made it clear that Liberal M.P.s were voting for the Second Reading on the clear understanding that the Bill would be altered fundamentally in Committee 'and that if the Bill is to succeed and to make progress through the House the Government must approach these issues with the utmost flexibility'.[12] The government, however, knew that if it began to show the kind of flexibility desired by Mr. Steel, it would lose the support of its back-bench loyalists, especially those from constituencies in the North who had voted for Second Reading less out of a passionate commitment to devolution than out of an unwillingness to embarrass the government on a major item of legislation.

V

The government, therefore, decided to offer a political concession to Labour dissidents in the form of referendums to be held in Scotland and Wales after the Bill received Royal Assent. This would enable opponents of the Bill to vote for it, but then to press the electorate in Scotland or Wales to reject it in the referendum.

In earlier statements to the Commons, Mr. Michael Foot, the Lord President of the Council, had refused to hold a referendum on the grounds, first, that there had been sufficient opportunity for public debate on the issue of devolution to Scotland and Wales; and second, that devolution was a manifesto commitment and the government therefore had a mandate to carry it through.

The commitment to the referendum was made on the final day of the Second Reading debate by Mr. John Smith, the Minister of State at the Privy Council Office, and the government's proposal was embodied in new clause 40 introduced in the Committee stage of the Bill on 10 February 1977. In the view of one M.P., this new clause was introduced 'amid scenes of procedural shambles, the likes of which I cannot remember in some years in this House'.[13] For the government's proposed new clause, eventually ruled as in order by the committee chairman, established two new precedents.

The first was that a proposal for a referendum could be introduced as an amendment to an already published Bill. This raised the spectre of a government introducing a proposal for a referendum at any stage during a bill's passage through the Commons so as to overcome resistance by its own back-benchers by bringing in 'another authority to overpower resistance within the House'.[14] Mr. Higgins thought that this was 'an issue which could turn out to be far more important than the Scotland and Wales Bill itself'.[15] And Mr. Mendelson claimed that 'we should be changing our constitution into a Swiss constitution if we adopted this course'.[16]

The second innovation in the new clause was that the referendums in Scotland and Wales would be mandatory, and not consultative as in the case of the referendum on Britain's membership of the E.E.C. Previous attempts to propose mandatory referendums had been ruled out of order as, in the words of Erskine May, 'proposing changes in legislative procedure which will be contrary to constitutional practice'.[17] When he ruled that the new clause was in order, the committee chairman was making it possible for an Act of Parliament to become operative solely *ad referendum* to the people. But on 15 February, Mr. Foot announced that the referendum would, after all, be consultative. So an awkward precedent was created for no particular purpose.

The right to vote in the referendum was to be restricted to residents of Scotland and Wales, a provision which offended many M.P.s who argued that devolution altered the constitution of the United Kingdom as a whole, and that therefore the whole U.K. electorate ought to have the right to express an opinion on the Bill. The government's case was that an intolerable situation would be created if Scotland and/or Wales voted for the Bill only to be overruled by an English majority. The implication of this argument was that Scotland and Wales could themselves determine the terms of their membership of the United Kingdom. Yet many M.P.s held that the Bill would adversely affect the rights and material interests of English taxpayers so that the terms affected England as well as Scotland and Wales.

The various constitutional and procedural irregularities involved in the referendum clause strengthened the feeling amongst many M.P.s that the Scotland and Wales Bill was so confused that it was probably unworkable. The feelings of the House were well expressed by Mr. John Mackintosh, a fervent supporter of devolution, who argued nevertheless that the Bill was so bad that if the referendum result was 'Yes' the 'appalling difficulties' inherent in the Bill 'could . . . endanger the unity of the country'.

Seldom have I seen the House or the Government in quite such a mess or in such difficulties as we are in over this Bill . . . What has happened is that this House does not contain a majority for this Bill. As a person who has supported devolution for twenty years, I would rather see this House have the courage of its convictions and reject the Bill. It should be thrown out and the electorate should make their views known at a General Election, so that the Government can come back with a better Bill at a later stage.[18]

At this stage, only three clauses and the new referendum clause had been debated in a Bill of 115 clauses. Debate on such important matters as the powers of the Assemblies, the reserve powers of the Secretaries of State, and the financial provisions, had not yet begun. The government therefore proposed an allocation of time amendment—a guillotine—seeking to ensure that discussion on the Bill would be completed within the session.

The government, however, was unable to attract its own dissidents back to the fold; nor could it make any concessions to retain the support of dissident Conservatives; and the Liberals refused to continue supporting a Bill which did not include provisions for electing the Assemblies by proportional representation or the devolution of revenue-raising powers. The Conservatives voted against the guillotine therefore; and eleven of the thirteen Liberals, excluding the two Welsh members, also voted against it. The government's only supporters outside the Labour Party were now the nationalists. Mr. Steel claimed that

The whole exercise started off as a ploy to keep the nationalist wolves from the door, but the Government find that they have ended up in bed with them. The Government have as their non-Labour supporters only those people in the House who know that the Bill will not work and hope that it will not.[19]

On 22 February 1977 at 10 p.m. the guillotine motion was defeated by 312 votes to 283, and the Scotland and Wales Bill was, in effect, dead. Twenty-two Labour M.P.s voted against the guillotine motion and twenty-three Labour M.P.s abstained; of these forty-three, nine were from the North of England and seven from Wales.

VI

The defeat of the government's major piece of legislation for the session had a shattering effect on the Labour Party. In Scotland, opinion polls showed that the S.N.P. was now the largest party in Scotland, with the support of 36 per cent of the electorate. The nationalist parties withdrew their support from the government in an attempt to precipitate a general election and the government would therefore need the support of the Liberal Party if it was to survive. But part of the price of that support seemed to be a new and improved devolution Bill.

The government's response to the failure of the guillotine motion was to offer all-party talks. The Conservatives agreed to these, but wanted these talks to consider 'proposals for the better government of Scotland and Wales within the United Kingdom, including . . . the Scotland and Wales Bill and federalism . . .' (28 May 1977). But the government indicated that it was only prepared to discuss its Bill, which it suggested 'might be referred to a Select Committee of the House'.[20] In the face of this disagreement, Mr. Foot announced on 14 June 1977 that there would be no further talks with the Conservatives.

In March 1977, however, the government had secured a parliamentary pact with the Liberals, and interest now centred on the shape of the new legislation which would result from the pact. But the Liberals were unable to secure significant improvements. They were in an unenviable position. They had opposed the guillotine on the Scotland and Wales Bill primarily in order to secure two improvements to the Bill—proportional representation and revenue-raising powers. Yet even if the government were to recommend proportional representation to its supporters in the Commons, it had no means of securing their votes. This was shown in the Bill on direct elections to the European Parliament where proportional representation was rejected by the Commons against the advice of the government. On revenue-raising powers, the government was adamant in refusing to make any concessions. This left the Liberals impotent, for they could hardly break the pact on so esoteric an issue. They were therefore handicapped throughout the negotiations by having no sticking point, no point at which they were prepared to bring down the government.

In a speech made to the annual conference of the Scottish Liberal Party on 19 June 1977, Mr. Steel made a significant concession on revenue-raising powers.

. . . we cannot accept a system of annual decision by the Treasury on the Scottish Assembly's budget. There must be either a power of revenue-raising within Scotland *or at least a set formula for finance on a more long-term basis independent of regular Treasury intervention.* (My italics)

It was perhaps of some significance that the formula approach was the one actually chosen by the government in the revised legislation. Otherwise the main alteration between the first exercise and the second was the division into two of the Scotland and Wales Bill; and Mr. Foot who, on 18 January, had argued that 'It was logical that the matter should be dealt with in the same Bill'[21] now claimed on 26 July that 'the House would welcome the separate consideration of what are dissimilar proposals'.[22] This alteration was, ironically, unwelcome both to the Welsh Liberal M.P.s, who had supported the guillotine on the first Bill, and to the Liberal Party organization, which believed it 'a major tactical blunder which is bound to endanger the Welsh Bill': and if the Welsh Bill was rejected, this 'would completely scupper any chance of pressing the case for a measure of regional government in England. A Scottish Assembly would be seen as *sui generis* and not inviting parallels elsewhere.'[23] Thus the separation of the Welsh Bill from the Scottish Bill seemed to put the federal idea even further into the distance. Nevertheless, the Liberals had to support the Scotland and Wales Bills unless they wished to force an election on tactically unfavourable ground.

The Scotland and Wales Bills were given Second Readings in the Commons on 14 and 15 November respectively, and both were immediately guillotined after Second Reading. The success of these guillotine motions was due not only to the accretion of Liberal support, but also to the return of Labour dissidents. Of the forty-three who had abstained or voted against the guillotine on the Scotland and Wales Bill, only sixteen were still prepared to withhold their support.

It was not that there had been significant conversions in the Labour Party to the cause of devolution. Rather the consequences of the defeat of the first Bill, and the realization that the government could be driven from office, persuaded doubters to conform. Besides, there was always the possibility, especially in Wales, that the Bills would be defeated at the referendum stage. Mr. Eric Heffer rationalized his support for the Bills in these terms:

I am in favour of sustaining the Government. Therefore if I do vote for the Government it will not be because I agree with the proposals, but merely to help sustain it. I have not become converted to devolution. I think it is unnecessary and a great mistake, and if the proposals are accepted, could lead to the break-up of the United Kingdom and ultimately of the Labour movement.

If the Bills do go through I shall offer my services to those in the Labour and trade union movements in Scotland and Wales who oppose the proposals and speak and campaign in the referendums against the legislation. I hope that at that stage the people will vote the proposals down.[24]

In a speech at Bexhill on 25 November, Mr. Enoch Powell referred to this tactic as 'without precedent in the long history of Parliament', and claimed that 'the House of Commons has trampled on its own authority, by treating the function of legislation as a mere device for getting responsibility, which its constituents have vested in it, transferred back again to an instant vote of the electorate'. But if Labour back-benchers found themselves in an unenviable position, the bulk of the Conservative Party were also guilty of insincerity. For Labour M.P.s opposed to devolution were willing to speak against it, and campaign against it in a referendum, but not to vote against it in the Commons: while the Conservatives, who were against devolution, were willing to speak and vote against the Bills, but not to admit that they were, in reality, opposed to any serious measure of devolution.

There can be little doubt that, in a secret ballot, the Scotland and Wales Bills would not have passed Second Reading, but the government's skilful tactics ensured that these two Bills, fundamental to the constitutional and political future of the United Kingdom, came to be passed by a House of Commons which was opposed to devolution.

But the government's troubles were not yet over. For on the first day of the committee stage of the Scotland Bill, the first Clause declaring that the Bill did not affect the supreme right of Parliament to make laws for the United Kingdom as a whole was thrown out, and the government was to lose another clause during the committee stage requiring the Assemblies to comply with national pay policy. The government conceded the loss of the equivalent clauses on the Wales Bill.

More seriously, the government was forced to accept three new provisions to the Scotland Bill. The first, proposed by Mr. George Cunningham, a Labour back-bench opponent of devolution and an expatriate Scot, proposed that if less than 40 per cent of the electorate were to vote 'Yes' in the referendum, an Order repealing the Scotland Act was to be laid before Parliament. The second was a new clause providing that if a general election were to be held before the referendum had taken place, the referendum would have to be postponed until at least three months after the election. Equivalent provisions were added to the Wales Bill. The third provision was to the effect that Orkney and Shetland could opt out of the Scottish Assembly if they voted 'No', but this was circumvented by Parliament agreeing to give the Secretary of State for Scotland special powers of override to defend the islands if in his view their interests were adversely affected after devolution. Also a constitutional commission was to be set up to review the future of the islands.

The House of Lords voted for proportional representation in the elections to the Assemblies, but the Commons rejected the Lords amendments on both Bills. The most important Lords amendment which was accepted by the Commons against the government's advice was one proposed by Lord Ferrers, a Conservative front-bench spokesman. This provided that if any Commons vote on a matter devolved in Scotland was passed through the votes of Scottish M.P.s, an Order could be laid before the House requiring a second vote to be taken two weeks after the first. The purpose of this amendment was to deal with the so-called 'West Lothian question', named after the M.P. for West Lothian, Mr. Dalyell, who had pressed it with much pertinacity in the Commons. The West Lothian question asked whether it was fair that Scottish M.P.s could vote in the House of Commons on matters such as housing, health, and education, which in Scotland were devolved. In such a situation English, Welsh, and Northern Irish M.P.s would be disfranchised from voting on Scottish domestic affairs, although Scottish M.P.s could vote on English, Welsh, or Northern Irish domestic affairs. It will be remembered that this is the same issue of the future representation at Westminster of a devolved area which Gladstone had found to be an insoluble one.

Under the terms of the Ferrers amendment, which the Commons finally accepted by one vote, pressure would no doubt be exerted upon Scottish members not to participate when a second vote had been called for. If that was the case, the House of Commons would become, for part of its life, an assembly for England, Wales, and Northern Ireland only. This could have profound consequences for the future of British government, especially when a government depended upon Scottish M.P.s for its majority. When that happened, the ministers responsible for matters which were devolved to Scotland, such as the Secretary of State for Education and Science or the Secretary of State for Health and Social Security, would find that their majority in Parliament had disappeared. There would be, in fact, a bifurcated executive, and it is not easy to imagine how a government could continue under such circumstances. It is not surprising that Mr. Pym described the effects of the Ferrers amendment as 'seismic'.

Despite these reverses for the government, however, the structure of the two Bills remained broadly intact. For the changes made to it by Parliament, although important, did not affect the fundamental basis of the proposals. The Bills received the Royal Assent on 31 July 1978, to await acceptance or rejection in referendums. If they are accepted, they will make fundamental changes in the government of the United Kingdom as a whole, and not just of Scotland and Wales. It is to an analysis of these changes that we now turn.

7 The Scotland and Wales Acts

As a nation the British have no great interest in either the institutions or the principles of law which determine the structure of their society and the means whereby it may change and develop.

Lord McDermott

I *The basic structure*

The central constitutional principles underlying the government's approach to devolution were succinctly laid out in Clause I of the Scotland and Wales Bills which the Commons, in a fit of irritation, threw out.

The following provisions of this Act make changes in the government of Scotland [Wales] as part of the United Kingdom. They do not affect the unity of the United Kingdom or the supreme authority of Parliament to make laws for the United Kingdom or any part of it.

Clause I rejected separatism, by implication since that would clearly affect 'the unity of the United Kingdom'; and also federalism since that would affect 'the supreme authority of Parliament to make laws for the United Kingdom or any part of it.' The clause therefore reflected the government's view that the Bills preserved parliamentary supremacy intact, so that Parliament could continue to legislate on matters devolved to the Scottish Assembly should it so wish; and, even though Parliament may not wish to exercise this right, it is nevertheless by convention and not as a matter of law that it refrains from doing so.

The clause also asserted what to many M.P.s was highly contentious, that the Acts 'make changes in the government of Scotland (Wales) as parts of the United Kingdom', the implication being that the Acts affected Scotland and Wales only, and not England or the U.K. as a whole. The government's view was that safeguards in the Bill prevented the constitutional changes in Scotland and Wales from affecting either the unity or the form of government of the United Kingdom. These safeguards were, firstly, the supremacy of Parliament; secondly, the provisions preventing the devolved administrations from influencing the administration of reserved subjects in a manner harmful to the public interest; thirdly, the financial sections of the Bill which made no provision for independent revenue-raising powers for the Assemblies, and, specifically, ruled out the assignation of oil revenues to the Scottish Assembly; and finally the 'guidelines' regulating the exercise of the devolved industrial powers, to ensure that they would not disturb the balance of regional policy.

The Scotland Act proposed the establishment of a Scottish Assembly directly elected by the first-past-the-post method, and consisting of between 145 and 150 members. There is to be a separate Executive headed by a First Secretary, nominated by the Assembly but appointed by the Secretary of State. The Assembly will have a fixed term of four years, except that if two-thirds or more of the members seek a dissolution, the Secretary of State is obliged to grant it.

The Assembly will not, in contrast to Stormont, be called a Parliament; and the First Secretary, although he may come to be regarded as Prime Minister of Scotland, is not, again in contrast to Stormont, to be given that title. The Northern Ireland experience no doubt predisposed the government against bestowing the titles of 'Parliament' and 'Prime Minister' so that the Scottish Assembly would be under no illusion that sovereignty had been transferred.

A related difference between Stormont and the proposed Scottish Assembly is that in place of a Governor exercising the functions of the Crown, the vice-regal functions will be performed by the Secretary of State for Scotland as a member of the Cabinet. He will have the power to reject, subject to the approval of Parliament, any Bill, action, or subordinate instrument of the Assembly on the ground that it would or might affect a reserved matter, *and* that it would not be in the public interest. This control is of a type which could not be applied to a local authority acting *intra vires*, and it represents something novel in British constitutional experience.

The Secretary of State also retains, as will be shown below, important executive functions in Scottish government. This will undoubtedly make him a factor of far greater weight in the affairs of the Assembly than the Governor was in Stormont. Here again, the intention was probably to ensure that the supremacy of Westminster could be made more effective.

The Scottish Assembly will have power to legislate for a broad range of social and environmental functions, including health and the social services (though not cash social security benefits), education (excluding the universities), housing, planning, transport (excluding rail), roads, and various Home Office functions relating to the courts, the legal profession, crime, and the fire services. It will also have power to legislate over most matters connected with local government in Scotland, specifically with the formation and pattern of local authorities, and the allocation of functions between these layers and the Assembly itself. It will take over responsibility for the Scottish Development Agency and the Highlands and Islands Development Board, but it will have only executive powers over the industrial development functions of these bodies to be exercised within statutory guidelines set by central government, and it will not be given functions in the field of selective regional assistance to industry.

The Assembly will have no independent taxing powers, and its finance will be derived from a block fund paid annually by the government. But since the Assembly will be responsible for the distribution of rate support grant to the Scottish local authorities, it would be able to increase its own revenue by distributing less grant to local authorities. It will not be able to abolish the rating system, although it will have the power to replace rates by an alternative local tax based on the principle of property rating. It would thus be able to replace local rates with a tax on site values or on capital values, but not with a local income tax; and it could alter the provisions concerning derating.

The Assembly's legislation will be subject to judicial scrutiny before the Royal Assent is given to its Bills and to post-assent judicial review. Before Assent, the Secretary of State must send a Bill to the Judicial Committee of the Privy Council if he believes it to be *ultra vires;* although if he believes it to be *ultra vires* because it contravenes international or E.E.C. obligations, he can himself refuse to submit the Bill for Assent, since the nature and extent of these obligations are for the government and not the courts to determine.

With post-assent review, the enactments of the Scottish Assembly will be in the same position as those of any other statutory body in that its legislation can be reviewed by the courts unless there is express provision to the contrary. Anyone with an interest to challenge it may therefore do so in the ordinary courts, although the ultimate authority on the interpretation of the Act will be the Judicial Committee of the Privy Council.

The Wales Act differs fundamentally from the Scotland Act in that it proposes a novel form of devolution, and one hitherto untried in the United Kingdom. It confers executive but not legislative functions on a Welsh Assembly of some eighty members, which will operate, like local authorities, through a committee system, without a separate Executive or the power of dissolution. Apart from the brief experience of the power-sharing executive in Northern Ireland from January to May 1974, there is no precedent in British constitutional experience for powers of so wide a scale and scope, including subordinate legislation, to be exercised by this form of administration.

The committee system of the Assembly must reflect, as far as possible, the party balance in the Assembly, except in the case of the Executive Committee, which will be the chief policy-making committee of the Assembly, corresponding to the Policy and Resources Committee in a local authority. The Executive Committee will be composed of the leaders of the other committees, and its leader will be in effect leader of the Assembly. The Assembly will not be able to spend any money except with the consent of the Executive Committee, which will be responsible for the allocation of resources from the block fund to the different subject committees of the Assembly, and provide central co-ordination and leadership to the Assembly.

The executive functions devolved to Wales are broadly similar to those devolved to Scotland, although because there is no separate Welsh legal system, fewer Home Office functions are devolved. The Welsh Development Agency is treated similarly to the Scottish Development Agency, so that devolution of industrial development powers will be subject to statutory guidelines, and powers of selective industrial assistance will not be devolved.

Two provisions of the Wales Act have no parallel in the Scotland Act. First, the Assembly is placed under a statutory duty to review the structure of local government in Wales and to report its findings to the Secretary of State; however, any changes must be made by Parliament and not by the Assembly, since reorganization would require legislation. The devolved Scottish administration does not need this power since it can alter local government through its own legislation. Secondly, the Assembly can also, with the consent of the Secretary of State and the approval of Parliament, be given responsibility for nominated bodies in Wales, for example the Wales Tourist Board or the Welsh Health Authority. This comes near to giving the Welsh Assembly some legislative competence.

Scotland and Wales will retain their existing representation at Westminster; this means that they will continue to be over-represented in relation to population. Scotland returns 71 members, whereas representation in accordance with population would give her only 57 seats; while Wales returns 36 members, although representation according to population would give her only 32. The offices of Secretary of State for Scotland and Wales will remain, and there will be no separate Scottish or Welsh civil service.

II *The allocation of powers*

Ministers seem to have decided at an early stage that the method of distributing powers adopted in the 1920 Government of Ireland Act, which established the Parliament of Northern Ireland, was inappropriate to the modern world, and that the relative success of devolution in Northern Ireland was not a pointer to the correct method of devolving powers to Scotland or Wales. Since Northern Ireland is separated by sea from the rest of the United Kingdom, devolution to Northern Ireland was less likely to affect the material interests of other areas of the U.K. than would devolution to Scotland and Wales. Nor would policy divergences in Northern Ireland be as politically visible as in Scotland and Wales.

Ministers faced a more complex and sophisticated world in the 1970s than their counterparts had done in 1920. It made little sense to devolve completely industrial and agricultural powers to Scotland and Wales since, even in Northern Ireland, the develop-ment of U.K. regional policy and national policies of agricultural support had shifted powers from Stormont to London. Nor did problems connected with energy loom so large in 1920 as they did in the 1970s. Moreover, it made little sense to break up the nationalized industries, and establish Scottish or Welsh units, where scope for the development of separate policies was small. In general, there was a strong argument against the transfer of meaningless powers, and it made sense to transfer powers only where there was a real possibility of policy divergence. Thus devolution of industrial and agricultural powers could be on a limited basis only, and the real question to be answered was whether any division of powers in these areas could meet Scottish and Welsh grievances as well as remaining compatible with both economic efficiency and fairness between different regions.

In allocating powers to the Scottish Assembly, therefore, the government decided not to follow the precedent of the Government of Ireland Act of 1920, but to ennumerate transferred powers. The Report of the Kilbrandon Commission on the Constitution recommended that this alternative method of defining transferred powers be adopted for Scotland and Wales, on the grounds that it produced the 'greatest clarity and precision'[1], and was better adapted to the need for flexibility, as periodic adjustments would need to be made from time to time in the list of powers transferred. This was because the development of new and unforeseen governmental functions such as those relating to atomic energy and space exploration, and of new constraints, especially those imposed by the requirements of E.E.C. membership, would require the harmonization of policy in matters already devolved. If, for either of these reasons, the U.K. government required to take back powers which had been transferred to Scotland and Wales, then, according to Kilbrandon, this would lead to considerable political embarrassment.

Moreover, the method of reservation of power had worked in the case of Northern Ireland, precisely because Stormont had been unwilling to challenge Westminster, so that powers could, as in the field of agriculture, be re-transferred to the U.K. government without difficulty. This might not be the case in Scotland and Wales, for, as we have seen, the pressures for devolution there are centrifugal and not, as in Northern Ireland, centripetal by nature. Therefore co-operation between the devolved administrations and Westminster could not be relied upon, and it would be best for the

U.K. government to be aware of precisely which powers it was surrendering.[2]

In deciding to adopt the method of enumerating transferred powers, ministers faced the problem that the complexity of modern legislation made it difficult to divide powers on an all-or-nothing basis. If education, for example, was devolved, should student grants, where divergence of policy would probably be harmful, also be devolved? If transport was devolved, would that mean that British Rail also would be devolved, entailing a separate administration of the railways on either side of the Scottish border?

Thus what purported to be a specification of transferred powers would in reality be a specification of *both* transferred *and* reserved powers. For it was impossible to specify the devolved subjects without at the same time specifying exceptions to them or qualifications of their scope.[3] Often these exceptions were specified not only by naming groups of subjects—education, health, etc.—but in terms of listing specific matters dealt with in existing statutes and even existing provisions in these statutes. In the Wales Act, the specification of what was to be devolved was achieved in an even more detailed way. For since Wales, unlike Scotland, has no separate legal system, there are few specifically Welsh Acts of Parliament, and only occasionally are there Welsh sections of general legislation. Consequently, there was no existing corpus of Welsh legislation to guide the draftsmen in deciding what was to be devolved.

One consequence of the method of allocation of powers chosen by the government is that the working of devolution may be constrained by the very detailed division of powers. For political systems in which governmental power is divided need to display considerable flexibility if they are to survive through changing social and economic circumstances. We have already seen that, however defective the division of powers embodied in the 1920 Government of Ireland Act, the Act itself allowed for change. The danger with the Scotland and Wales Acts is that even the most minor alteration in the allocation of functions will require legislation at Westminster, and the battles over devolution could be fought again and again with tedious regularity.

Moreover, given the very detailed listing of statutes and provisions, it will be extremely difficult for either the Assembly, or the ordinary litigant in Scotland and Wales, to discover simply by inspection of the Acts precisely what is being devolved. And even when the devolved powers have been ascertained it will not be easy to discern any clear line of principle demarcating the subjects devolved from the subjects retained.

Mr. Edward Short argued in the Commons on 3 February 1975 that the Scottish Assembly 'should have a legislative role and legislative power within fields within which separate Scottish legislation already exists'. But the Scottish Law Commission found it

difficult to take this announcement at its face value, because, except possibly in certain areas of public and administrative law, it is based on no discernible principle. It is often merely a matter of accident whether legislation affecting Scotland is contained in United Kingdom enactments or in separate Scottish enactments or, indeed, in both. The decision whether to present a Scotland-only or a United Kingdom measure has . . . frequently been the result of accidental constraints deriving from the nature of Governmental legislative programmes and the availability of Parliamentary time.[4]

A more promising approach to the demarcation of powers might have been to devolve all the functions which had been administratively decentralized to the Secretaries of State in Scotland and Wales, on the grounds that if a subject was suitable for separate Scottish or Welsh administration, it must be a Scottish or Welsh, and not a United Kingdom function. But the government was unwilling to adopt this approach since it considered some of the powers of the Secretary of State not suitable for devolution. In particular, in 1975, in response to political pressures, it had decentralized fairly wide economic powers to Edinburgh and Cardiff, and believed that devolution of these powers would threaten the economic integrity of the country. It was also unwilling to devolve electricity, which in Scotland was the responsibility of the Secretary of State, since that would militate against a common energy policy.

The result, however, was that in the absence of a powerful ministerial voice laying down clear principles of policy, the actual demarcation of powers depended upon a process of inter-departmental bargaining in Whitehall. This led to many anomalies. In its memorandum on the Scotland and Wales Bill, the Law

Society of Scotland drew attention to some of them: why, if partnership was devolved, was company law reserved; why, if bankruptcy was devolved, was liquidation retained? This according to the Law Society made it difficult to develop Scots law as a coherent system.[5] The Scottish Law Commission felt that there was a danger of 'a branch of a legal system' being 'severed from its roots',[6] since the Scotland Bill extended only to a part even of private Scottish law, so that the Assembly would not be a legislative authority for the whole of Scottish law.

Mr. John Mackintosh gave a graphic account of the confusions engendered by the government's approach:

I recall being visited not long ago by the people who run the Scottish college of agriculture. They said 'For certain purposes we are agricultural and undevolved. For other purposes we are educational and devolved. Some of our students are getting what is, strictly speaking, agricultural training, others are getting university degrees in agriculture, and others still are getting educational diplomas. We think that our educational functions are devolved. Our agricultural functions stay with the Secretary of State. Our research functions we do not know about, but we think that the land we farm—because land tenure and management are devolved— is devolved.'[7]

The method chosen to allocate powers, therefore, was not, as Mr. John Smith, the minister in charge of the Bills claimed, a mere 'choice of presentation and technique'.[8] On the contrary, it was a choice which revealed the nature and limits of the government's commitment to devolution.

III *The Secretary of State*

Because the Scotland Act subdivides powers currently exercised by the Scottish Office, devolution will lead to there being a four-fold division of governmental powers in Scotland. There will be reserved powers exercised by ministers with overall U.K. responsibilities, as well as reserved powers exercised by the Secretary of State. Then there will be powers, primarily in the industrial field, where Parliament retains responsibility for legislation but there is executive devolution to the Assembly; and, finally, there are those matters where there is full legislative and executive devolution to the Assembly.

The Secretary of State will remain responsible for the four

disparate and unrelated subjects of industrial development, agriculture, electricity, and the police; his primary role after devolution will be as Scotland's economic Minister. But his position will not be an enviable one: he will also have to perform the difficult task of representing the views of the Scottish Executive to the Cabinet, and the views of the Cabinet to the Scottish Executive. He will have to reconcile this task with his functions as a Cabinet minister representing a particular political standpoint.

It would require an exceptional individual to fulfil such a combination of roles successfully. The most likely result is that, in the words of Mr. David Price M.P., he will become 'the butt in between, in the continual argument between the Scottish Executive and Assembly and the Treasury here, for the United Kingdom. At best he will be a go-between.'[9] If the political composition of the Executive is different from that of the Cabinet, the Secretary of State will be under pressure from his supporters to curb the Executive; but he will also be under pressure from the Executive to press Scotland's views more forcefully in the Cabinet.

There will thus be two voices speaking for Scotland—the Executive and the Secretary of State. It is not difficult to imagine which voice will be the louder. The Executive will claim to be the genuine representative of Scotland, and when contentious issues arise will not be content to have its views represented by a minister who, because of his reduced role, carries little weight in Cabinet discussions. 'If there is a crucial shut-down of a major industrial plant he [the First Secretary] will go to No.10 Downing Street about it. He will not walk over the corridor to see the Secretary of State, whose clout in the Cabinet will depend on administering half the Department of Agriculture and half the Department concerned with economic affairs.'[10]

The most logical way of solving this dilemma is to abolish the office of Secretary of State for Scotland and transfer his functions to United Kingdom departments; for either a function is Scottish, in which case it should be transferred to the Assembly, or it is not, in which case it should be with a United Kingdom department. The vice-regal functions could then be performed by a non-party commissioner as has been suggested by John Mackintosh;[11] and the override powers, if not either abolished or entrusted to the Courts, could also be transferred to the relevant minister.

The proposed division of powers in Scotland is unlikely, therefore, to be a stable or permanent one. For either the Assembly will successfully demand the powers, especially the economic powers, at present with the Secretary of State, or alternatively these powers will gravitate back to London. In either event, the post of Secretary of State for Scotland will lose its importance. It was, indeed, an appreciation of this logic that led many Scottish Labour M.P.s to resist first devolution, and second the transfer of economic powers to the Assembly, since they believed that Scotland gained more from its separate representation in the Cabinet than it would from an Assembly.

IV *Override and the courts*

Since devolution is intended to affect only the government of Scotland and Wales, and not that of the United Kingdom as a whole, some method must be found of preventing the Assemblies from using their powers to affect reserved matters. The government sought to vindicate Westminster's supremacy by giving the Secretaries of State the power to override the Assemblies if they used their powers in such a way as to affect a reserved matter in a manner contrary to the public interest. Thus the Assemblies will not, for example, be able to use their planning powers to prevent the construction of military airfields, since defence is a reserved matter; although, if their use of planning powers is held to have undesirable repercussions on English planning matters, the override weapon cannot be used, since planning is a devolved matter. A Secretary of State's use of his override power will be subject to the negative vote procedure of both Houses of Parliament, and will, presumably, be reviewable by the courts analogously to delegated legislation.

The experience of Northern Ireland shows how difficult it was to use the Governor's reserve powers in opposition to the wishes of a responsible elected body. The same may be true of the use of the override power by the Secretary of State. It will normally be a risky weapon to use, since it will put the U.K. government into direct conflict with the Scottish or Welsh Assembly. The Assembly may well claim that it represents the feeling of Scotland or Wales on the issue in question, and it may persuade Scottish or Welsh

M.P.s of all parties not to support the action of the Secretary of State in using override. There is bound to be great danger of a confrontation which arouses Scottish or Welsh national feelings against Westminster. The Scottish Executive may even threaten to resign, as Sir James Craig did in 1922, if it is not allowed to pass its own legislation.

It is likely, then, that use of the override provisions will be confined to pathological political situations of the kind that afflicted Northern Ireland after 1968. Under normal circumstances, the government will be unable to use the weapon of override to secure acceptance of its point of view, and its influence upon the Scottish or Welsh Assembly will depend upon the more subtle financial controls, and upon appeals to party loyalty. When the override power has to be used, it will be a sign that the relationship between London and Edinburgh or Cardiff is beginning to break down.

The provisions for resolving disputes concerning the *vires* of Scottish enactments are likely to prove much more important, and the scope for litigation will be much greater in the case of the Scotland Act than it was in the Government of Ireland Act. In Northern Ireland there were only a small number of cases dealing with the division of powers partly because Stormont had an incentive to avoid friction with London; but primarily because the enumeration of transferred powers is bound to be less clear-cut than the enumeration of reserved powers.

The detailed categories of powers enumerated in the Scotland Act leave great opportunity for dispute as to their precise scope. The government's aim was to achieve the maximum possible precision through the detailed enumeration of powers; but paradoxically the effect may well be the opposite. Indeed the framers of the 1920 Act quoted a judgement of Lord Watson's that

The world is not big enough to hold the book which would have to be written to contain a precise and exact enumeration of all the things relating to the complexity of human affairs which you meant or did not mean to hand over to any legislative assembly.[12]

The division of powers in the Scotland Act may not, therefore, be as precise as it appears, for British law 'is not in the form of codes strictly limited to particular subject matters and without overlap on other domains'.[13] The enactments of the Assembly will not bear a label indicating the category to which they belong, and it will often be a matter for argument whether an enactment relates to a devolved or a reserved matter. The Assembly might, for example, claim that a particular enactment deals with health which is a devolved matter, while the government claims that in reality it deals with drugs or social security which are reserved subjects. These are just the kinds of questions which confront judges interpreting the constitutions of federal states, and they have led to a vast amount of case-law which will, no doubt, be brought to bear on litigation concerned with devolution issues.

In the Scotland Act, provision is made for both pre-assent scrutiny of Scottish legislation, and for post-assent review. At the pre-assent stage, the Secretary of State can send any proposed enactment to the Judicial Committee of the Privy Council if he believes that it would be *ultra vires;* and the Judicial Committee will be placed in the position, hitherto uncongenial to British courts, of deciding 'questions of legal *vires* in the abstract rather than in the context of concrete cases'.[14] If the Judicial Committee agrees with the Secretary of State that the Bill is *ultra vires*, then he will refuse to submit the Bill for approval. But if the Judicial Committee regards the Bill as *intra vires* the Secretary of State retains, presumably, the option of using the override power.

With post-assent review, Acts of the Scottish Assembly can be challenged in any court, but the Judicial Committee may again be used as the final Court of Appeal on constitutional questions. To determine the validity, as opposed to the construction, of legislation within the United Kingdom will be a novel function for a British court—always excepting the Northern Ireland experience—and it will mean that an Act of the Scottish Assembly will be law only insofar as a court has ruled that it is valid, or if it has not yet been challenged.

Moreover, under its present constitution, the Judicial Committee of the Privy Council may not be fully accepted as a reasonable arbiter of constitutional cases arising under the Scotland Bill, since there is no legal obligation for Scottish judges to be members of the Privy Council, or for them to sit on particular cases heard by the Committee. It is perhaps surprising that no provision was made in the Scotland Act for regulating the constitution of the Judicial Committee so as to include a given number of Scottish judges. In the kind of politically charged situation which could so easily arise, it is not difficult to see how Scottish sensibilities might be offended by any imagined under-representation on the Committee.

It is not easy to predict how the Judicial Committee will interpret the division of powers in the Scotland Act, because the Act itself does not, as we have seen, provide a publicly intelligible guide for adjudication. The Council of the Law Society of Scotland claimed that since it was difficult to 'trace any discernible principle of rationale upon which the subjects to be devolved have been selected . . . this will cause difficulty to the Judicial Committee of the Privy Council, or any other court in attempting to provide a corpus of consistent rulings on the legislative competence of the Assembly'.[15]

This lack of logic in the allocation of powers in the Scotland Act means that the basis for adjudication remains uncertain, and the actual division of powers will depend upon judicial interpretation. Judicial decisions could therefore amend the distribution of powers very considerably, as has occurred in federal states such as the United States and Canada. The future evolution of government in Scotland may well depend as much upon judges as it will upon politicians.

V *The Welsh model*

At first sight, the Welsh model of devolution appears as merely a weaker variant of the Scottish model: for while the Scottish Assembly is to be a law-making body, the Welsh Assembly would be purely an executive body with powers only over subordinate legislation such as statutory instruments and orders. But what seems a difference in degree is in fact a difference in kind. For devolution in Wales would involve the introduction of a wholly new set of governmental relationships, hitherto untried in the United Kingdom.

Whereas legislative devolution involves only a decision whether or not to transfer responsibility for a particular field of policy, for example education, to an Assembly, executive devolution involves the additional decision of *how much* responsibility for policy should be transferred, and this involves the question of how legislation is to be drafted. If Parliamentary draftsmen draw legislation loosely, they will leave considerable scope for the Assembly's executive role; but if legislation is drawn up tightly, the Assembly may enjoy little power.

It would therefore be perfectly possible for a government to limit the autonomy of the Welsh Assembly by passing legislation which left it with little scope for independent action. Indeed a Conservative government in London faced with a Labour Assembly in Cardiff might well be tempted to act in this way if the alternative was to allow the Assembly to frustrate the government's policy on a politically contentious issue, such as the setting of council house rents.

There is, then, a crucial difference between the Scotland Act, a model of 'vertical' devolution of the Canadian type, and the Wales Act, a model of 'horizontal' devolution of the West German type. For if one wants to ascertain the precise powers which Edinburgh will enjoy after devolution, one can do so by inspecting the provisions of the Scotland Act and looking at the statute book to see which statutes have been devolved. But the powers which Cardiff would enjoy are dependent not only upon the provisions of the Wales Act, but also upon the way in which future legislation for Wales is framed at Westminster, and the degree of discretion which Westminster thinks it right to confer upon the Welsh Assembly.

If there is to be effective devolution in Wales, therefore, principles will have to be devised to regulate the character of primary legislation for Wales. In the Federal Republic of Germany, where such principles have been developed, there has been the advantage of a structure of public law which 'displays a relatively high degree of coherence and homogeneity' so that 'it is possible . . . to achieve a consistency of principles . . . which is unattainable within the traditions of pragmatic positivism which have shaped both the Common Law and the statutory public law in Britain.' This would involve for Britain, however, 'the review and re-writing of major slices of public law, and with the express intention of removing numerous powers from the hands of ministers.'[16] Even so, there would be no way in which Parliament could bind itself to observe any principles which were developed. Moreover, in West Germany the federal system is buttressed by a constitutional court which ensures that the demarcation lines are observed.

Thus the Welsh model is derived from a country with a very

different system of public law and very different ideas about the role and scope of central government. It is not clear how it can be made to work in a country in which neither Parliament nor ministers have been very willing to adopt a policy of self-abnegation in the exercise of their powers.

In Britain, constitutional practice has hitherto been based upon a fusion of legislative and executive powers. Indeed, so closely are these powers fused that, in the words of the Royal Commission on the Constitution, the division between them 'is not a precise one, and under the present arrangements they are not clearly separated' (para. 828). The division does not correspond to the political importance of the issue concerned, and past legislation does not seem to have been guided by any very clear principles in this respect, since the division between types of legislation was never intended to provide the basis for a division of powers. For some extremely important matters of policy are dealt with by executive action; other more trivial matters may be dealt with by primary legislation.

With regard to existing legislation, therefore, the Assembly would find that its powers are of uneven scope and depth, since there is no reason why the division between primary and subordinate legislation in one area, for example health, should match the division in another, for example education. Thus the initial powers of the Assembly would have no clear rationale. In its response to the government's devolution proposals, Plaid Cymru commented that the Welsh Assembly would suffer

from an uneven degree of decision-making power in all devolved areas . . .· In each field of policy, different acts permit varying degrees of secondary decision-making. It is likely that the Welsh Assembly will have to spend its first two years reviewing past Westminster legislation in order to assess precisely what it is and is not allowed to do. Therefore an integrated approach to solving problems in a particular field of policy, or in a particular locality, will be rendered virtually impossible.[17]

What would be the basis for the division between legislative and executive powers with respect to legislation for Wales? According to the Report of the Royal Commission, the division would be bound to be on an *ad hoc* basis. 'The division would be an arbitrary one in that the range of powers conferred on the assemblies would depend upon a *political* judgment of the extent of the control it was necessary to retain at the centre.'[18]

Moreover, if devolution is to work successfully in Wales, primary legislation for Wales would have to be drawn up more loosely than primary legislation for England, so as to allow scope to the Assembly without giving ministers with responsibilities confined to England, for example the Secretary of State for Education and Science, wide delegated powers. This means that future statutes would have to be framed differently for England and for Wales. If they were to be framed similarly, either they would be very loosely drawn both for England and for Wales, in which case the Assembly would have considerable scope, but 'English' ministers would be given too wide a discretion; whereas alternatively if the legislative framework were drawn up tightly for both England and Wales, the powers of the Welsh Assembly would be severely constrained.

But if devolution in Wales requires that statutes be framed differently for England and for Wales, there will be extra work for the parliamentary draftsmen and an unwelcome addition to Parliament's already heavy legislative burden. This might well disappoint those who are hoping that it will lead to a genuine dispersal of power, a lightening of Parliament's burden, and a solution to the problem of governmental 'overload'. The Cabinet may be put in a more difficult position as a result of devolution in relation to primary legislation for Wales, since it will have lost its contact with the local authorities who actually administer services there. Deprived of its Welsh case-load, Whitehall may be less informed about the needs of Wales. The Welsh Assembly which would, of course, be in a better position to appreciate Welsh problems will have no legislative role, and it will therefore have to rely upon the co-operation of the Secretary of State for Wales to promote Welsh legislation. Since the Secretary of State may belong to a different party from that of the majority in the Assembly, this may lead to difficulties, especially on such sensitive issues as the status of the Welsh language and the reform of local government.

It will be difficult to give the Welsh Assembly the power to comment on draft Bills before they are published, since this would be a breach of confidentiality; and, after publication of Bills, the Assembly will be free to comment upon them like any other body or individual. There can therefore be no more requirement that the government take notice of the Assembly's deliberations than that it take notice of the deliberations of any other body; but the hope must be

that the Assembly's views will carry more weight than those of most other bodies. First, the Assembly will represent the people of Wales and will speak with a virtually unique political authority on matters affecting the Principality. Second, the Assembly will be responsible for implementation of legislation on devolved matters in Wales; it will know the situation 'on the ground' and will speak with knowledge on proposals relating to that situation. In reality, therefore, the Assembly's *influence* on legislation could be substantial.[19]

However influence on Bills already published is not likely to be a good substitute for genuine influence upon policy-making. For the vast majority of policy decisions take place at the pre-legislative stage well before Bills are actually published. The Welsh Assembly, however, will have no formal representation on the policy-making bodies of central government, and therefore it will have to rely upon pressures exerted upon Westminster and Whitehall during this pre-legislative stage.

The danger would be that, lacking political space in the legislative sphere, the Assembly will encroach upon the sphere of Welsh local government. For most of its functions will involve the supervision of services administered by local authorities, and it will also be responsible for the distribution of rate support grant to local authorities in Wales. Since a large portion of the block fund which the Welsh Assembly will receive from the government will be pre-empted by the requirements of primary legislation and by the statutory obligations placed upon local authorities and other public bodies, the Assembly may seek to trespass upon the autonomy of local authorities so as to ensure that its own order of priorities rather than that of the local authorities themselves is made effective.

There is moreover a danger that issues of housing and educational policy will have to pass through three layers of government—local authorities, Welsh Assembly, and Whitehall—rather than two, after devolution. That would be a recipe not for the dispersal of power but for a system of government in which it is difficult to get anything done. Thus devolution in Wales might well lead not to separation—for which there is little demand—but to a confused system of government without clear demarcation of responsibility between different layers of administration.

VI *Devolution and local government*

A prime argument for devolution is that it will lead to a dispersal of power from Westminster and Whitehall. Yet this will not be achieved simply by setting up Assemblies in Edinburgh and Cardiff, unless they have a positive desire to decentralize. If the Assemblies were to seek to dominate local government and to take away its powers, then devolution would lead to the centralization of power and not to its dispersal. An examination of the relationships between the Assemblies and local government is therefore crucial to any consideration of whether devolution will lead to decentralization.

In drawing up its devolution plans, the government undoubtedly inherited a difficult situation since it faced both in Scotland and in Wales a newly reorganized local government system, which had taken no account of the possibility of devolution. In Wales, this was because both the Labour government in the late 1960s, and the Conservative government which succeeded it, had come to believe that Welsh local government must be reformed on the same basis as in England. In Scotland, local government was reorganized differently, although still on a two-tier model. The upper tier consisted of regional authorities, geographically larger than their English counterparts, and, arguably, more suitable as strategic planning bodies. For this reason, no doubt, the Scottish regions, unlike the English and Welsh counties, were given responsibility for administering water and sewerage. But the largest of these regional authorities, Strathclyde, contained over one-half of the population of Scotland, and would obviously co-exist uneasily, if at all, with a Scottish Assembly. Neither in Scotland nor in Wales would the new structures have been chosen if devolution had been intended at the time of reorganization.

The Scottish Assembly will have the power to alter both the structure and the functions of local government; it could also alter the basis of distribution of grant to local authorities; indeed, it could abolish local government in Scotland entirely if it so wished. In Wales, the Assembly will be under an *obligation* to review the structure of local government, an obligation which Mr. Gervas

Walker, Chairman of the policy committee of the Association of County Councils, has described as 'an open invitation to the Welsh Assembly to initiate further reorganization of local government in Wales only four years after the extensive upheaval of 1974'.[20]

It would be natural for the Assemblies to seek to eliminate one of the local government tiers. But to eliminate the districts—the lower tier—would make government unacceptably remote, especially in Scotland, If, however, the upper tier—the counties in Wales and the regions in Scotland—were to be eliminated, the district authorities would probably be too small to carry out functions such as education and the social services. If, therefore, new all-purpose local authorities are to be established by the Assemblies, there will have to be a complete reorganization of local government so as to create unitary authorities midway in geographical size between the existing two tiers. Such a task is likely to be wasteful both of time and expense. Indeed, Harold Wilson speaking as Prime Minister to a Labour Party local government conference in Cardiff in January 1976 argued that 'To impose yet another reorganization would be a burden not easily to be tolerated. We will not throw the whole of local government again into the melting-pot.' The government's consultative document, *Devolution, The English Dimension* argued that if devolution to the English regions entailed a further reorganization of local government, it should be rejected, since coming 'so soon after the last one [it] would be bound to create confusion in the minds of the average elector. Probably he would feel more remote from the affairs of a local government body administering services over a much wider area' (para. 83).

The government also began by taking the view that the functions performed by local authorities would not be affected by devolution. In its White Paper, *Our Changing Democracy*, it argued that devolution did not entail 'any removal of current tasks or powers from local government' (para. 235), because devolution involved the transfer of functions from the centre and not from local government. But this view ignored the fact that devolution proposes a new territorial division of power. If we seek to discover what functions are best exercised at each of three different levels of government in Scotland and Wales, it becomes clear that there is no particular reason why some functions at present exercised by local authorities might not be better exercised at Assembly level. For it might well be that functions such as strategic planning and parts of the education service are at present exercised at local level only in the absence of an intermediate tier of government, and should be transferred upwards when that intermediate tier comes into existence. Indeed, the government in its Consultative Document directed at England, *Devolution, The English Dimension,* recognized as much since it argued the case against devolution to the English regions, on the grounds that 'Many functions of the Counties would need to be raised to the new regional authorities' (para. 54). But if this would be so in England, why not also in Scotland and Wales?

The existence of the Assemblies may also affect the financing, and therefore the pattern of local government services, through the new arrangements by which rate-support grant to the local authorities will be distributed, as responsibility for the distribution of grant will be transferred to them from the Secretaries of State for Scotland and Wales. For the Assemblies will be composed of elected representatives with their own distinctive views as to the proper shape of local government spending: in the view of the Association of County Councils, members of the Assembly

will have their own geographical and functional interests to press and it is possible that in seeking to safeguard those interests the latitude previously enjoyed by local authorities within their total resource allocations may be curtailed.

The danger is that in performing this task, it may well overstep the mark and seek to reduce local authorities to be merely executants of its policy thus reducing local choice and determination and imposing a uniformity which precludes local representatives from responding to the needs and wishes of a local electorate.[21]

Since the amount to be distributed to local authorities will not be an earmarked part of the block fund, it will be for the Assemblies to decide how much is to be distributed. According to Mr. Millan, the Secretary of State for Scotland, the Scottish Assembly 'will alter the balance between what is raised by local taxation and what is paid out of the block fund. The Assembly may be more generous— that is reduce the rate and pay more out of the block fund—or less generous'. When asked by a Conservative M.P. whether this meant that the Assembly 'will be able to spend more than is expected on one part of its functions and make up the shortfall by forcing local authorities to raise rates at a higher level', Mr. Millan replied, 'This fact has been clear all along . . . The negotiations on rate support grant, and therefore the ultimate impact on ratepayers, will pass to the Scottish Executive.'[22] Thus if the Assemblies decide to withhold grant from local authorities, they will be able to secure extra finance for themselves, and force local authorities to raise their rates to maintain an equivalent standard of service. There is to be no obligation upon the Assemblies to consult local authorities on the allocation of grant between England and Scotland (or Wales), on the allocation of grant between local government and other services, or on the distribution of the block fund allocated to the Assembly among the various devolved services, most of which are actually administered by local authorities. The Assemblies will decide how much is needed for local government services in Scotland and Wales, and they will make their bids accordingly. They will thus have discretion upon the amount and distribution of grant to local authorities, and may be able to exert a powerful influence upon their spending programmes should they choose to use the weapons which they will undoubtedly possess.

It does not, of course, follow that these weapons will in fact be used to limit local autonomy. Indeed, it might be argued that local authorities will be in a stronger position in dealing with an Assembly than with central government. For such consultation as they at present enjoy over the distribution of rate-support grant does not in practice give them great influence over the distribution, which is a matter for the Cabinet. It might well be that local authorities can more easily make their wishes known and secure attention to these wishes when dealing with directly elected Assemblies than with the Whitehall machine.

What must be clear, however, is that devolution will only lead to decentralization if it is accompanied by what the Royal Commission on the Constitution called 'a new style of thinking, positively favourable to devolution and based on co-operation rather than the exercise of central authority' (para. 282). Thus the attitudes of the Assemblies to local authorities in Scotland and Wales will be a vital element in determining whether devolution leads to 'over-government' or to a genuine dispersal of power.

VII *Economic and industrial powers*

The most complex of the issues facing the government with regard to the distribution of powers lay in the field of economic and industrial policy. For the government had to balance its conception of economic unity against a widespread demand in Scotland for the devolution of economic powers—the demand in Wales was far weaker since Wales is more integrated into the English economy, and, lacking North Sea oil, finds herself more dependent than Scotland upon the success of the U.K. economy as a whole. Many in Scotland, however, sought to use devolution to diversify the industrial structure and to increase employment. These policies could, in the view of many Scots, be financed from the oil revenues which should also be under the control of the Assembly.

In the government's view, however, these claims sought the advantages of separate statehood while retaining the benefits of U.K. regional policy. For economic development in Scotland would depend not only upon the positive inducements to industry offered by a Scottish Assembly, but also upon U.K. policies of industrial assistance, and, more particularly, upon the government's success in steering firms away from London and the South East through the use of industrial development certificates and other methods of persuasion.

What then did economic unity entail? Clearly it meant that the central tools of demand management and macro-economic policy in general were to be retained by Westminster. But the government also argued that it was the only body constitutionally empowered to determine a fair balance between the different regions of the U.K. Such a balance could not be determined by the regions themselves, for then the allocation of resources would depend upon the political bargaining power of the regions, and not upon considerations of genuine social need. In the government's view, it would be wrong for Scotland and Wales to benefit economically just because they were given devolution if the needs of other parts of the country were more pressing. Such a policy would militate against the government's whole conception of devolution as relating 'to matters which primarily affect people living in Scotland and Wales and which can be administered separately in either country without side-effects for those living in the rest of the United Kingdom.'[23] Moreover, a process of competitive bidding up of regional incentives, such as might be engendered by the wide devolution of economic powers, would benefit neither Scotland and Wales, nor any other part of the U.K.

It is true that the Northern Ireland example was at hand to illustrate the possibility of a generous devolution of industrial powers. But as with the method of allocation of powers, ministers did not believe that the Northern Ireland example offered a useful analogy for devolution to Scotland or Wales. Moreover, it could be argued that Northern Ireland was a 'special case' since her rate of unemployment was far higher than in any other part of the U.K., while Scotland has a lower level of unemployment than Merseyside; and there were, fortunately, no problems of internal security in Scotland or Wales which might be used to justify special treatment.[24] Therefore the government was not disposed to accept the Northern Ireland solution for Scotland or Wales, and the legislative devolution of industrial functions was rejected as being incompatible with economic unity and the maintenance of a regional balance.

But the government recognized that it must respond to the political pressures in Scotland, and it decided to go beyond the Royal Commission's recommendation that there should be no devolution of trade and industry functions at all. The industrial development functions of the Scottish and Welsh Development Agencies and the Highlands and Islands Development Board would be placed under the control of the Assembly, but they would be required to operate within statutory published guidelines which would be binding upon the devolved administrations. These guidelines would cover such matters as ensuring that loans are made at broadly commercial rates of interest and that the Agencies have regard to the profitability of the firms in which they invest; and the Agencies will, in general, be required to operate in a commercial manner. Statutory responsibility for them will remain with Parliament and they will be required to present annual reports to Parliament on matters covered by the guidelines which 'No doubt . . . will be carefully scrutinized by Members representing other parts of the United Kingdom.'[25]

In this way, some limited industrial powers could be devolved without distortion of competition or conflict between the operation of the Agencies and the government's regional policy.

Politically, the government's solution might render the devolution of industrial powers palatable to English public opinion. For, although much of the criticism of the government in Scotland was to the effect that the government was devolving too little, the political acceptability of the package would depend crucially upon whether English M.P.s could be persuaded to vote for it; and this depended in turn upon the reaction of their constituents, especially in the North, who were being asked to concede devolution to Scotland and Wales. Their reluctant acquiescence to this request could probably not be secured if the Agencies were to be devolved without the guidelines.

Any judgement as to the success of the government's strategy in the devolution of economic and industrial powers must ask two questions: first, would it satisfy Scottish grievances; and second, would it undermine the principle of a fair allocation of national resources? As we have seen, the government was faced with a complex problem in balancing different objectives; a solution to the problem could not, therefore, have consisted in the absolute satisfaction of one set of claims, but rather in finding the best balance between them.

If the grievances giving rise to a demand for devolution in Scotland are primarily economic in nature, it may seem that the Assembly will be able to do little to remedy these grievances. Certainly the existing system under which Scotland has its own territorial representation on the Cabinet has been of considerable benefit to her in securing industrial aid—especially perhaps when the pressure of the Secretary of State has been backed up by a belief that seats will be in danger if aid is not given.

There may also be a risk that, if wide industrial powers are devolved to Scotland, the office of Secretary of State will disappear, and then the Department of Industry, which will be responsible for industrial assistance in Scotland, may be tempted to ignore Scottish interests, using the argument that industrial policy has already been devolved in Scotland, and that its task is to assist the English regions. Yet, as we have seen, a successful industrial policy must depend upon the sharing of power between different levels of government, and Scotland relies heavily upon central measures such as regional development grants and industrial development certificates.

For supporters of Scottish devolution, however, all these objections are outweighed by one crucial factor. The Scottish Assembly, they believe, will be so powerful a pressure group upon Westminster and Whitehall as to ensure that economic and industrial policy is fashioned with greater regard to Scottish needs. In a sense, therefore, the influence of the Assembly may depend less upon the precise powers that it wields, and more upon its being *the* political body which represents Scotland. That, at least, is the fear of many in the North, and, to the extent that this fear is justified, the government will be compelled to make further concessions to the North of England, perhaps including the establishment of a Northern Development Agency or even an Assembly for the North. It may therefore be unable to limit devolution to matters domestic in Scotland.

To what extent would devolution of industrial powers actually provide scope for Scotland to modify current policies? As we have seen, the government does not intend that Scotland should obtain extra resources from Whitehall as a result of devolution, so the issue must be the extent to which Scotland's present resources can be reallocated to assist industrial development.

The example of Northern Ireland shows that a policy of industrial development undertaken by a provincial government can within limits be successful. It would, of course, require Scotland to be willing to devote more resources to industrial development at the expense of services such as education and housing.

But the basic case for devolving rather more industrial powers to Scotland and Wales than the government has done must be that putting the onus of responsibility upon those most closely concerned with the success of industrial policy is likely to improve its effectiveness. For those living in Scotland and Wales will, so it may be argued, be more likely than Whitehall to appreciate the particular needs of their countries; and devolution will lead as it did in Northern Ireland to speedier administration and decision-taking, without the need for continual reference back to London. More intangibly, it might be claimed that the devolution of decision-making to Scotland and Wales may release the latent energies of their workforces; managers and workers who find it difficult to identify with a country of fifty-five million people, may be able to identify with Scotland and Wales; that perhaps is the reason for the success of so many small countries in achieving industrial growth. Generally, then, the case for a wider devolution of industrial powers is no different from the case for devolution itself—that the effectiveness of government is increased through the dispersal of power: and if the main grievances in Scotland are economic, it is hardly likely that a model of devolution which excludes real industrial powers will prove stable for very long.

VIII *The E.E.C. dimension*

As we have seen, the government has treated international and E.E.C. obligations alike in the Scotland and Wales Acts. In each case, the government remains responsible for policy-making, and it retains the power, through the override provisions, to ensure that the implementation of E.E.C. directives is in accordance with government policy. The case for this arrangement is that the government is legally liable for international and E.E.C. obligations, and that it is therefore for the government and not for the Assemblies to determine their nature and extent.

But, it is very doubtful whether it makes sense to think of European Community affairs as an aspect of Britain's international relations. The Dean of the Faculty of Advocates in Scotland wrote to the Secretary of State for Scotland after the publication of the White Paper, *Our Changing Democracy*, to say that 'no lawyer familiar with the concepts and working of European law could possibly subscribe to such a proposition'.[26] For the European Community is itself a novel type of institution, intergovernmental rather than international in the traditional sense. The activities of the E.E.C. may well come to permeate almost every aspect of British life, so that a scheme of devolution which made every E.E.C. matter a reserved one might not allow for any devolution at all.

At present, however, the E.E.C. is mainly concerned with issues of industrial, trade, and agricultural policy which have not been devolved to the Assembly. The retention of these powers by the government means that the E.E.C. dimension will not loom large during the early stages of devolution; and it might, perhaps, be an argument for the government's 'minimalist' view of devolution, that it involves less complications as far as the E.E.C. is concerned. Nevertheless, it would be wrong to believe that the E.E.C. can be ignored in any account of the implications of devolution, for it is very likely to extend its concern into the devolved areas. Therefore if policy-making in matters affected by the E.E.C. is to remain a responsibility of central government, the Scottish Assembly will suffer from continually increasing constraints upon its actions through a process of 'creeping reservation'.

The E.E.C. dimension, then, is bound to become more important as devolution proceeds. We have already shown that Scotland benefits at present from its representation in the Cabinet and in Parliament, which has been designed to ensure that policy-making takes some account of the Scottish legal system and the institutional differences between Scotland and England. In Brussels, however, there will be no equivalent to the Scottish Office or the Scottish law offices in the European Commission, and no equivalent to the Scottish Grand Committee in the European Parliament. There must, then, be a danger that the European policy-making process will take insufficient account of the implications of Community legislation upon Scots law. Some way must therefore be found by which the Scottish Assembly and its Executive may be able 'to bring the Scottish aspects of Community affairs to the attention of the Government'.[27] This implies some formalized method of consultation between the Executive and the government, to discuss both the implications of proposed E.E.C. legislation upon Scottish law, and also the practical implementation of E.E.C. regulations and directives in Scotland.

The need for such consultation is particularly pressing since, as we have seen, the override weapon is likely to prove a blunt one, to be used only in pathological political circumstances. In practice, the government is bound to depend upon the willing co-operation of the Assembly and the Executives in the implementation of E.E.C. legislation, and this co-operation is more likely to be secured if the Assemblies feel that they have been given a full voice in the policy-making process. Indeed the Scottish Law Commission concluded that there was

a need to embody in the Devolution Act reciprocal duties of consultation between the United Kingdom Government and the Scottish executive in matters both of legislation and administration where legislative or administrative action proposed by one body is likely to be of concern to the other . . . The need for an appropriate machinery is particularly important . . . in the context of European Community and international matters . . .

While it would not be feasible to envisage sanctions for a failure to consult, the requirements might be so drafted as to have the effect of a constitutional convention, making it difficult for either side to ignore its existence.[28]

The failure to consider institutional arrangements for dealing with E.E.C. matters is, however, symptomatic of a wider deficiency in the devolution legislation—and an extremely serious one: the underplaying of the inter-governmental relationships which will be necessary between Parliament and the Assemblies. For while the Scotland Act divides powers between two distinct layers of government in Scotland, it makes no provision for establishing the inter-governmental institutions which will be needed if there is to be mutual accommodation between the government and the devolved administrations. If we are right in our view that the legal machinery in the Scotland Act and the override powers given to the Secretary of State can be used only as constitutional long-stops, then in practice the two layers of government can work successfully only through such a process of mutual accommodation and good-will, and not through the exercise of Westminster's supremacy.

In most federal systems, very sophisticated mechanisms for the conduct of inter-governmental relationships have been developed, embracing both politicians and civil servants, and frequently involving regular conferences between state and federal leaders, as well as departmental heads. For in the modern world, it is impossible to maintain a rigid demarcation between different levels of government. Rather than remaining separate, powers inter-penetrate different areas of social and economic life, just as the influence of the E.E.C. is seen less in the form of a division of powers than as one aspect of an inter-governmental penetration of power.

After devolution, there will be a number of occasions when inter-governmental co-operation will be of vital importance. For example, consultations between the devolved administration in Scotland and the government in advance of the introduction of Bills into the Scottish Assembly might help to avoid serious dispute, and the need for the use of the override provisions. Inter-

governmental co-operation will also be required when it becomes
necessary to redefine the spheres of action of the government and
the Assemblies—and, in view of the highly specific nature of the
powers devolved, the need for such redefinition may be very
frequent; and it may become desirable for the Scottish administration
to act as the agent for the government in some matters, as the
Northern Ireland government acted as the agent for the government
in the administration of measures of agricultural support. There
may, furthermore, be a need for co-operative or joint action on
some devolved matters if the devolved administrations decide that
common standards of service in a particular area are required; and
the devolved administrations may also seek to make arrangements
with the government for the provision of administrative, professional, or technical services. This will involve links between the
executive departments of the Assembly and corresponding Whitehall departments.

But such inter-governmental links will be important not only on
matters connected with the distribution of powers. They will be
especially crucial in the area of financial relationships. Probably
the most important single decision affecting the operation of the
Assemblies will be the determination of the formula for the allocation of expenditure on devolved services. In the financial field, the
government has recognized that it would be against the spirit of
devolution 'to settle unilaterally the procedures to be followed in
its dealings with the devolved administrations on financial matters
. . . the views of the devolved administrations will themselves be
one of the main determinants'. Exchanges between government
and the devolved administrations 'are intrinsically desirable as a
way of ensuring that both the Government and the administrations
take account of the possible effects of their plans on other parts of
the country, or on national policies. They will not be a basis for
intervention by the Government in decisions by the administrations,
but will be a part of the background to the determination of
devolved expenditure, ensuring that the Government has a fair
understanding of the policies and programmes to which it relates.'[29]
What is necessary is that this understanding of the way in which
devolution can be expected to work, should be extended to other
areas of policy.

In Wales, where devolution would be of the 'horizontal' type involving a division between primary legislation, which remains the responsibility of Westminster, and secondary legislation which will be the responsibility of the Assembly, inter-governmental relationships would have a special role to play. For it would be necessary to develop principles upon which the distinction between primary and secondary legislation can be based; and the Welsh Assembly would surely wish to be represented in the discussions leading to the adoption of these principles. It might also exert influence as a pressure group upon the government so that it comes to be consulted about primary legislation for Wales before such legislation is introduced into the Commons.

Moreover, since the Secretary of State for Wales would no longer be responsible for secondary legislation in housing and education, and would no longer be in contact with local authorities in these fields, he may be handicapped in Whitehall discussions on primary legislation for Wales, by the loss of his departmental case-load. To avoid this, the Secretary of State would need to co-operate closely with the Assembly if he is to be kept fully informed of Welsh needs, and there would also have to be close co-operation between the Welsh Office and the civil servants staffing the Assembly.

More generally, the government, in the Welsh model of devolution, would depend upon the Assembly to implement its policies in Wales, and the Assembly would depend upon the government to draw up primary legislation sufficiently loosely so as to allow scope for Welsh autonomy. A state of inter-dependence between two layers of government is created—even more obviously than in the Scottish model—and devolution in Wales would only prove effective if it operated upon a basis of co-operation and reciprocity between the devolved administration and the government.

It can be seen then that devolution, if it works successfully, will establish not independent, but interdependent, bodies in Scotland and Wales. In this, it will follow in the footsteps of most federal states, where a 'co-operative' federalism between the units and the federal government has long replaced the 'dual federalism' of two layers of government each with its own carefully defined sphere of action.

Such a structure, however, raises problems of political accountability which have nowhere been fully solved. To whom will the inter-governmental layer be responsible? Political decisions may come to be taken as the result of a complex process of bargaining, which will occur at one remove from the electorate. When unpopular decisions are made, each side will claim that the other side was responsible, as occurs at present when local authorities are asked by central government to make cut-backs in essential services. The new structure of government in Scotland and Wales would, therefore, allow a good deal of room for obfuscation and buck-passing on the part of politicians, and the electorate will not find it easy to pinpoint the responsibility for decisions.

The structure of government in Scotland and Wales, then, would inevitably become more complex after devolution. If it is to work successfully, the new system would require its practitioners to display to a high degree those qualities of tact and harmony which go to build a political consensus.

IX *Finance*

Finance is the spinal cord of devolution, for it is the financial arrangements which will largely determine the degree of autonomy enjoyed by the devolved administrations; the financial settlement, therefore, will exert a dominant influence on whether the aims of devolution are sustained or frustrated.

Post-war experience did not augur well for supposing that the financing of devolution would necessarily be consistent with the policy aims of government. For, over the past thirty years, the allocation of functions to public authorities and the pattern of public finance have come to be increasingly divorced from each other. The result has been that finance has frequently frustrated, and rarely sustained, broader policy aims. Local authorities in particular have suffered because their main source of revenue—rates—has not been sufficiently buoyant to accommodate the expansion of public services. Local government has thus lost functions such as health and water to central government, and the result has been a decline in local democracy and an increase in centralization. Moreover, the 1974 reorganization of local government was carried out without being accompanied by any reconsideration of local authority finance, and so it proved impossible to restore any major responsibilities to local authorities. For this reason, reorganization has been unable to secure any very great advance in local autonomy, and the state of local government finance remains the main hindrance to effective decentralization.

Two factors have been responsible for the increasing drift to the centre in the U.K. The first has been that, in the words of the government's White Paper *Our Changing Democracy* (Cmnd 6348), distribution according to relative need is the 'cardinal fact about our whole system of allocating public expenditure. Resources are distributed not according to where they come from but according to where they are needed' (para 20). On this view, the danger of any significant devolution of the taxing power, is that the richer parts of the country will be able to benefit at the expense of the poorer. According to Sir George Godber, a former Chief Medical Officer at the Department of Health and Social Security,

Anyone familiar with the pattern of development of local authority health services before 1948 . . . knows well that the wealth of an authority has a direct bearing on the quality of the service provided. This was not the sole factor, but it was, in my belief, the most important. A county like Surrey, for instance, was able to recruit doctors for its public health services in the 1930s much more easily than a county borough like, say, Bootle, for the simple reason that it offered £600 a year as compared with £500 a year, which was the minimum negotiated rate.[30]

Many politicians and civil servants retain, of course, powerful memories of the 1930s, and the evils of that period have legitimized the dominant contemporary philosophy of social democracy, held not only by most Labour M.P.s, but by Liberals and Conservatives also. This philosophy requires the central determination of the allocation of public expenditure, on the ground that the central government is the only body able to secure the equitable distribution of public resources on the basis of need.

The second source of resistance to devolved taxation lies in the fact that the central government's approach to finance must always be different from that of the devolved administrations. The administrations need revenue to finance expenditure plans: central government needs revenue to stabilize the economy. The Treasury's fear is that the dispersal of revenue-raising powers will make the processes of economic management more difficult. For the greater the amount of public expenditure which lies outside the direct control of the government, the greater the scope for evading measures of economic control. For example, in carrying out its public expenditure cuts after 1975, the government was handicapped because some local authorities refused to comply with government requests and, instead of cutting services, raised the rates in order to finance them. Such a policy, in the Treasury's view, damages the chances of success in counter-inflation policy, and so the revenue-raising power of local authorities is, for the Treasury, a loophole in the system of control of public finance; indeed a Treasury official at a press briefing on the 1976 Public Expenditure White Paper, described the present structure of local authority finance as the 'Achilles Heel' of the government's policy of restricting public spending. How much more difficult it would be if the Government was also confronted with powerful Assemblies with their own taxing powers, bodies with more political weight than local authorities, and therefore better able to resist government requests for restraint.

The government would thus need to retain control not only of the global totals of expenditure in Scotland and Wales after devolution, but also of the balance between private and public expenditure which could be altered through decisions taken by the Assemblies. The Treasury would therefore have to interest itself in the way in which expenditure in Scotland and Wales was financed. For if the Assemblies decided to increase public expenditure as a proportion of total expenditure in Scotland and Wales, this might have deleterious effects upon industrial investment and growth; it might also lead to pressures for wage increases, and thus fuel inflation, if wage demands were to be based not on the overall standard of living but on post-tax incomes. For, if private consumption is squeezed, 'There is some evidence to show that when you get to a certain degree of constraint the public—at least the public in this age—will not take it, and they try to get out from under. This was what happened in 1970; and this was a very severe lesson.'[31] Here also, then, only the government can assess the competing claims on national resources which expenditure by the devolved administrations might generate.

For these reasons, the government at an early stage in the process of policy formulation, decided not to allow the devolved administrations substantial tax-raising powers. Instead their major sources of finance would be derived from a block fund, annually negotiated between the government and the devolved administrations but subject to an annual vote in the Commons. The Scottish and Welsh Offices did not fight against this decision as much as might have been expected, since, for them, the block fund, departing as it did from a service-by-service determination of public expenditure, was a significant improvement in the financial arrangements for Scotland and Wales.

In its first attempt to deal with the problems of financing the Assemblies, the White Paper *Our Changing Democracy*, published in November 1975, proposed that, in addition to the block fund, the Assemblies would be able to secure extra finance by imposing a surcharge upon local authority rates. However, as David Heald has commented, such a proposal seemed 'to be more likely a piece of black humour than a serious suggestion'.[32] For if the rates were insufficiently buoyant even to sustain the existing pattern of local authority services, how could they also provide a source of revenue for the Assemblies? It would be difficult indeed to imagine a proposal more likely to cause ill-will between local authorities and the Assemblies, than to require the former to raise their rates to pay for the excesses of the latter; and the suggestion was quietly dropped the following year.

Our Changing Democracy rejected the proposal by the majority of the Royal Commission, that the amount of the block fund be determined by an independent Joint Exchequer Board, on the ground that 'No neat formula could be devised to produce fair shares for Scotland (and for England, Wales, and Northern Ireland) in varying circumstances from year to year. The task involves judgments of great complexity and political sensitivity' (para. 100). The White Paper also rejected the suggestion that the Scottish Assembly be financed from the revenues derived from North Sea Oil, since the government

believe that oil must be treated in the same way as other natural resources (like the big coal deposits recently found in England, and the natural gas off its shores) and the benefits brought into the national pool for distribution in accordance with relative needs. Any other course could destroy not only economic unity but also political unity. Those who wish to reserve to Scotland oil or other revenues arising there are, in effect, demanding a separate Scottish state. The circle cannot be squared: it is not possible for Scotland—or any other part of the United Kingdom—to enjoy rights which can only go with separation yet not to have separation itself. (Para. 97)

The government's approach in the White Paper was severely criticized because it proposed to establish directly elected bodies with wide powers, yet unable to raise their own revenue. The Assemblies would, therefore, be in a weaker position than the local authorities subordinate to them. The government began, therefore, to claim that its objection to revenue-raising powers for the Assemblies was based not on principle, but upon the practical difficulties of finding taxes suitable for devolution. In September 1976, Mr. Millan, the Secretary for State of Scotland, provoked astonishment at the International Congress of the Institute of Public Finance, when he asked for their suggestions as to appropriate revenue-raising powers, saying 'if any of you here today from the United Kingdom or elsewhere can produce a solution to this problem we would be very grateful to you';[33] and Mr. Callaghan speaking in the Second Reading debate of the abortive Scotland and Wales Bill, claimed 'We are not against it [i.e. revenue-raising powers] in principle. We have simply not yet found a scheme which would be satisfactory.'[34]

This position, however, did not seem very plausible in the light of the fact that so many other countries had managed to solve a similar problem without too much difficulty. Indeed, as Lord Crowther-Hunt and Professor Peacock put it in their Dissenting Memorandum to the Royal Commission's Report, the Treasury argument

prompts one to ask the question why it happens to be the case that major countries with devolved systems of government manage to be at least as successful (and in some cases more successful) at stabilising their economies with high rates of employment and a lower rate of inflation . . .[35]

The briefest inspection of the tax systems of federal countries shows that provincial units enjoy a considerable diversity of revenues, but this does not seem to inhibit policies of economic stabilization. Indeed, the U.K. government already has far more of the country's gross national product under its control than many other countries where governments are well able to control aggregate demand. Moreover, the Treasury's argument implies that control of aggregate demand is far more precise than is in fact the case. The Memorandum by the Chief Secretary to the Treasury 1978/9 (Cmnd 7159) admitted that total expenditure on Supply in the financial year 1976/7 had amounted to £37,012m. as compared with an estimate of £26,488m. (Table 2). And in evidence before the Trade and Industry Sub-Committee to the House of Commons Expenditure Committee, Sir Douglas Wass, the Permanent Secretary to the Treasury, confessed that

> the injection of £100m. or £200m. into an economy whose gross national product is nearly £100,000m. is almost insignificant in relation to the rate of inflation. . . If one were thinking of an injection of demand—that is to say, expenditure on resources—of the order of £1,000m., at that order one would admit that it had some effect on the rate of cost inflation. . .[36]

It would therefore be perfectly possible for the Treasury to retain its control over the economy while still devolving taxing powers to the Assemblies, so long as it insisted upon a certain global limit to the total expenditure of the Assemblies, and a limit upon the permissible rate of change of Assembly taxation in any one year. These restrictions would not prove particularly onerous to the Assemblies.

A natural candidate for a devolved tax is income tax, although it would have to be supplemented by an equalization grant, since Scotland and Wales would almost certainly generate insufficient revenue to finance public services to a standard comparable to that enjoyed in the rest of the United Kingdom. The government, however, continued to maintain that it was unable to find a tax suitable for devolution. But it showed itself willing to compromise in order to meet two further criticisms directed against its financial proposals: that the block fund would allow detailed central scrutiny of the proposed programmes of the Assemblies; and that the annual vote in the Commons, on the proposed allocation, would become an occasion for territorial conflict, when English M.P.s would have to justify to their constituents why Scotland and Wales received higher allocations of public spending than England, and Scottish and Welsh M.P.s would have to explain why they had not asked for more, in view of alleged inadequacies in the state of public services in Scotland or Wales.

The government therefore issued a further White Paper, *Devolution: Financing the Devolved Services* (Cmnd. 6890) in July 1977, and proposed that the block fund be based upon a non-statutory formula, which would be calculated by relating 'the total of devolved public expenditure in Scotland or Wales to comparable expenditure elsewhere in the country on the basis of relative need' (para. 76). The formula would be maintained for a period of four years, and it might therefore obviate the need for annual consideration of the size of the block fund. The aim of the formula, presumably, would be to limit the range of conflict between the government and the devolved administrations. Instead of the block fund being determined through a programme-by-programme comparison of Scottish or Welsh, and English needs, a global formula would be calculated. The four-year period would, it was hoped, provide a period of stability and certainty during which the Assemblies would be able to plan their future expenditure.

It is not clear, however, how the formula approach will achieve these effects. For, not only will the Assemblies lack revenue-raising powers, they will also lack any *automatic* right to revenue, such as would be given by statutorily assigning the proceeds of specific taxes, e.g. excise duties, to them. And if the formula has no statutory basis, it will, presumably, still depend upon an annual vote in the Commons. Whether a satisfactory four-year formula can be calculated at all must depend first upon whether objective criteria of need can be drawn up; and secondly whether it will be sufficiently flexible to survive short-term economic fluctuations. Neither of these requirements seems likely to be met.

The formula will be constructed on the basis of the relative needs of Scotland and Wales, as compared with England. It seems, however, judging from the role played by the concept of need in the calculation of rate support grant paid to local authorities, that it is not a very precise concept. Indeed, according to the Department of the Environment in its evidence to the Layfield Committee, '. . . assessments of need often involve subjective judgements; many aspects of need cannot be measured; indicators may sometimes be misleading; and averages can conceal wide local variations. Variations in the quantity and quality of the available stock of social and environmental investment pose a particular problem.' For this reason '. . . because the varying expenditure needs of individual authorities cannot all be identified objectively or measured precisely, it can never be shown that the financial arrangements are completely equitable'.[37] There is no reason to believe that the formula for the allocation of the block fund will be any less subjective.

The method of calculating rate-support grant in England and

Wales which may well be used to calculate the block fund to the Assemblies also, is to use a regression equation 'embodying the assumption that the present pattern of expenditure is an accurate reflection of need'. The equation thus 'applies sophisticated methods to dubious material',[38] because it does not take account of the fact that current expenditure patterns may well not reflect current needs. The formula will thus have conservative implications because it will imply that existing expenditure patterns should be maintained. Yet part of the case for devolution is just that Scotland and Wales 'need' different patterns of public spending from those prevailing in the rest of the United Kingdom. The distribution of rate-support grant in Scotland, which is the responsibility of the Scottish Office, is already significantly different from that in England and Wales. The Assemblies might well seek to alter the pattern of public expenditure in Scotland and Wales. If they do so, this will redefine the need. Thus the issue of how the formula is drawn up will be a *political* one, depending upon a judgement of how much Scotland or Wales are entitled to, and the determination of the formula is likely, in the absence of independent revenue-raising powers for the devolved administrations, to draw Westminster into conflict with the Assemblies.

An alternative way of calculating the formula which does not make the assumption that current expenditure patterns reflect need, might be to consider whether indicators of need could be constructed. The attempt has been made to construct such indicators to determine the regional distribution of expenditure on the health service. It is possible, but perhaps unlikely, that an agreed formula could be calculated on this basis such as would satisfy Westminster, Edinburgh, and Cardiff as well as the poorer English regions. At any rate one need not envy those statisticians called upon to attempt the task.

A further difficulty with the formula approach is that it may not be sufficiently flexible to cope with short-term economic fluctuations. Suppose that in the second year of operation of the formula, the government faced a crisis on the lines of that in 1976, calling, in its view, for a rapid reduction in public spending. Such a crisis would be bound to call into question the agreed allocation to Scotland and Wales. Since 1974, the needs element in rate-support grant has been determined annually, rather than on a two-year basis, and it has fluctuated considerably with changes in the economic climate. During the panic which followed the financial crisis of 1976, the government used the weapon of cash limits to cut public expenditure, so that if inflation rose by more than had been expected, programmes were automatically cut. In such circumstances, it is difficult to see the formula remaining unaffected, and therefore a period of continuing inflation will be bound to call into question the value of the formula.

Even though the proposed formula represents a modest advance upon the government's previous position, it does not meet the central criticism of the government's financial proposals, that an Assembly without revenue-raising powers will be financially irresponsible, and that this will lead at best to confused government, and at worst, in Scotland, give an impetus to the forces of separatism.

That the power to raise money should be vested in the same hands as the power to spend it has long been thought of as a fundamental tenet of responsible government. In its report to the Cabinet in 1911, the Committee on Irish Finance, set up to consider the financial relationships of Home Rule, claimed that it was

a first principle of sound government that the same authority that has the spending of revenue should also have the burthen, and not infrequently the odium of raising that revenue. That one should have the unpopular duty of providing the same, and another the privilege of expending them, is a division of labour that leads to disaster.[39]

Over sixty years later, the Layfield Committee on Local Government Finance echoed the report of this Committee when it declared: 'whoever is responsible for spending money should also be responsible for raising it so that the amount of expenditure is subject to democratic control'.[40]

For Scotland and Wales, failure to devolve revenue-raising powers will fundamentally affect the character of the devolved administrations. Since they will have the power to spend but not to tax, there will be an incentive for them to bid high for funds from London. Since they will not have to balance their spending by raising the taxes to pay for it, the only constraint upon the spending of the devolved administrations will appear to be the lack of generosity of the government. There would be no incentive, for example, for a Conservative administration in Scotland to economize since, instead of reducing taxes, such economies would serve only to swell the funds of a Labour government in London. The devolved administrations will thus be subject to little financial discipline or accountability. The political debate in Scotland and Wales, therefore, instead of being concerned with competing economic and social philosophies, such as Socialism or Conservatism, will increasingly be orientated around the single issue of which party can squeeze the most out of London. As the economist, Lord Vaizey has argued, candidates for the Assemblies will not say—I want to increase health spending and raise council house rents to pay for it; instead they will say—I will press Westminster to alter the formula.[41] The devolved administrations will thus take on the character of pressure groups focused on London rather than independent responsible political bodies.

Moreover, the nature of the pressure group relationship must inevitably be an unstable one. For the demand for improved public services in Scotland and Wales is not one that can easily be satisfied; it is a demand that is nearly infinite. Whenever the standard of roads, or hospitals, or schools in Scotland or Wales is held to be inadequate, London will be blamed, and deficiencies in public services will be attributable not to bad government in Scotland and Wales, but to the meanness of government in London. The electors themselves will be unable to decide whether these deficiencies are due to incompetent administration in Edinburgh or Cardiff, or meanness in London. Each side will attempt to pass the buck to the other, and the elector will not be able to decide who is accountable.

The U.K. government, in turn, will find itself drawn into discussion of the proposed expenditure plans of the Assemblies. The government in calculating a sum for the total of devolved expenditure, will scrutinize carefully the components of that total to ensure that it can be related to comparable expenditure in England. Despite the intentions of the government, this will inevitably involve it in the scrutiny of specific projects proposed by the devolved administrations. The administrations will have to justify themselves to the government, and will find it difficult to justify departures from patterns of expenditure determined by Whitehall. Moreover if the negotiations between government and the devolved administrations are carried out by civil servants rather than by elected members, they may share two 'noticeable features of the rate support negotiations . . . their secrecy and the lack of any involvement of elected members until the very last stage. . .'[42] This also would import a centralist bias into the final settlement.

Thus, the financial relationship between the Assemblies and the government will conflict with the political aims of devolution. The financial arrangements will counteract tendencies leading to a dispersal of power; and conflict over finance will prevent the Scotland and Wales Acts from being final settlements of the constitutional issue, but will introduce an element of instability into the settlement.[43]

The S.N.P. and Plaid Cymru will benefit the most from this instability. For they alone will not be constrained in bidding for funds from London, by the fear of damaging their London-based party headquarters. A Conservative administration in Scotland will not wish to appear profligate at a time when a central policy of the Conservative Party is to restrict public expenditure; and a Labour administration will be under some pressure from a Labour government in London not to damage its economic policy by going in for a spending spree. The S.N.P. and Plaid Cymru, however, will be continually seeking to show their electorates that it is only London's parsimony which is preventing them from improving public services. In Scotland, the S.N.P. will be greatly assisted in this enterprise by being able to use the specious, but nevertheless politically effective, argument that London is taking Scotland's oil, but refusing to finance any improvements in her public services.

A further serious defect in the government's financial proposals is that they take no account of the changed psychological and political climate in Scotland resulting from North Sea Oil, which has made it appear to many Scots that they could be better off as an independent country than as a part of the United Kingdom. According to D.I. and G.A. Mackay in their book, *The Political Economy of North Sea Oil*, the continuation of current U.K. energy policies means that the benefits to Scotland from the commerical exploitation of oil are likely to be extremely small. The Mackays divide the economic effects into direct effects upon employment and income, and indirect effects from increased revenues and an improved Balance of Payments. The direct effects will accrue to Scotland but, according to the Mackays, they will be comparatively small, and counterbalanced by environmental spoliation in the North East of Scotland. It is the indirect effects which will be the important ones, but these will accrue to the United Kingdom as a whole. Scotland will benefit only to the extent that an improvement in the United Kingdom's Balance of Payments and government revenue is used to rejuvenate the Scottish industrial structure.

The interesting point is that an independent Scotland, with control of the oil revenues, could hope to secure the indirect as well as the direct benefits of the oil. She could therefore gain a strong Balance of Payments position for herself, and this 'would allow the pursuit of more expansionary economic policies aimed at increasing the productive capacity of the economy'.[44] The oil, in other words, offers to Scotland the possibility of rejuvenating her economy, and so any devolutionary settlement must offer Scots visible evidence that their economic position is benefiting from the discovery of oil.

As we have seen, the government in its White Paper, *Our Changing Democracy*, insisted that energy was not be to devolved, and that ceding control of the oil revenues was tantamount to setting up a separate state in Scotland. This was a perfectly understandable position to take. On grounds of equity, there could be no reason why Scotland should gain as a result of a windfall, when other areas of the United Kingdom with high indices of deprivation, were to receive little benefit, because they lacked the advantage of a nationalist movement fighting on their behalf. Moreover, Scotland has been a continuous beneficiary of U.K. regional policy over the past fifteen years.

Yet, although the government's position was a sound one in terms of strict equity, it seemed to lack sufficient foresight and flair to accommodate a changed situation in Scotland. It would have been perfectly possible to use a portion of the oil revenues for a Scottish Development Budget, as suggested by Christopher Smallwood in *New Edinburgh Review*, February 1976; or, alternatively, to have accepted the proposals put forward by the Outer Circle Policy Unit, and the Liberal Party in its negotiations with the government, that the Scottish Treasury be given the royalties of 12½% on oil brought ashore in Scotland. Such a proposal might have been the means of providing credibility to the government's argument that Scotland could benefit as much from remaining in the United Kingdom, as by choosing independence.

The financial proposals thus remain the weakest part of the government's devolution package. They reflect an approach to devolution which insists upon maintaining the reins of centralized power while conceding as little as possible to centrifugal pressures. It is difficult to disagree with Dr. Jeremy Bray, who claimed in the Commons debate on revenue-raising powers:

> The economic arguments have been mistaken by those who argue that it is essential to maintain the central management of the United Kingdom economy. That is an important argument, but it is like arguing that because one wants to keep a motor car in one piece one must bolt the wheel axles onto the chassis. The one sure thing is that, if one does that, the car will shake itself to bits.[45]

Even if—to change the metaphor—the devolution settlement does not hit the rocks as a result of the inadequacies of the financial proposals, it must at least be clear that they 'mark the beginning and not the end of the debate on how to finance the Assemblies'.[46] They represent the most serious source of instability in the Scotland and Wales Acts.

X *The English dimension*

England is hardly mentioned in the Scotland and Wales Acts, and yet she is, in many respects, the key to devolution. This is partly because in order to secure the parliamentary passage of the Scotland and Wales Bills, the government was forced to make concessions to ensure that the package was acceptable to English M.P.s who constitute the vast majority of the Commons; but, more importantly, because the success of devolution to Scotland and Wales will depend upon the extent to which English opinion believes it to be a fair and equitable settlement. For although much of the debate on devolution has concerned itself with whether the government's package can satisfy opinion in Scotland and Wales, it is of at least equal importance to ensure that the settlement is palatable to an England reluctantly conceding devolution. If, therefore, the Scotland and Wales Acts are to secure a permanent settlement, they will have to be accepted as fair not only by the Scots and Welsh, but also by the English, who after all constitute eighty-five per cent of the population of the United Kingdom.

Lord Crowther-Hunt, the Labour Government's constitutional

adviser during 1974-75, was, in the Memorandum of Dissent, an enthusiast for a broad scheme of executive devolution applied to Scotland, Wales, and the regions of England alike. It is reasonable, therefore, to conjecture that this option was considered carefully by the government's Constitution Unit. But it soon became apparent that Scotland was determined to have legislative devolution together with a Cabinet-type structure of government; and that opinion in England was by no means desirous of any further reorganization of government. The government, therefore, while producing its proposals for Scotland and Wales, delayed reaching conclusions on policy for England until it could obtain a clearer view of the form which they should take.

It was, nevertheless, essential to ensure that devolution to Scotland and Wales did not lead to adverse effects in England; and the government hoped to avoid an English backlash by confirming that its legislation for Scotland and Wales related only to the domestic concerns of Scotland and Wales, and did not affect the position of the English regions. In a letter to the Chairman of the Merseyside County Council, Mr. Foot, the Lord President of the Council, claimed that 'a great deal of thought had been given . . . in drawing up the powers of the proposed assemblies to ensure that the interests of other parts of the United Kingdom would not be adversely affected. In particular, in the economic and industrial fields, detailed provision is made to maintain parliamentary control and the continued allocation of resources throughout the United Kingdom on the basis of need.'[47] The philosophy behind the Scotland and Wales Bills was contained in their Long Titles, which stated that they were Bills making changes in the government of Scotland (Wales), and *not* changes in the government of the United Kingdom as a whole. It was for this reason that the government was determined to retain control, first over regional policy and the central instruments of economic management; second over the block funds to be allocated to the devolved administrations, and the total capital expenditure which they were authorised to borrow; and finally, through the statutory guidelines for the Scottish and Welsh Development Agencies, ensuring that they could not offer investment incentives denied to the English regions.

The government's consultative document, *Devolution, The English*

Dimension (1976), therefore concluded that the constitutional implications of devolution were confined to Scotland and Wales, and that
fears 'expressed that devolution will lead to an accretion of powers
and influence to the devolved administrations of a kind likely to
prejudice the interests of England and, more particularly, the less
prosperous regions of England', were 'in fact, groundless' (para. 22).

These assurances were, however, received with considerable
scepticism both by local authorities in the North, and by academic
commentators. Indeed, *Devolution, The English Dimension* was given
a scathing reception. Lord Crowther-Hunt, now out of office,
argued in *The Times* (21 December 1976) that the document 'has all
the characteristics of a false prospectus', since 'it plays down the
extent of the devolution of power now actually proposed for Scotland and Wales; inevitably, therefore, it gives the false impression
that England has nothing to worry about'. He contrasted the
soothing language of the Consultative Document, with the promise
in *Our Changing Democracy*, addressed to Scotland and Wales, that
devolution would involve 'a massive handover to the new elected
Assemblies of responsibility for the domestic affairs of Scotland
and Wales'.

The document failed to come to grips with the fact than an
already existing constitutional imbalance in favour of Scotland
and Wales would be accentuated by devolution. Scotland and
Wales already had their own Secretaries of State pressing their
case at Cabinet level, which was why they benefited more from
public spending than English regions whose needs were as great
but who had no territorial representation in the Cabinet; they were
also over-represented in Parliament in proportion to population
when compared with the English regions.

Yet the Scotland and Wales Acts proposed the continuance of
the offices of Secretary of State for Scotland and Wales, as well as
the continued over-representation of Scotland and Wales in the
Commons. Moreover, after devolution, Scottish M.P.s would be
able to vote on matters of English domestic concern, such as
schools, housing, health, etc. and perhaps even determine the
political colour of the government which would make these decisions
for England, while English M.P.s would be unable to vote on
Scottish domestic matters. *The English Dimension* did not so much as
mention these factors, which meant that, in the words of a Liberal

Party publication: 'U.K. citizens resident in England, already second class in terms of representation, are to be third class since they will have no assemblies. Why should any English person be expected to support such treatment?'[48]

This constitutional imbalance would thus cease to be tolerable if Scotland and Wales were to enjoy the additional advantage of directly elected Assemblies to press their claims upon Westminster. As Professor J. A. G. Griffith argued in the *New Statesman*, 17 December 1976, '. . . the fears of the North West and North East are not founded on a misunderstanding of the statutory powers of the Government. They are founded on the belief that the political clout which Scotland and Wales can deliver through their Assemblies will enable them to obtain a greater share of regional aid than at present'. Mr. Tom Urwin, a member for a Northern constituency and a former junior minister, who for the first time in his political career rebelled over devolution, believed that devolution would give Scotland even 'greater influence at cabinet level through its Secretary of State prodded by a Scottish Assembly'.[49] The English regions, lacking representation in the Cabinet, and lacking powerful nationalist parties which could act as pressure groups, would be unable to counteract this influence.

Devolution, The English Dimension, failed to satisfy local authority leaders in the North, and their anxieties were reflected in seminars organized by the Tyne and Wear and Merseyside County Councils. Mr. William (now Lord) Sefton, then Chairman of Merseyside County Council, sent a letter to the Prime Minister and the leaders of the Conservative and Liberal Parties protesting that: 'It is totally wrong for the question of possible Devolution to Scotland or to Wales to be discussed by Parliament before the implications for England and the United Kingdom as a whole had been totally thought through'.

For devolution would 'lead to a serious economic imbalance between the North East and other regions favourable to Scotland at the expense of ourselves'.[50] Thus, for the first time since the war, a powerful regional lobby in England had been generated, in order to campaign against devolution to Scotland. In the Labour revolt on the guillotine motion on the Scotland and Wales Bill in February 1977, the Northern Group of M.P.s provided a disproportionate share of the rebels. '18.2 per cent of the Labour opponents and 25 per cent of the Labour abstainers were members of the Northern group, which accounts for only 9.1 per cent of all Labour M.P.s.' The government was compelled, therefore, to make concessions to its Northern supporters, if it wished to secure a majority for devolution; and on 8 November 1977 in the debate on the Address, Mr. Varley, the Secretary of State for Industry, announced that the National Enterprise Board was to set up regional boards for the North East and North West; and, whether by coincidence or not, 'Department of Industry figures for the second quarter of 1977 show that the North received a higher proportion of regionally relevant public expenditure per head than any other U.K. region.'[51]

Regional feeling in the North has been primarily directed at preventing devolution. It is not to be interpreted as a demand for devolution to the North, a claim which would probably not have been put forward if the Scotland and Wales Bill had not been brought before Parliament. Nevertheless, once the Assemblies are set up, the strategy of the Northern protestors might well become the more constructive one of seeking to establish a Northern regional assembly. It is difficult to see any other way in which the North will be able to protect its interests.

XI *English regionalism*

The passage of the Scotland and Wales Bills, therefore, is unlikely to mark the end of the process of devolution, and increasingly the case for devolution to the English regions, especially to the Northern regions, is likely to be heard. *Devolution, The English Dimension*, was cautious about the possibilities of devolution in England, on the ground that the desire for change in England was less strong, and that those who sought change were unclear as to the form it should take.

This view, although attacked by constitutional zealots, was in reality the only possible one for the government to take. It would have been politically foolish to attempt an overall constitutional settlement at a time when the pressures for change were felt with such different intensity in different parts of the United Kingdom. An overall approach would have meant either that England would have regional assemblies forced upon her, simply because Scotland and Wales wanted devolution; or, alternatively, that Scotland and

Wales should be made to wait for their Assemblies until English opinion had been converted to devolution. The government had to walk a tightrope if it was both to secure an equitable settlement, and also contain the forces in Scotland seeking separation.

Instead of making firm proposals, therefore, the government invited various interested bodies as well as private individuals to express their views as to the desirability of constitutional change in England. But the response from members of the public to *Devolution, The English Dimension* was extremely disappointing. A mere seventy replies were received from individuals, and, surprisingly, only a handful of these were from the North, the vast majority being from the Home Counties. These were, as might be expected, wholly against further change. The local authority associations were, admittedly, in favour of devolution, but to local government rather than to regional authorities. In particular, they wanted health and water functions restored to local government; but they did not consider how this could be done in the absence of a reform of local government finance; nor whether local government units were large enough to handle successfully matters such as river pollution and health care.

Faced with so negative a response, Mr. Foot, in a Commons written answer on 15 November 1977, announced that 'a broad consensus of popular support' would be necessary 'if a regional structure of government were to be established in England', but this consensus 'as is clear from the consultations, does not exist at present'. The consultations had, however, 'revealed support for limited change within the local government system', to which the government was giving further consideration.[56] (Col. 5.)

But interest in English regionalism was developing from another source, as a result of an internal Labour Party debate on local government reform. As early as February 1973, Harold Wilson in a speech to the annual Local Government Conference of the Labour Party at Newcastle, had argued that if local government reorganization was to achieve a genuine decentralization of power it had to be accompanied by elected regional authorities.

Instead of transferring functions from local to central government, or proceeding with one after another *ad hoc*, more or less appointive body covering wide areas of the country, we need, not only to halt this process, but to do two other things. First, to decentralize and democratize more and more work presently undertaken by central government either from Whitehall or through their own regional machinery, and, second, to create democratic regional authorities accountable to the people of the area they serve, to deal with those services for which existing local authorities are too small.

Regional authorities, Harold Wilson went on, were 'needed for more of the strategic decisions on planning and land-use, transport and road-building, the environment, water, and sewerage. A great part of the central Government's function here can be devolved.' They would also inherit the functions of the Regional Economic Planning Councils set up in 1965 and would be given executive powers, so that they would become strategic planning authorities for their regions.

The Conservative Government which reorganized local government had not denied the existence of the regional dimension. The White Paper on *Local Government in England* (Cmnd. 4584), published in February 1971, admitted that 'none of these proposed metropolitan counties can practically contain the solution of all the planning problems of the conurbations . . . There are functions of both central and local government which need to be considered in a regional provincial context . . . The most important of these is the formulation of the broad economic and land-use strategy which would be the regional framework within which services would be provided' (paras. 32, 35). The Conservatives, however, intended to delay decisions on the constitution of regional bodies and the range of functions they might carry out, until the Commission on the Constitution had reported.

Nevertheless, it would appear that the insertion of a regional tier of government in England would mean, as in Wales, a further reorganization of local government. For a three-tier structure below central government level would 'unquestionably . . . be totally unacceptable to public opinion and would be destroyed by angry public reaction immediately it was reorganised'.[52] Indeed, one of the arguments deployed by regionalists is that regional government would make possible an improved local government structure, by eliminating one tier of local government—the county tier—so that the new structure would comprise a regional layer of government responsible for broad strategic planning, and a local government layer responsible for the provision of services. Such an approach was also suggested in the report of the inquiry into Greater London by Sir Frank Marshall, formerly the Conservative leader of Leeds City Council. This report, published in 1978, proposed that the G.L.C. be accepted as the regional authority for London, responsible for strategic decisions, while the London boroughs would be responsible for the day-to-day provision and administration of services. Sir Frank was in favour of the creation of a Regional Health Authority for the whole G.L.C. area, and expressed himself 'wholeheartedly' in favour of 'the G.L.C.'s long term policy for the unification of the Health Service at a regional level under the democratic control of the Council'.[53] He also favoured the devolution of functions from central government, if the G.L.C. was to act as a genuinely strategic authority.

When the Labour party was returned to power in 1974, however, it found its regionalist policy pre-empted by the Conservative reorganization of local government, and was wary of proposing a further reform so soon after the last one. Indeed Mr. Silkin, the Minister for Planning and Local Government, was reported as having said that the only thing worse than the last reorganization of local government would be another one; and Harold Wilson told the Labour Party's Local Government Conference at Eastbourne in 1975: 'To import the regional issue is very long-term, because no one sees a further major change in local government in the years immediately ahead'.

The Labour Party's response to this impasse was twofold. First, the Labour Party's policy committee continued its investigations into the potential support for a regional solution; but this served only to confirm the government's finding. For, in the words of a National Executive policy statement presented to the 1978 Annual Conference, the idea of regionalism was 'not yet sufficiently supported or even understood by many people involved in local government, or by the public at large'. Therefore the regional solution might remain as an ideal; it could not be an immediate policy aim.

The second element in Labour's approach was the proposal by Mr. Shore, Secretary of State for the Environment, for 'organic change' in local government, through which functions such as education, the social services, highways, and non-strategic planning, would be transferred to the nine major cities which had lost them in the 1974 reorganization. This was seen by many in the Labour Party, though not by Mr. Shore, as a prelude to the gradual phasing out of the counties, which would clear the way for the introduction of regional authorities.

It can be seen, therefore, that there are two different factors at work forcing consideration of devolution in England. The first is what might be called the backlash resulting from devolution to Scotland and Wales, and the lop-sided constitutional structure which that will create; and the second is the pressure for a modernized system of local government suited to the realities of modern social geography. The Scotland and Wales Acts, therefore, are unlikely to mark the end of the debate on devolution, for they may well lead through a process which the Opposition spokesman on devolution, Mr. Francis Pym, called in a speech at Manchester in July 1978, 'federalism by stealth', to the adoption of a quasi-federal system of government for the United Kingdom as a whole.

8 Conclusion: Federal devolution

England, having no constitution at all, has no excellent, no matchless constitution; for nothing has no properties.

Bentham: *Constitutional Code*

I

It is time now to draw together the threads of our discussion on the Scotland and Wales Acts, and attempt some general appraisal of the structure that will result. What will the future government of the United Kingdom look like if the Scottish and Welsh Assemblies come into being and how stable is the resulting settlement likely to prove?

Any assessment of the implications of devolution must begin with a realization that it is *political* rather than *constitutional* factors which will determine the success or failure of the policy. For many, if not all, successful constitutions display logical defects which are difficult to defend; conversely, that most logical constitution of all, the constitution of the Weimar Republic, proved unworkable, because the political will to work it did not exist. We need to concentrate, then, less on the formal structure of devolution, and more on the political reality beneath.

Politically, devolution may be understood as the placing of a weapon in the hands of the Scots and Welsh; and just as one cannot be sure that a weapon will be used only for the specified purposes for which it was given, so also one cannot predict the use which the Scots and Welsh would make of devolution. For the Assemblies would represent areas of the United Kingdom with long histories of local identity and pride, and it would be the reaction of these psychological factors upon the new institutions which would determine their path of development. The life of the Assemblies, then, may take a very different course from that expected by their creators. This will especially be the case in the future relationships between London and Edinburgh.

We have seen that the government went to great lengths to ensure that Westminster's supremacy over the Assemblies was not jeopardized. The Scottish Assembly was to be a strictly subordinate body. Westminster's supremacy over the Assembly in Edinburgh was to be buttressed in three ways; first by severely limiting the latter's area of legislative competence so that it could deal only with social and environmental and not with economic affairs; secondly, by providing that even within its area of legislative competence, the government retained a power of override; and finally, by denying the Assembly revenue-raising powers, the intention being to ensure that if dependent upon government for finance, the Assembly would be safely confined to a subordinate position.

In the face of these restrictions, it was natural for critics of the Scotland Act to argue that little was being conceded. The powers being transferred were, it was suggested, so hedged by qualifications, and by the supervision of central government, that they would be insufficient even to sustain a viable system of devolved government in Scotland, let alone threaten Westminister's supremacy. Power devolved, according to this view, was power retained.

If, however, we look at devolution through political rather than constitutional spectacles, we can see that this view is likely to prove profoundly mistaken. For in reality a new locus of political power would be established both in Scotland and in Wales. The Assemblies would be the only elected bodies to represent Scotland and Wales; they would claim to represent Scottish and Welsh opinion at least as effectively as Scottish and Welsh M.P.s; and they would provide a powerful base for ambitious politicians who are likely to seek to use their powers to the full and extend them if possible.

Thus the seemingly all-powerful restraints in the Acts can only be brought into play by Westminster at the expense of considerable political disaffection in Scotland and Wales. It would be difficult to imagine an issue which would unite Scottish or Welsh opinion more fervently than conflict between their own elected Assemblies and a London-based government. In practice, therefore, the powers retained by Westminster might be very difficult to exercise, and in particular, the override weapon is unlikely to prove a viable means for securing Westminster's supremacy.

We have already seen how difficult it was for Westminster to exercise its supremacy over Northern Ireland; and on the one occasion upon which the U.K. government sought to exercise its reserve power to withhold assent to proposed legislation from Northern Ireland, it was met with a threat of resignation by the government of Northern Ireland, and was forced to give way. But the U.K. government's problems are bound to be greater in the case of Scotland and Wales, who will be in a far stronger position than Northern Ireland, since their Assemblies, unlike Stormont, will represent not an artificially created province, but nations, and the Scottish nation in particular has a history of statehood and a national tradition embodied in concrete and ever-present institutional form.

The position of Scotland under devolution might come to bear a very close resemblance to that of a province in a federal state. For the Scotland Act will in practice divide legislative power between London and Edinburgh. Wheare, in *Federal Government*, finds the distinguishing mark of federalism to lie in a constitutionally guaranteed division of powers between co-ordinate and independent levels of government. Clearly, neither the Scottish and Welsh Assemblies would have such a constitutional guarantee, as they would be subordinate bodies. But Scotland, and to a lesser extent Wales, would enjoy a division of powers, guaranteed by the support of Scottish public opinion, and perhaps Scottish M.P.s also, against any attempt by Westminster to vindicate its supremacy.

For if the new arrangements work as intended, the Scottish Assembly will be the supreme authority over Scottish domestic affairs—it will be the Scottish Parliament. The normal convention will be that Westminster ceases to legislate for Scotland, or intervene in Scottish domestic affairs.

It is then in constitutional theory alone that full legislative power remains with London; and it is only in constitutional theory that the unitary state is preserved. In practice, power will be transferred, and it cannot, except under pathological circumstances, be recovered. The formal assertion of parliamentary supremacy as 'the supreme authority to make laws for the United Kingdom or any part of it' in the deleted Clause 1 of the Scotland Bill, becomes an empty assertion because it will no longer be accompanied by a real political supremacy. In Scotland, at least, the supremacy of

Parliament will bear a different and a more attenuated meaning after the setting up of the Assembly.

Westminster, instead of enjoying a regular and continuous exercise of supremacy, will possess merely a nebulous right to supervise the Assembly. But political authority depends upon its regular and continuous exercise; it is not the mere incursion of legislative authority once every ten, fifteen, or twenty years. In these circumstances the assertion of supremacy would become in Enoch Powell's words, 'so empty that it could eventually be given effect only by what would in reality be a revolutionary act'.[1] Thus Wesminster's supremacy in Scotland, which was once a real power to make laws affecting Scotland's domestic affairs, would become merely the power to supervise *another* legislative body which would make laws over a wide area of public policy.

The Scotland Act will thus establish, if not a federal *constitution* regulating the relationship between England and Scotland, a quasi-federal form of *government*, to adapt Wheare's description of the Canadian structure of government.[2] Moreover, it will buttress this division of powers through an embryonic constitutional court in the form of the Judicial Committee of the Privy Council. Indeed, we have seen that the Scotland Act may prove particularly susceptible to the process of constitutional adjustment through judicial interpretation because of the way in which it divides powers between London and Edinburgh. Admittedly, the Judicial Committee can pronounce only on Scottish and not on West-minster's legislation. Nevertheless, if it decided a dispute over the division of powers in Scotland's favour, it would be difficult to imagine Westminster deliberately choosing to legislate for Scotland on a matter which a court had ruled was devolved. In practice, therefore, the Judicial Committee may well come to assume something like the role of a constitutional court with respect to Scotland.

Thus the Scotland Act not only effectively limits the power of Parliament, but it also introduces a judicial element into the defining of the limitation. It proposes, therefore, what amounts to a written constitution for the United Kingdom, establishing a quasi-federal system of government with a politically sanctified division of powers and a court to act as arbiter of the division.

II

To what extent is the new constitutional situation created by the Scotland and Wales Acts likely to prove a stable one? In introducing the Government of Ireland Bill—the first Home Rule Bill—in 1893, Gladstone argued that a *sine qua non* of its success was that it 'should be in the nature of settlement, and not of a mere provocation to the revival of fresh demands.'[3] Mr. Callaghan, introducing the ill-fated Scotland and Wales Bill into the Commons, expressed the hope that it would prove 'an enduring framework for reconciling legitimate demands for Scottish and Welsh control over their own affairs within the unity of the United Kingdom government'.[4] If these hopes are realized, the Scotland and Wales Acts will yield a genuine settlement in Gladstone's sense, but if they are not, the result will be merely a staging post on the road to further constitutional evolution.

The government was, as we have seen, faced with the cruel dilemma of balancing centrifugal with centripetal political forces. It had to take account both of the new political forces in Scotland and Wales, and the danger of arousing an English backlash if devolution was seen as giving unfair advantages to Scotland and Wales. If it conceded too much, it might stimulate the growth of an English nationalism hostile to the devolution settlement; but if it conceded too little, it would fail to conciliate Scottish opinion, and it might put the unity of the state itself at risk.

Nevertheless, the government rejected three proposals which might have given stability to the new structure. The first of these (proposed by Norman Buchan, a Scottish M.P., and supported by the Labour Party's Scottish Council), that there should be a second question in the referendum on whether the Scots wanted independence, might have succeeded in demarcating Labour's position from that of the S.N.P. The argument against the proposal was that, by bringing the issue of independence out into the open, it would make it a more credible option: but it could have provided a valuable safeguard to prevent Assembly politics being dominated by the independence issue; and it would have ensured that the Scots did not find that they had accidentally given the S.N.P. a mandate to seek independence, as a result of protest votes against Labour and Conservative candidates. We have already noticed that the life of Stormont was bedevilled by the issue of the border, and in Scotland, too, the work of the Assembly could be totally undermined if the S.N.P. decided to use it purely as a forum for seeking independence without seeking to make a constructive contribution to its work.

If, however, there can be some scope for dispute as to the advisability of the second question in the referendum, it is difficult to find a rationale for the rejection of proportional representation in the elections to the Scottish and Welsh Assemblies. The arguments for the first-past-the-post system of election are at their strongest where there is a two-party system, and the need is for strong government capable of swift executive action. Neither of these considerations prevails in Scotland and Wales where the two-party system has broken down, and the need for a powerful executive cannot be as strong in a subordinate government as it is in Westminster. In Wales, the failure to secure proportional representation in elections to the Assemblies will mean that the Welsh Assembly would be dominated by a Labour caucus from South Wales, whose methods in local councils may not inspire confidence that the Assembly would be an effective advertisement for devolution. In Scotland, the consequences are likely to be even more serious, since in a party system where three parties compete on reasonably equal terms, the relationship between seats and votes may come to resemble a lottery. It would be perfectly possible for the S.N.P. to win an absolute majority of the seats in the Scottish Assembly with only thirty-five per cent of the vote, and to interpret this as a mandate for independence. Proportional representation, on the other hand, would have forced the S.N.P. to decide whether or not it wished to play a constructive role in the Assembly. If it did not, it would be entirely excluded from the process of government in Scotland; but if, as is more likely, it agreed to participate in a coalition, it would be compelled to present responsible policies, and would cease to be a party whose whole *raison d'être* was to use devolution as a staging-post to independence. Indeed, in such circumstances the S.N.P. might well split between a Left wing and a Right wing as other territorially based parties have done in similar situations.

The third proposal for stability which the government rejected was to give the Assemblies revenue-raising powers. We have already analysed the consequences of this rejection, and it remains only to repeat that the financial arrangements remain the weakest part of the devolution proposals, and may lead to a system of irresponsible government in which Westminster will be blamed for deficiencies of public services in Scotland and Wales, and the S.N.P. will acquire a further argument to support its case that an independent Scotland would be a wealthier Scotland.

It is particularly regrettable that the government should have rejected so many lifelines, since our analysis has shown that the Scotland and Wales Acts are unlikely to yield a stable constitutional settlement.

The main reason for instability is the very great contrast between the constitutionally subordinate role of the Assemblies and their powerful representative position, for this will give them an incentive to expand their powers. For, as our analysis of the background to devolution in Scotland has shown, many of the causes of grievance in Scotland are economic rather than social or environmental in their origin, and much of the resentment against London government flows from a feeling that Westminster and Whitehall have ignored Scotland's economic problems. Therefore, devolution will be judged according to whether or not it assists in solving Scotland's economic problems. The government's devolution package gives Scotland power to deal with issues on which there is little discontent, while denying her the power to deal with those issues where discontent is strongest. That cannot be a recipe for stability.

It is of course not possible to predict with any precision the future course of events in Scotland since there are a number of possible outcomes. One possibility is that the Scottish Assembly, far from defusing discontent with government, provides legitimacy for Scottish national claims, and therefore stimulates the demand for independence. The Assembly may claim to be the sole body capable of interpreting the wishes of the Scottish people, and refuse to accept that legislative power for Scotland can be divided at all. In that case, the Scottish Assembly will itself be the forum within which the demand for independence will be made, and it will act as the embryonic legislature of an independent Scotland. Such a development is particularly likely to occur if the economic prospects for Scotland fail to improve, for devolution will be blamed for

Scotland's economic plight, and also provide the fulcrum for the transition to independence.

An alternative possibility, equally depressing from Westminster's point of view, would be that devolution leads to a confused system of government which becomes too complex for electors in Scotland and Wales to understand. Devolution may seem to be adding an extra layer of politicians and administrators to an already complex two-tier system of local government, in which electors may not find it easy to locate responsibility for public services. Responsibility for the administration of services will appear divided, and it may prove difficult to secure an ordered set of priorities for the government of Scotland and Wales. 'Whatever happens', the late Lord Selwyn-Lloyd has argued, 'another layer of officialdom, or elected representatives must not be introduced . . . If obligations are imposed on new bodies, others must be relieved of them.'[5] Otherwise the result of devolution will be popular alienation from government, and this too may help the S.N.P. in Scotland.

Neither of these eventualities is inevitable however. The Assemblies and Westminster might well find a way to live together. Much may depend upon the first elections to the Scottish Assembly, and the strength of S.N.P. representation in the first Assembly. Much also will depend upon the practical interpretation in Edinburgh and Westminster of the devolution settlement. Both sides will have to operate according to the spirit rather than the letter of devolution. Westminster will have to resist the temptation to use its financial powers to control the priorities of the Assembly; and the Assembly will have to act responsibly, and not succumb to the temptation of attributing all the evils of Scotland to Westminster's malign influence. If that happens, a new equilibrium will be found, balancing the centrifugal pressures in Scotland against the centripetal forces in London.

A fourth prognostication, and perhaps the most likely, is for the government's devolution package to evolve even further in a federal direction. It is indeed in this direction that many of the most enthusiastic supporters of devolution, such as the late Professor John Mackintosh, and Mr. Alick Buchanan-Smith, a former Shadow Secretary of State for Scotland, have foreseen the likely path of constitutional development. Mrs. Thatcher, who opposed the Scotland and Wales Acts, has been quoted as saying that 'she expected an Assembly to be established eventually, but that there might have to be a quasi-federal solution to achieve this',[6] and Mr. Pym in the speech in which he referred to the government introducing 'federalism by stealth' argued that a properly thought-out federal scheme 'would be far more stable for the whole U.K. or Scotland alone than one based on the Government's Scotland Bill.'

Federal devolution may occur if the Scottish, and perhaps the Welsh Assembly also, are seen by their electors as *the* bodies responsible for Scottish and Welsh affairs; they will then come to be held responsible by their electorates even for non-devolved matters. If there is a proposal to close a steel mill in Wales, or a shipbuilding yard in Scotland, there will be a demand that the Assembly 'does something about it'. The Assemblies will be regarded as the domestic goverments of Scotland and Wales, just as the Secretary of State for Scotland was regarded as Scotland's minister, and therefore as responsible for all Scottish affairs, long before he was given the economic powers which could make the title of Scotland's minister a reality.

After devolution, the Secretary of State will become, in effect, a minister for Scottish economic affairs, for most of the functions which he is to retain lie in the economic sphere. But, in the eyes of the Assembly, he may not have the political weight to make it worthwhile negotiating with him on crucial economic issues. The Scottish administration is likely to seek direct access to Whitehall. It would demand that it be given revenue-raising powers and the economic and industrial powers necessary to deal with Scotland's problems and to bring its power into line with the way in which its responsibilities are seen by the electorate. If the Scottish Assembly succeeded in acquiring these powers, the Welsh Assembly would probably not be slow to follow Scotland's lead.

The evolution of government in Scotland and Wales to a federal relationship with Westminster may have profound effects upon British politics, and especially upon the relationships between the central party machines and their Scottish and Welsh counterparts. For, where federal states have succeeded in dispersing power, this has been less the result of constitutional provisions than of a federal type of party system, in which either parties come to be confined to a particular state and do not involve themselves in the competition for power at the federal level at all, as with the *Parti Québecqois*; or the parties themselves come to be organized on a state/provincial basis, as in Australia and the United States. Indeed, in the case of the United States it has been argued that there are in reality 100 parties and not two, since the parties, being organized on a state basis, only come together as national parties once every four years at the time of the Presidential elections. Since the administrative and technical pressures for centralization are so great in the modern world, it may be that only powerful countervailing *political* pressures, in the form of a decentralized party system, can hope to ensure a genuine dispersal of power of the kind advocated by proponents of devolution.

It is difficult to predict the extent to which the Labour and Conservative parties in Scotland and Wales will remain subordinate to their London headquarters. Will they seek to press the claims of Scotland and Wales even when such pressures prove embarrassing to their national leadership? Would a Conservative administration in Scotland scale down its bid for funds when a Conservative Opposition at Westminster was calling for reductions in public spending? Would a Labour administration in Wales embarrass a Labour Government by refusing to retrench at a time when the Government believed that public expenditure cuts were essential?

These are, of course, imponderable questions, and answers to them can only be speculative. We are unlikely to see a fully developed federal party system in the U.K. in the near future; but we already have state parties in Ulster (Ulster Unionists), Scotland (S.N.P.) and Wales (Plaid Cymru). It is also worth remembering that political issues in Northern Ireland during the period of devolution—1921 to 1972—bore little relationship to the debate in the rest of the United Kingdom; for in Northern Ireland, the Unionist/Republican conflict over-shadowed the conflict over socio-economic philosophy which animates the British parties.

What is most likely to happen is a loosening of the ties between the Scottish and Welsh parties and their London counterparts, so that the Scottish and Welsh parties gain for themselves a greater degree of autonomy. There may also be a subtle alteration in the role of Scottish and Welsh M.P.s, whose status is likely to decline. They will lose contact with much of the day-to-day work in the devolved areas, and they may well find themselves under pressure at Westminster to abstain from participating in debates on matters such as education, health, and housing, especially when Scottish or Welsh M.P.s hold the balance of power in the Commons.

The role of Scottish and Welsh M.P.s may alter in another respect; for they may come to be used by the Assemblies to press acceptance of a particular Scottish or Welsh point of view upon the government. The Assemblies may then seek to mobilize Scottish or Welsh M.P.s to support their case, so that these M.P.s come to assume the role of territorial delegates, and this will set them even further apart from their English colleagues. Devolution may therefore have very profound effects upon the role of Scottish and Welsh M.P.s, and Westminster will have to accommodate federal elements which coexist uneasily within its traditional structure.

III

These pressures for devolution may be strengthened by events in England. We have already seen that the Scotland and Wales Acts would create a lop-sided structure of goverment, and this has given rise to new regional coalitions in England, fearful that devolution to Scotland may divert resources from the North of England. If the Scottish and Welsh Assemblies work successfully, they may well stimulate demands for replicas in England; and, as we have seen, demands for regional assemblies might conveniently dovetail with pressures for local government reform.

If there is a possibility, then, of the introduction of regional government in England, it is worth asking whether the insertion of a regional tier would lead to better government or merely involve another layer of bureaucracy and longer delays in decision-making. The answer to this question also must be speculative since, as we have seen throughout this book, the success of different structures of government depends as much upon political factors as upon institutional arrangements. To believe that a structure of federal devolution would of itself lead to a dispersal of power from Westminster and Whitehall would clearly be to over-estimate grossly the influence of institutional change. If the establishment of elected regional authorities were not to be accompanied by a change in political habits, the centre would still insist upon supervising and controlling the regions, and the result would only be a more confused system of government. Regionalism would lead to the dispersal of power only if the will to decentralize were present amongst leading decision-makers. If such a will were present, however, the gains from decentralization might be very great, and it is worth concluding by rehearsing what these gains would be.

A properly conceived programme of decentralization could do much to make government accountable, and to alleviate the dangers of corporatism in Britain. A corporate system of government is characterized by a transfer of power from representative institutions to the leaders of the great corporations such as the T.U.C. and the C.B.I., and the civil service. Decisions come to be made through a process of bargaining between different groups, and the result is presented to Parliament for what is often only a formal ratification.

Such a structure of government leads to alienation, because it implies that individuals can have no influence upon government except insofar as they belong to one of these corporations. But the leaders of the corporations themselves come to lose touch with the interests of their members, and to identify the interests of their organization with those of government itself. The corporations, therefore, begin to assume a *collusive* role as collaborators with government, and they lose sight of their function as representative organizations whose job it is to articulate the grievances of their members.

Since the Second World War, Parliament in Britain has signally failed to make the institutions of the state properly accountable, nor has it been able to counteract successfully the centralist and corporatist tendencies of the age. In an attempt to increase the responsiveness of government, new methods of administration have been tried such as the 'hiving off' of institutions from Whitehall and the establishment of new *ad hoc* bodies. But they have not succeeded in stemming the tide. They have succeeded only in making government seem more complex and remote from the citizen.

Devolution, however, offers an opportunity of controlling corporate power, because it seeks to reduce the scale of government. 'The difference between Scottish T.U.C./government negotiations on Scottish economic matters and an explicit system of devolved government is as much a difference between corporate and electoral politics as between a unitary and a federal constitution.'[7]

If technical and economic forces seem to act as inexorable pressures towards centralization and bigness, the demand that government be made responsive, a demand expressed particularly strongly in Western democracies by an affluent and well-educated population increasingly sceptical of the claims of authority, offers a hope of reversing the trend.

But the dispersal of power offers advantages to central government as well, for it offers relief from the strain of overload. Increasingly it is becoming evident that the growth of government actually impedes its effectiveness, for the central institutions of government come to be so over-burdened with detailed work that they are unable to devote their energies to the major decisions of the day. What seems most lacking in government is energy—'Energy in the executive' which was for Alexander Hamilton 'a leading character in the definition of good goverment . . . But energy is the first quality to disappear when the workload becomes too heavy. Energy and creativity.'[8]

There is considerable evidence both in the writings of ex-ministers and of academic commentators that the existence of overload offers a serious impediment to the successful operation of modern government in Britain. The Crossman Diaries, for example, show how, on a number of occasions, a minister responsible for the housing drive was forced to divert his attention to matters such as the treatment of gypsies in Essex and Kent, a brick kiln in Apsley Guise, and the condition of the toilets in Bladon village adjacent to Churchill's grave. In any rational system of administration, such matters would not be the responsibility of central government.

Lord Hailsham has commented that

When I was a minister and visited opposite numbers abroad, I was always amazed at the amount of leisure they seemed to possess in contradistinction to myself. I put this down to the appalling over-centralisation of government in the United Kingdom, which combines the maximum hours of work for ministers with the minimum period of reflection, not in my view, a good administrative arrangement.[9]

Another Conservative ex-Cabinet minister, Mr. Peter Walker, has written 'Looking back upon the Conservative government of 1970–4, one of my regrets is that we did not as a Cabinet find the time to stand back from the day-to-day pressures and talk over the long-term strategy we wished to pursue.'[10]

The consequence is that power seeps away from elected politicians to the civil service, since ministers are unable to oversee their vast empires—the needs of bureaucracy, rather than the choices of elected politicians come to determine priorities; and the conglomertion of responsibilities makes it extremely difficult for departments to plan coherently for the future at all. Therefore important decisions of policy come to be crowded out in favour of what is of immediately pressing importance. Lord Crowther-Hunt, a former Minister of State at the Department of Education and Science, has argued that in central government

. . . policy-making (in departments), especially long-term thinking and planning, is the responsibility of officers over-burdened with more immediate demands arising from the parliamentary and public responsibility of ministers . . . civil servants, particularly members of the administrative class, have to spend a great deal of their time preparing explanatory briefs, answers to Parliamentary Questions and Ministers' cases . . . In the press of daily business long-term policy-planning and research takes second place.[11]

Central government is too preoccupied with its traditional controlling, regulating, and inspecting functions to devote much time to those broad issues of policy-making which are essential if planning is to be successful.

Thus in the field of town and country planning the central government has been so busy approving development plans and their five-yearly revisions, processing planning appeals and exercising call-in powers that it has never had time to produce the national land-use plan which should have logically underpinned its decisions on individual development plans. Similarly, in the field of transport any notion of a total view of national communications has until recently languished in the shade of the vast bureaucratic tree that is required to maintain close control of highway maintenance and traffic management.[12]

Since the major problems of government in the future will not be those of inspection or regulation, but will involve planning for the future, a dispersal of power from the centre might actually improve the effectiveness of government by strengthening its central directing organs.

The House of Commons in turn suffers from over-centralization. It works longer hours than legislatures in other democratic countries without being as effective in holding government accountable. It is so over-burdened with detailed constituency problems that it does not find time to give proper scrutiny to the mass of legislation which pours from the government machine. Its weaknesses in this respect have been highlighted by the difficulties involved in scrutinizing E.E.C. legislation, a task which is bound to strain the energies of the Commons to breaking-point. Here, too, Parliament is only likely to be able to resume its function of scrutinizing legislation if there is a real dispersal of power from the centre.

IV

If it is successful, devolution will, in the long run, give rise to a new style of politics in Britain, one based less upon party conflict and adversary politics than upon mutual accommodation and bargaining between different layers of government. A devolved system of government is undoubtedly more difficult to operate successfully than a unitary one, precisely because it involves co-operation between separate layers. The political consensus required for policy-making will need to be constructed and not assumed. But it could be argued that the decisions resulting from such a process of mutual accommodation would, for that very reason, acquire more authority than decisions which had been taken by central government alone. Devolution might make for stronger government, therefore, if it succeeded in securing a wider basis of agreement for legislation.

Nor need devolution necessarily weaken national unity. Given that there are powerful centrifugal forces at work in Britain today, it might be that the best way to strengthen national unity is to give way to these forces a little the better to disarm them. Then those deep underlying causes which make for national unity can be allowed to operate without giving rise to unnecessary conflict or antagonism.

Political science has been much concerned with the key question of how political societies are held together. To that question, the British answer has hitherto been to concentrate responsibility and political authority in one undivided central Parliament. But the case that centralization makes for national unity is something that needs to be argued for, and not simply asserted. This book has attempted to show that an alternative answer is possible—that a society may be held together through what Gladstone called a 'recognition of the distinctive qualities of the separate parts of great countries'.[13] If this answer is correct, devolution will strengthen national unity, not weaken it.

Notes

The following manuscript collections were consulted in the preparation of this book.

Asquith Papers, Bodleian Library, Oxford.

Gladstone Papers, British Museum (BM).

Diary of Sir Edward Hamilton, BM.

Harcourt Papers, Bodleian Library, Oxford.

Lloyd George Papers, House of Lords Record Office.

All references to Hansard are to the 5th Series unless otherwise indicated.

PRO is used to indicate Public Record Office.

CHAPTER 1

1 *Speeches and Letters on American Affairs*, Everyman, 1961, p. 60.
2 James Cornford: Introduction p.11 in *The Failure of the State*, ed. Cornford, Croom Helm, 1975.
3 Suzanne Berger: 'Bretons and Jacobins' in *Ethnic Conflict in the Modern World*, ed. Milton. J. Esman, Cornell University Press, 1977, p. 175.
4 Martin Kolinsky: Introduction in *Divided Loyalties: British regional assertion and European integration*, ed. Kolinsky, Manchester University Press, 1978, p. 11.
5 Alexandre Sanguinetti quoted by Berger, p. 167.

CHAPTER 2

1 Gladstone Papers: May 1886, BM Add. MS. 44772, f. 82.
2 ibid: BM Add. MS. 44631. Sir R. Hamilton's Memo, February, 1885, fs. 122-128.
3 ibid: BM Add. MS. 44772, ff. 58–60; and H. C. Debs, 3rd Series, Vol. CCCIV, Col. 1043.
4 ibid: BM Add. MS. 44672, f. 95.
5 H. C. Debs, 3rd Series, ibid., Col. 1082.
6 A. W. Hutton and H. J. Cohen (Eds.): *The Speeches and Public Addresses of the Right Hon. W. E. Gladstone M.P.*, Methuen, 1894, Vol. IX. 1886–1888. Speech on Welsh and Irish Nationality at Swansea, June 4, 1887, p. 226.
7 Gladstone: *Special Aspects of the Irish Question*, John Murray, 1892, p. 133.

8 H. C. Debs, ibid., Col. 1081.

9 ibid., Cols. 1544–5.

10 Speech on American Taxation in *Speeches and Letters on American Affairs*, pp. 59–60.

11 Gladstone Papers: Notes for Speeches, 8 April 1886, BM Add. MS. 44672, f. 21.

12 *Special Aspects of the Irish Question*, pp. 218–9.

13 H. C. Debs, 3rd Series, Vol. CCCV, Col. 585.

14 Gladstone Papers: BM Add. MS. 44772, ff, 131–2.

15 *Special Aspects of the Irish Question*, p. 47.

16 Memo to the Queen, March 1886: Gladstone Papers, BM Add. MS. 44772 ff. 64–5.

17 *Special Aspects of the Irish Question*, pp. 47 and 49.

18 Gladstone to Peel, 17 Oct. 1841, BM Add. MS. 40469, f. 20.

19 Gladstone Papers: BM Add. MS. 44672 f. 122.

20 Lord Thring: 'Home Rule and Imperial Unity' in *Contemporary Review* Vol. 51, p. 315. Lord Thring was chief parliamentary draftsman when the 1886 Bill was being drawn up.

21 Gladstone Papers. BM Add. MS. 44772, f. 51.

22 ibid., f. 103.

23 Gladstone to the Queen, 2 April 1886, PRO CAB 41/20/13.

24 Gladstone Papers: BM Add. MS. 44255. f. 178.

25 L.P. Curtis Jnr.: *Anglo-Saxons and Celts*: New York U.P., p. 103.

26 Quoted in A. B. Cooke and J. R. Vincent: *The Governing Passion*, Harvester Press, 1974, p. 419.

27 Gladstone Papers. Notes for Speech, 8 April 1886. BM Add. MS. 44672, f. 27.

28 H. C. Debs. 3rd Series, Vol. CCCIV. Col. 1055.

29 H. C. Debs. 3rd Series, Vol. CCCIV. Col. 1056.

30 Gladstone Papers, ibid. 8 April 1886.

31 ibid. BM Add. MS. 44772, ff. 47 – 8.

32 Granville to Hartington, 20 Dec. 1885 in Lord Edmond Fitzmaurice: *Life of Earl Granville*, Vol. 2, Longmans Green, 1905, p. 468.

33 Speech at Newcastle, 22 April 1886, quoted in A. V. Dicey, *A Leap in the Dark*, John Murray, 1893, p. 43.

34 Gladstone Papers, 8 April 1886, BM Add. MS. 44672 f. 28.

35 5 May 1886. ibid., BM Add. MS. 44772, ff. 103 – 4.

36 Lord Thring: 'Ireland's Alternative' in *A Handbook of Home Rule*, ed. James Bryce, Macmillan, 1887, p. 204.

37 Gladstone Papers, 5 May 1886, BM Add. MS. 44772, f. 101.

38 ibid., BM Add. MS. 44771, f. 81.

39 W. R. Anson: 'The Government of Ireland Bill and the Sovereignty of Parliament' in *Law Quarterly Review*, Vol. 2, p. 442.

40 F. S. L. Lyons: *Charles Stewart Parnell*, Collins, 1977, p. 449.

41 H. C. Debs. 4th Series, Vol. VII. Col. 260.

42 Lyons, p. 451.

43 Memorandum by the Committee of the Irish Parliamentary Party on

the Contribution by Ireland to Imperial Charges, 13 January 1893, p. 9. PRO CAB 37/33, No. 7.

44 Report of Committee on Irish Finance (Primrose Committee), 1911, p. 18. PRO CAB 37/108. No. 132.

45 E. W. Hamilton, Finance Brief, 17 July 1893: Harcourt MS., Box 160, f. 277.

46 Hamilton Diary, 14 January 1893, BM Add. MS. 48659, f. 81, and 20 March 1893, BM Add. MS. 48660. f. 19.

47 Hamilton Memorandum: Gladstone Papers, BM Add. MS. 44631 f. 124.

48 Childers to Gladstone, 18 March 1886, Gladstone Papers, BM Add. MS. 44132, f. 227.

49 *Special Aspects of the Irish Question*, p. 4.

50 H. C. Debs, 3rd Series, Vol. CCCIV, Col. 1536.

51 *A Leap in the Dark*, p. 107.

52 Memorandum by the Chancellor of the Exchequer on the financial arrangements proposed in the Government of Ireland Bill, 16 January 1893, p. 4, PRO CAB 37/33, No. 4.

53 Harcourt to Ripon, 19 January 1893, quoted in D. R. Brooks: Gladstone's Fourth Ministry 1892-94. Policies and Personalities, Ph.D., Cambridge, 1975, p. 99.

54 PRO CAB 37/108. No. 132., p. 18.

55 Harcourt to Gladstone, 15 February 1893, BM Add. MS. 44203 f. 52.

56 Harcourt MS., Box 160 f. 97.

57 Primrose Committee, PRO CAB 37/108, No. 132, p. 26.

58 Gladstone to the Queen, 25 May 1886, PRO CAB 41/20/11.

59 H. C. Debs. 4th Series, Vol. XII, Col. 477.

60 ibid. Vol. X, Col. 1629.

61 PRO CAB 37/108, No. 132, p. 22.

62 *What Federalism is Not*, John Murray, 1914, p. 119.

63 H. C. Debs, Vol. 116, Col. 1930.

64 ibid., Col. 1898.

65 H. C. Debs, 3rd Series, Vol. CCCIV, Col. 1211.

66 Report of a Joint Deputation from the Houses of Parliament to the Prime Minister on Federal Devolution, 26 June 1918, Lloyd George Papers, F/74/26/3.

67 Quoted in R. J. Lawrence: *The Government of Northern Ireland*, Oxford University Press, 1965, p. 188.

68 A.V. Dicey: *England's Case Against Home Rule*, 1886, 1973 Edition, Richmond Publishing Company, p. 178.

69 A. V. Dicey: *Unionist Delusions*, Macmillan, 1887, pp. 34 – 5.

70 Letter from Mr. Speaker to the Prime Minister, Cmd. 692, 1920.

71 Lord Salisbury to Rev. M. MacColl 12 April 1889 in G. W. E. Russell (ed.): *Malcolm MacColl: Memoirs and Correspondence*, Smith, Elder, 1914, p. 137.

72 J. E. Cairnes: 'Fragments on Ireland' in *Political Essays*, Macmillan, 1873, p. 198.

73 *Contemporary Review*, Vol. 51, p. 325.
74 N. Mansergh: *The Government of Northern Ireland: A Study in Devolution*, Allen and Unwin, 1936, p. 16.

CHAPTER 3

1 N. Mansergh, p. 93.
2 Letter from Lloyd George to Bonar Law, November 1918, Lloyd George Papers F/68/1.
3 Cabinet Committee on Ireland 1919-20, 1st Report, p. 5. PRO CAB 27/68.
4 Mansergh, pp. 236–7.
5 Buckland: *Ulster Unionism and the Origins of Northern Ireland*, 1886–1922, Gill and Macmillan, 1973, pp. 116–7.
6 H. Calvert: *Constitutional Law in Northern Ireland: A Study in Regional Government*, Stevens, 1968, p. 3.
7 F. H. Newark: 'The Law and the Constitution' in Thomas Wilson (ed.) *Ulster Under Home Rule*, Oxford University Press, 1955, p. 31.
8 *The Law and the Constitution*, Fourth edition, University of London Press, 1952, p. 158.
9 *A House Divided*, Collins, 1973, p. 23.
10 *The Autobiography of Terence O'Neill*, Faber, 1972, p. 147. Broadcast 9 Dec. 1968.
11 (1937) A.C. 863. See Sir Arthur Quekett: *The Constitution of Northern Ireland*, Part 3, 'Validity of Laws', HMSO, 1946, pp. 35–7.
12 *Ulster at the Crossroads*, Faber 1969, pp. 76–7.
13 The Protection of Human Rights in Northern Ireland (Standing Advisory Committee on Human Rights), HMSO, 1977, para. 2:11.
14 Meeting of the British co-signatories of the Irish Treaty, 7 September 1922, PRO CAB 43/1.
15 Quoted in Paul Arthur, Devolution as Administrative Convenience: A Case Study of Northern Ireland, *Parliamentary Affairs*, Vol. XXX, No. 1, Winter 1977, p. 98.
16 Mansergh, p. 138.
17 ibid, p. 143.
18 H. C. Debs, Vol. 163, Cols. 1624–5.
19 H. C. Debs, Vol. 698, Col. 1151.
20 H. C. Debs, Vol. 707, Cols. 79–80.
21 H. C. Debs, Vol. 718, Cols. 45–6, 58.
22 *A House Divided*, p. 66.
23 PRO CAB 24/137, CP 4081.
24 R. J. Lawrence: 'Devolution Reconsidered': *Political Studies*, Vol. IV, No. 1, 1956, p. 8 fn.
25 ibid.
26 H. C. Debs, Vol. 335, Cols. 1708–9.
27 Minutes of Evidence to the Commission on the Constitution, Vol. III: Northern Ireland, HMSO 1971, para. 88.

28 Martin Wallace: 'Home Rule in Northern Ireland: Anomalies of Devolution' in (1967) 18: *Northern Ireland Legal Quarterly*, p. 161.

29 Lawrence, p. 49.

30 F. H. Newark: Review of Lawrence: *The Government of Northern Ireland* in (1966) 17: *Northern Ireland Legal Quarterly*, p. 346.

31 Minutes of Evidence, op. cit., p. 176.

32 Written Evidence, op. cit., para. 3.

33 ibid., para. 245.

34 Minutes of Evidence, op. cit., para. 245.

35 See the Note by the Home Office: The Status of Northern Ireland within the United Kingdom: Written Evidence to the Commission on the Constitution, Vol. 3, HMSO 1969, para. 26.

36 Garret FitzGerald: *Towards A New Ireland*: Charles Knight, 1972, p. 77.

37 O'Neill: *Ulster at the Crossroads* p. 81.

38 ibid., paras. 150, 151.

39 Minutes of Evidence, op. cit., p. 71.

40 D. P. Barritt and Charles F. Carter: *The Northern Ireland Problems: A Study in Group Relations*, 2nd Edition, OUP, 1972, p. 112.

41 Cmnd. 4178, para. 21.

42 See M. N. Hayes: 'Some Aspects of Local Government in Northern Ireland' in *Public Administration in Northern Ireland*, Ed. Edwin Rhodes, Magee University College, Londonderry, 1967, especially pp. 88–97.

43 Ulster Year Book 1971, HMSO Belfast, p. 219.

44 Calvert, pp. 381–2.

45 Report on Disturbances in Northern Ireland (Cameron Report), Cmd. 532, HMSO Belfast 1969, para. 229(a)(6).

46 A Background to Constitutional Reform: Presidential Address to Holdsworth Club, University of Birmingham, 1975.

47 Lawrence, p. 34.

48 Report of the Royal Commission on the Constitution, para. 1253.

49 Report of the Convention: HMSO, London, 1975, para. 35.

CHAPTER 4

1 G. S. Pryde: *The Treaty of Union, 1707*, Nelson, 1950, pp. 25 – 6.

2 J. D. Mackie: *A History of Scotland*, Penguin, 1969, pp. 8 – 9.

3 Pryde, p. 21.

4 R. S. Rait: *The Parliaments of Scotland*, MacLehose and Jackson, 1924, p. 9.

5 Pryde, p. 37.

6 T. C. Smout: 'The Road to Union' in G. Holmes (Ed.) *Britain after the Glorious Revolution*, Macmillan, 1969, p. 191.

7 J. D. B. Mitchell: *Constitutional Law*, 2nd Ed., W. Green, 1968, p. 91.

8 A. Taylor Innes: *The Law of Creeds in Scotland*, Blackwood, 1902, p. 58.

9 R. King Murray: The Anglo – Scottish Union in *Scottish Law Times*, 4 November 1961, p. 162.

10 Pryde, pp. 48 – 9.

11 Sir R. Coupland: *Welsh and Scottish Nationalism: A Study*, Collins, 1954, p. 109.

12 A. V. Dicey and R. S. Rait: *Thoughts on the Union between England and Scotland*, Macmillan, 1920, pp. 252 – 3.

13 ibid., p. 319.

14 H. C. Debs, 3rd Series, Vol. CCCIV, Col. 1044.

15 Commission on the Constitution: Written Evidence, Vol. II, HMSO 1969: Memorandum by Scottish Office, paras. 15, 16.

16 Report of Royal Commission on Scottish Affairs, Cmd. 9212, para. 13.

17 Col. 458.

18 Technical Report No. 12: Public Expenditure in the Northern Region and other British Regions 1969/70 – 1973/74, pp. 41 – 52.

19 Minutes of Evidence, op. cit., para. 773.

20 Select Committee on Scottish Affairs: Minutes of Proceedings, 24 March 1970, para. 3129.

21 Commission on the Constitution: Research Paper No. 5: The Mechanism of Scottish Government by J. S. Berridge and J. Kellas, para. 38.

22 K. C. Wheare: *Government by Committee*, Oxford University Press, 1955, p. 161.

23 G. E. Edwards: The Scottish Grand Committee, 1958 to 1970 in *Parliamentary Affairs*, 1972, p. 322.

24 Emrys Hughes: *Parliament and Mumbo-Jumbo*, Allen and Unwin, 1966, p. 127.

25 First Scottish Standing Committee, 6 March 1973, Cols. 868 – 9.

26 Michael J. Keating: 'A Test of Political Integration: The Scottish Members of Parliament', *Studies in Public Policy No. 6*, University of Strathclyde, 1977, p. 31. This and the preceeding paragraphs are based on Keating.

27 James Cornford: 'Anglo – Scottish Relations since 1880', Unpublished Paper for CPS/Norwegian Conference 1975, p. 5.

28 ibid., p. 2.

29 Lady Sinclair of Duntreath quoted on p. 170 of J. N. Wolfe: *Government and Nationalism in Scotland*, Edinburgh U.P., 1969.

30 'Statement of Scotland's Claim for Home Rule', Scottish Home Rule Association, Edinburgh, 1888, pp. 5, 10–11.

31 Peter G. J. Pulzer: *Political Representation and Elections in Britain*, Allen and Unwin, 1967, p. 98.

32 William L. Miller with Bo Sarlvik, Ivor Crewe, and Jim Alt: 'The Connection Between S.N.P. Voting and the Demand for Scottish Self–Government' in *European Journal of Political Research*, Vol. 5, 1977, p. 90.

33 Ian Budge and D. W. Urwin: *Scottish Political Behaviour*, Longmans, 1966, p. 134.

34 Miller *et. al.*, p. 99.

35 Scottish Government: Draft Discussion Paper, Scottish Labour Party, n.d.

36 James Kellas: *The Scottish Political System*, 2nd Ed., Cambridge University Press, 1975, p. 210 fn.
37 William Wolfe: *Scotland Lives*, Reprographia, 1973, pp. 39–40.
38 Neil MacCormick (Ed.): *The Scottish Debate*, Oxford University Press, 1970, p. 2.
39 Michael Steed in Butler and Kavanagh op. cit., p. 403.
40 *Scotsman*, 15 December 1977.
41 *Scotland and Nationalism*, pp. 182, 184.
42 Scotland's Government: The Report of the Scottish Constitutional Committee, Edinburgh, 1970, p. 62.
43 Sir William McEwan Younger in *New Scotland*, No. 15, Summer 1970.
44 Scotland's Government, Preface, p. v.
45 ibid., pp. 65, 41.
46 Quoted in J. P. Mackintosh: The Report of the Royal Commission on the Constitution, 1969 – 73 in *Political Quarterly*, 1974, p. 116.
47 K. O. Morgan: *Wales In British Politics*, Revised Edition, University of Wales Press, 1970, p. 199.
48 *Memories*, Collins, 1952, p. 69.
49 Cited in Michael J. Keating: Nationalism in the Scottish Labour Movement 1914 – 74, Unpublished Paper prepared for Political Studies Association Conference, Aberystwyth, September 1977, p. 17.
50 Minutes of Evidence, Vol. 2, paras. 70, 126.
51 *Diaries of a Cabinet Minister* Vol. 3, Hamish Hamilton and Cape, 1977, p. 106.
52 H. M. Drucker: *Breakaway*, EUSPB 1978, p. 28.
53 Tam Dalyell: *Devolution: The End of Britain?*, Cape, 1977, p. 106.
54 Drucker, p. 29.

CHAPTER 5

1 Coupland, p. 44.
2 Quoted in Council for Wales and Monmouthshire: Report on The Welsh Language Today, Cmnd. 2198, 1963, para. 21.
3 Quoted in Coupland, p. 48.
4 Quoted in *Wales in British Politics*, p. 65.
5 Tom Nairn: 'Scotland and Wales: Notes on Nationalist Pre–History' in *Planet*, No. 34, November 1976, p. 8.
6 Engels: *The Magyar Struggle*, quoted by Christopher Harvie in *Scotland and Nationalism*, p. 26.
7 Henry Pelling: *The Social Geography of British Elections, 1885-1910*, Macmillan, 1967, pp. 368–9.
8 J. Vyrnwy Morgan: *The Philosophy of Welsh History*, John Lane, 1914, p. 154.
9 W. Llewellyn Williams: *Young Wales Movement: Cymru Fydd: Its Aims and Objects*, Roberts Bros., 1894, p. 3.
10 *Wales in British Politics*, p. 164.
11 ibid., pp. 107, 231.
12 Quoted in Neville Masterman: *The Forerunner: The Dilemma of Tom Ellis*, C. Davies, 1973, p. 256.

13 Coupland, p. 199.
14 *Wales in British Politics*, pp. 306–7.
15 K. O. Morgan: Introduction to *Lloyd George: Family Letters, 1885-1936*, University of Wales Press and Oxford University Press, 1973, p. 8.
16 Quoted in Ioan Bowen Rees: *The Welsh Political Tradition*, Caerphilly, 1975, p. 14.
17 Royal Commission on the Constitution, Report, para. 349.
18 Quoted in Coupland, p. 369.
19 Alan Butt Philip: *The Welsh Question*, University of Wales Press, 1975, p. 316.
20 Reprinted as 'The Fate of the Language' in *Planet* 4, February/March 1971, pp. 26–7.
21 *Plaid Cymru and Wales*, Llyfrau'r Dryw, 1950, p. 17.
22 At the Plaid Cymru Youth Conference, quoted in Butt Philip, p. 186.
23 Philip N. Rawkins: Minority Nationalism and the Advanced Industrial State: A Case–Study of Contemporary Wales, Ph.D., Toronto, 1975, p. 368.
24 ibid., pp. iv–v.
25 Gwynfor Evans, *Wales Can Win*, C. Davies, pp. 87 and 124.
26 Rawkins, p. v.
27 Notes for the President of the Board of Education 'What the Welsh Department has done for Wales since its creation' 29 November 1909. Quoted in P. J. Randall: The Development of Administrative Decentralisation in Wales, from the establishment of the Welsh Department of Education in 1907 to the creation of the post of Secretary of State for Wales in October 1964, M.Sc.Econ., Wales, 1969, p. 51.
28 ibid., p. 58.
29 Sir Percy Watkins, Permanent Secretary of the Department, 1925–1933, quoted in Randall, p. 45.
30 Notes for the President of the Board of Education, quoted in Randall, p. 51.
31 W. J. Braithwaite: *Lloyd George's Ambulance Wagon*, Methuen, 1957, p. 222.
32 Randall, p. 72.
33 Sir Henry Bunbury, Introduction to Braithwaite op. cit., p. 31.
34 Quoted in Randall, p. 101.
35 James Griffiths: *Pages from Memory*, Dent, 1969, p. 161.
36 H. C. Debs, Vol. 702, Col. 627.
37 Written Evidence, Vol. 1, paras. 41–5, Minutes of Evidence Vol. 1, para. 34.
38 Minutes of Evidence, Vol. 1, paras. 445–50.
39 Working Party on Housing Finance in Wales, First Report, HMSO, Cardiff, 1977, p. 2.
40 Supply Estimates 1976–7: Supplementary Estimates (Classes II–XVII: Civil), HC 10, December 1976, pp. 136–9.
41 P. K. Risko: Regional Government in Britain, B.Litt., Oxford, 1978, p. 141.

42 Quoted by Risko, p. 142, from interview with Owen Hooker, Senior Economic Adviser to the Welsh Office.

43 Edward Rowlands: 'The Politics of Regional Administration: The Establishment of the Welsh Office' in *Public Administration*, Autumn 1972, pp. 340–2, 345.

44 H. C. Debs, Vol. 697, Col. 755.

45 Minutes of Evidence, Vol. 1, para. 14.

46 R. L. Borthwick in *Parliamentary Affairs*, 1967–8, p. 275.

47 *Western Mail*, 5, 6 December 1969.

48 Welsh Council of Labour: Report to Annual Meeting, May 1974.

49 *Diaries of a Cabinet Minister*, Vol. 2. p. 344.

50 19 January 1968.

51 *Diaries of a Cabinet Minister*, Vol. 2, p. 771.

52 *Western Mail*, 24 March 1972.

53 'How Local Government?' in *Planet* 31, March 1976, p. 8.

54 House of Commons Standing Committee D, 1971–2, Vol. V, Cols. 2914, 2890.

55 'Why Devolution?', Labour Party in Wales, Cardiff, September 1976, p. 4.

CHAPTER 6

1 Pelling, p. 416.

2 *Nations and States*, Methuen, 1977, p. 445.

3 Cmnd. 5460–1, para. 1.

4 Cmnd. 5460, para. 13.

5 *Diaries of a Cabinet Minister*, Vol. 3, p. 252.

6 Jenifer Hart: 'Some Reflections on the Report of the Royal Commission on the Police' in *Public Law*, Autumn 1963, p. 303.

7 Para. 129, p. x and para. 126.

8 In *The Times*, 6 October 1976.

9 Quoted in 'The Devolution White Paper: Synopsis and Commentary', S.N.P. Research Department, January 1976, p. 5.

10 Mr. Kinnock, quoting a memorandum from the Law Society, H. C. Debs. Vol. 924, Col. 116.

11 Mr. Sillars, H. C. Debs, Vol. 922, Col. 1319.

12 ibid., Col. 1021.

13 Mr. Goodhart, H. C. Debs, Vol. 926, Col. 382.

14 Mr. Mendelson, H. C. Debs, Vol. 925, Col. 1679.

15 ibid., Col. 1683.

16 ibid., Col. 1679.

17 Ch. 21, p. 523. Cited by Mr. Maurice Macmillan, ibid., Col. 1674.

18 ibid., Cols. 1715–6.

19 H. C. Debs, Vol. 926, Col. 1273.

20 H. C. Debs, Vol. 933, Col. 226.

21 H. C. Debs, Vol. 924, Col. 221.

22 H. C. Debs, Weekly Hansard, Vol. 936, Col. 313.

23 The Government's Devolution Plans: A Note of Dissent from the United Kingdom Liberal Party's Machinery of Government Policy Panel, Autumn 1977.

24 *Guardian*, 14 November 1977.

CHAPTER 7

1 Para. 742.

2 ibid., paras. 737–745.

3 Scottish Law Commission: Memorandum No. 32: Comments on the White Paper: 'Our Changing Democracy: Devolution to Scotland and Wales', para. 11(3).

4 Memorandum by Scottish Law Commission to Lord Advocate on 'Devolution, Scots Law and the Role of the Commission', reprinted in Memorandum No. 32 supra., para. 58.

5 Memorandum on Scotland and Wales Bill, pp. 2–3.

6 Memorandum to Lord Advocate, para. 23.

7 H. C. Debs. Weekly Hansard, Vol. 941, Col. 1699.

8 ibid., Col. 1734.

9 ibid., Col. 1740.

10 John Mackintosh, ibid., Col. 1703.

11 The Power of the Secretary of State in *New Edinburgh Review*, February 1976, No. 31, pp. 9–16.

12 Notes on Amendments to Clause 4 of the Government of Ireland Act, 1920, PRO CAB 27/70, CI 64.

13 Scottish Law Commission: Memorandum No. 32, para. 13.

14 ibid., para. 20.

15 Memorandum by Law Society of Scotland on Scotland and Wales Bill, pp. 2–3.

16 Commission on the Constitution: Research Papers I: 'Federalism and Decentralisation in Germany' by Nevil Johnson, paras. 6, 134.

17 Plaid Cymru's Response to the Government's White Paper on Devolution, para. 13.

18 Para. 829. My italics.

19 Extract from a Cabinet paper written early in 1975, entitled 'The Role of the Welsh Assembly in Primary Legislation' quoted in John Osmond: *Creative Conflict*, Routledge and Kegan Paul, 1968, p. 153.

20 Reported in the *Western Mail*, 23 June 1978.

21 Association of County Council's Report, 'Devolution and Local Government', July 1976, pp. 3–4.

22 H. C. Debs, Vol. 942, Cols. 1300–02.

23 *Devolution: The English Dimension*, HMSO 1976, para. 23.

24 Brian W. Hogwood: 'Models of Industrial Policy: The Implications for Devolution', *Studies in Public Policy, No. 5:* University of Strathclyde, 1977, p. 11.

25 *Devolution: The English Dimension*, para. 37.

26 Quoted on p. 128 of T. St. John N. Bates; 'Devolution and the European Community' in J. P. Grant (Ed.) *Independence and Devolution: The Legal Implications for Scotland*, W. Green, 1976.

27 ibid., p. 135.

28 Memorandum No. 32, para. 29.

29 *Devolution: Financing the Devolved Services*, Cmnd. 6890, HMSO 1977, paras. 4, 73.

30 Regional Devolution and the National Health Service in *Regional Devolution and Social Policy*, Ed. Edward Craven, Macmillan 1975, p. 77.

31 Committee on Local Government Finance: Appendix 1: Oral Evidence by H.M. Treasury, p. 302.

32 Making Devolution Work, Young Fabian Pamphlet, No. 43, March 1976, p. 27.

33 *Scotsman*, 7 September 1976.

34 H. C. Debs, Vol. 922, Col. 990.

35 Cmnd. 5460–1, Appendix A, para. 27.

36 Fourteenth Report from the Expenditure Committee, 1974–5, HC 617, Vol. 11, pp. 2958, 2963.

37 Committee on Local Government Finance: Appendix 6, Evidence by Department of the Environment, paras. 30, 32.

38 David A. Heald: Financing Devolution in *National Westminster Bank Review*, November 1975, p. 13.

39 PRO CAB 37/108 No. 132, p. 36.

40 Chapter 15, p. 283, para. 2.

41 H. L. Debs. Vol. 391, Col. 330.

42 Heald: Financing Devolution, pp. 11–12.

43 G. W. Jones 'Central-Local Government Relations: Grants, Local Responsibility, and Minimum Standards' pp. 66–82 in *Policy and Politics* ed. D. E. Butler and A. H. Halsey, Macmillan, 1978.

44 Croom Helm, 1975.

45 H. C. Debs. Vol. 941, Col. 1591.

46 Diane Dawson: The Financing of Devolved Government: Paper presented to SectionF of the British Association for the Advancement of Science, September 1977, p. 3.

47 Quoted in letter to councillors from Secretary of Merseyside County Council, 4 May 1977.

48 The Government's Devolution Plans: A Note of Dissent from the United Kingdom Liberal Party's Machinery of Government Policy Panel.

49 'Is This a United Kingdom?', Tyne and Wear County Council, January 1977, p. 8.

50 Councillor M. Campbell, Leader of Tyne and Wear County Council, 'Is This a United Kingdom?', p. 4.

51 Roger Guthrie and Iain Maclean: Another Part of the Periphery in *Parliamentary Affairs*, 1978, pp. 196 and 199.

52 Devolution and Regional Government in England, A Discussion

Document for the Labour Movement, Labour Party, September 1975, p. 19.
53 Marshall Inquiry on Greater London, GLC 1978, p. 83, para. 4. 1.

CHAPTER 8

1 H. C. Debs. Vol. 924, Col. 458.
2 *Federal Government*, pp. 19–21.
3 H. C. Debs, 3rd Series, Vol. CCCIV, Col. 1536.
4 H. C. Debs, Vol. 922, Cols. 992–3.
5 Selwyn Lloyd: *Mr. Speaker, Sir*, Cape, 1976, p. 170.
6 *Scotsman*, 17 May 1977.
7 Miller *et. al.*, p. 85.
8 Daniel P. Moynihan: 'Imperial Government' in *Commentary* June 1978, p. 30.
9 *The Listener*, 28 October 1976.
10 Peter Walker: *The Ascent of Britain*, Sidgwick and Jackson, 1977, p. 199.
11 Lord Crowther–Hunt: 'Long–Term Planning Takes Second Place' in *Times Higher Education Supplement*, 7 May 1976.
12 L. J. Sharpe: British Politics and the Two Regionalisms in W. D. C. Wright and D. H. Stewart (Eds.) *The Exploding City*, Edinburgh University Press, 1972, p. 140.
13 W. E. Gladstone: Speech at Swansea, 4 June 1887, in Hutton and Cohen Vol. IX, p. 226.

Suggestions for further reading

Hugh Seton-Watson, *Nations and States*, Methuen, 1977, provides a general account of nationalism. A. V. Dicey's *England's Case Against Home Rule*, Richmond Publishing Company Edition, 1973, written in 1886 offers the best critique of Gladstone's proposals and is very relevant to the contemporary debate. Its arguments have never been effectively refuted.

On Northern Ireland, R. J. Lawrence, *The Government of Northern Ireland*, Oxford University Press, 1965, describes the development of public services, and Harry Calvert, *The Constitutional Law of Northern Ireland*, Stevens, 1968, is the best account of its subject if not also of the constitutional aspects of devolution as a whole.

James Kellas, *The Scottish Political System*, Second Edition, Cambridge University Press, 1975, offers a good introduction to modern Scottish politics; and K. O. Morgan, *Wales in British Politics*, Revised Edition, University of Wales Press, 1970, and Alan Butt Philip, *The Welsh Question*, University of Wales Press, 1975, perform the same function for Wales.

On devolution to Wales *Creative Conflict*, Routledge and Kegan Paul, 1978, by John Osmond, makes a powerful case. There is no equivalent for Scotland, but Tam Dalyell, *Devolution: The End of Britain?*, Cape, 1977, is a fiercely hostile polemic.

Harry Calvert (Ed.), *Devolution*, Professional Books, 1975, and Edward Craven (Ed.), *Regional Devolution and Social Policy*, Macmillan, 1975, are valuable collections of essays on current problems. James Cornford (Ed.), *The Failure of the State*, Croom Helm, 1975, shows the similarities and differences between the problems faced by Britain and by other European states.

Index

Heath, Edward, 42, 96, 108, 110–12, 143, 154
Heffer, Eric, 159–60
Hicks-Beach, Sir Michael, 34
Highlands and Islands Development Board, 86, 165, 186
Hogg, Quintin *see* Hailsham, Lord
Hughes, Cledwyn, 130, 141–2

Irish Home Rule Bills: first (1886), 4, 10–29 *passim*, 37, 55, 90; second (1893), 10, 23, 29–31; third (1912), 10, 23, 31–5, 43–4

Jennings, Sir Ivor, 50
Johnston, Tom, 114
Joseph, Sir Keith, 138

Kennedy, Ludovic, 103–4
Kilbrandon, Lord, 70, 147, 150

Lewis, Saunders, 127–8
Lloyd George, David, 4, 37, 39, 43–7 *passim*, 51–2, 122, 124, 125, 132, 144, 145

MacCormick, John, 91,
Mackay, D. I. and G. A., 204
Mackintosh, John, 111–12, 156–7, 171, 172, 222
Maclean, John, 114
Macmillan, Harold, 106, 134
Madison, James, 3
Marshall, Sir Frank, 213
Marshall, W., 115
Maxwell-Fyfe, Sir David, 133
Millan, Bruce, 183–4, 198
Miller, William, 94, 98
Morley, John, 10, 17, 21

Northern Ireland Constitution Act (1973), 71
Northern Ireland Constitutional Convention, 73
North Sea Oil, 80, 96–8, 100, 115, 127, 164, 185, 197, 204–5

Oliver, F.S., 36
O'Neill, Capt. Terence, 50, 51, 67
Our Changing Democracy,153, 182, 189, 195, 197–8, 205, 208

Parnell, Charles Stewart, 24, 28, 33, 37, 44
Parti Québecqois, 2, 223
Peacock, A. T., 148, 150, 198
P.E.S.C. (Public Expenditure Survey Committee), 136, 137
Plaid Cymru, 94, 95, 125, 126–31, 141–4 *passim*, 147, 151, 178, 204, 224
Powell, Enoch, 102, 160, 218
Price, David, 172
Primrose Committee on Irish Finance, 30, 35, 202
Pym, Francis, 112, 162, 214, 223

Redmond, John, 33, 44
Reid, George, 153
Renton, Sir David, 151
Rifkind, Malcolm, 111
Rosebery, Lord, 35
Ross, William, 83, 106, 115, 142
Rowlands, Edward, 137–8
Royal Commission on the Constitution (The Kilbrandon Commission), 5, 60–3, 66, 73, 83, 110–11, 115, 136, 139, 141, 142, 147–52, 168, 178–9, 184, 186, 197, 198; Memorandum of Dissent, 5, 148–51, 198, 207

Salisbury, Lord, 39
Scottish Development Agency, 81, 86, 97, 165, 166, 186, 207
Scottish Home Rule Association, 90
Scottish Labour Party, 100
Sefton, Lord, 209
Selwyn-Lloyd, Lord, 222
Shore, Peter, 213–14
Short, Edward, 170
Sillars, Jim, 99–100
Simon Declaration, 58
Sinn Fein, 44, 45, 47
Smith, John, 155, 171
S.N.P. (Scottish Nationalist Party), 83, 89, 91–105, 107, 108, 112–17 *passim*, 126–31 *passim*, 141, 147, 151, 153, 157–8, 204, 219–24 *passim*
Starforth, Michael, 104
Steel, David, 87, 104, 154–5, 157, 158
Steel, Sir James, 150–1
Street, Harry, 151